Windows Server®
Administration Fundamentals

Crystal Panek

Copyright © 2020 by John Wiley & Sons, Inc., Indianapolis, Indiana

Published simultaneously in Canada

ISBN: 978-1-119-65065-2
ISBN: 978-1-119-65775-0 (ebk.)
ISBN: 978-1-119-65068-3 (ebk.)

Manufactured in the United States of America

No part of this publication may be reproduced, stored in a retrieval system or transmitted in any form or by any means, electronic, mechanical, photocopying, recording, scanning or otherwise, except as permitted under Sections 107 or 108 of the 1976 United States Copyright Act, without either the prior written permission of the Publisher, or authorization through payment of the appropriate per-copy fee to the Copyright Clearance Center, 222 Rosewood Drive, Danvers, MA 01923, (978) 750-8400, fax (978) 646-8600. Requests to the Publisher for permission should be addressed to the Permissions Department, John Wiley & Sons, Inc., 111 River Street, Hoboken, NJ 07030, (201) 748-6011, fax (201) 748-6008, or online at http://www.wiley.com/go/permissions.

Limit of Liability/Disclaimer of Warranty: The publisher and the author make no representations or warranties with respect to the accuracy or completeness of the contents of this work and specifically disclaim all warranties, including without limitation warranties of fitness for a particular purpose. No warranty may be created or extended by sales or promotional materials. The advice and strategies contained herein may not be suitable for every situation. This work is sold with the understanding that the publisher is not engaged in rendering legal, accounting, or other professional services. If professional assistance is required, the services of a competent professional person should be sought. Neither the publisher nor the author shall be liable for damages arising herefrom. The fact that an organization or Web site is referred to in this work as a citation and/or a potential source of further information does not mean that the author or the publisher endorses the information the organization or Web site may provide or recommendations it may make. Further, readers should be aware that Internet Web sites listed in this work may have changed or disappeared between when this work was written and when it is read.

For general information on our other products and services or to obtain technical support, please contact our Customer Care Department within the U.S. at (877) 762-2974, outside the U.S. at (317) 572-3993 or fax (317) 572-4002.

Wiley publishes in a variety of print and electronic formats and by print-on-demand. Some material included with standard print versions of this book may not be included in e-books or in print-on-demand. If this book refers to media such as a CD or DVD that is not included in the version you purchased, you may download this material at http://booksupport.wiley.com. For more information about Wiley products, visit www.wiley.com.

Library of Congress Control Number: 2019952299

TRADEMARKS: Wiley, the Wiley logo, and the Sybex logo are trademarks or registered trademarks of John Wiley & Sons, Inc. and/or its affiliates, in the United States and other countries, and may not be used without written permission. Windows Server is a registered trademark of Microsoft Corporation. All other trademarks are the property of their respective owners. John Wiley & Sons, Inc. is not associated with any product or vendor mentioned in this book.

SKY10033271_021122

This book is dedicated to my loving husband, William Panek, and to my two wonderful daughters, Alexandria and Paige. Thank you all for your love and support. I love you all more than anything!

Acknowledgments

I would like to thank my husband and best friend, Will, because without him I would not be where I am today—thank you! I would also like to express my love to my two daughters, Alexandria and Paige, who have always shown nothing but love and support. Thank you all!

I would like to thank everyone on the Sybex team, especially my associate acquisitions editor, Devon Lewis, who helped make this the best book possible. I would like to thank Christine O'Connor, who was the production editor, and Kim Wimpsett for being the proofreader.

Finally, I also want to thank everyone behind the scenes who helped make this book possible. Thank you all for your hard work and dedication.

About the Author

 **Crystal Panek** holds the following certifications: MCP, MCP+I, MCSA, MCSA+ Security and Messaging, MCSE-NT (3.51 & 4.0), MCSE 2000, 2003, 2012/2012 R2, 2016, MCSE+Security and Messaging, MCDBA, MCTS, MCITP.

For many years she trained as a contract instructor teaching at such places as MicroC, Stellacon Corporation, and the University of New Hampshire. She then became the vice president for a large IT training company, and for 15 years she developed training materials and courseware to help thousands of students get through their certification exams. She currently works on a contract basis creating courseware for several large IT training facilities.

She currently resides in New Hampshire with her husband and two daughters. In her spare time, she likes to camp, hike, shoot trap and skeet, golf, bowl, and snowmobile.

Contents at a Glance

Contents

Introduction

What Does This Book Cover?

Chapter 1: Server Overview This chapter covers understanding server installation options, choosing the correct operating system version options, Server core vs. Desktop Experience, Nano Server installation, interactive installs, automated install using WDS, VHD/VHDX installation source, how to perform unattended installs, perform upgrades, clean installs, and migrations. This chapter also covers identifying application servers, mail servers, database servers, collaboration servers, monitoring servers, and threat management. You will learn to understand server virtualization, virtual memory, virtual networks, VHD and VHDX formats. This chapter delves into identifying major hardware components, memory, disk, processor, network, 32-bit and 64-bit architecture, removable drives, graphic cards, cooling, power usage, and ports. This chapter will also teach you how to work with updates, software, driver, operating systems, applications, Windows Update, and using Windows Server Update Service (WSUS).

Chapter 2: Managing Windows Server 2016 This chapter covers understanding device drivers, installing, removing, disabling, update/upgrade, rollback, troubleshooting, Plug & Play, IRQ, interrupts, driver signing, and managing devices through Group Policy. This chapter will also teach you how to understand services. It also covers which statuses a service can be in, startup types, recovery options, delayed startup, Run As settings for a service, stopping or pausing a service, service accounts, and dependencies. This chapter will also delve into understanding remote access. Also covered are remote assistance, remote administration tools, Remote Desktop Services, multipoint services, licensing, RD Gateway, VPN, application virtualization, and multiple ports.

Chapter 3: Managing Storage This chapter covers identifying storage technologies and their typical usage scenarios, the advantages and disadvantages of different storage topologies, local storage, network storage, Fibre Channel, and iSCSI hardware. This chapter also introduces using RAID redundancy, RAID 0, RAID 1, RAID 5, RAID 10 and combinations, hardware and software RAID. This chapter will also discuss understanding disk types, such as Solid State Drive (SSD) and Hard Disk Drive (HDD) types and comparisons, ATA basic disk, dynamic disk, mount points, file systems, mounting a virtual hard disk, and distributed file systems.

Chapter 4: Monitoring and Troubleshooting Servers This chapter covers understanding performance monitoring, methodology, procedures, effect of network, CPU, memory and disk, creating a baseline, Performance Monitor, Resource Monitor, Task Manager, performance counters, and Data Collector Sets. You will also learn to understand logs and alerts, Event Viewer, performance logs, and alerts. This chapter will cover the steps of the startup process, BIOS, UEFI, TPM, bootsector, bootloader, MBR, boot.ini, POST, and Safe Mode. Will delve into understanding business continuity, using backup and restore, disaster recovery planning, clustering, AD restore, folder redirection, data redundancy, uniterruptible power supply (UPS). You will also learn troubleshooting methodologies, processes, procedures, best practices, systematic vs. specific approach, Performance Monitor, Event Viewer, Resource Monitor, Information Technology Infrastructure Library, central logging, event filtering, and using default logs.

Chapter 5: Essential Services This chapter covers understanding accounts and groups, domain accounts, local accounts, user profiles, computer accounts, group types, default groups, group scopes, group nesting, and understanding AGDLP and AGUDLP processes to help implement nesting. You will learn about organizational units and containers, the purpose of OUs, purpose of containers, delegation, default containers, uses for different container objects, default hidden, and visible containers. This chapter will teach you about the Active Directory infrastructure, domain controllers, forests, child domains, operation master roles, domain vs. workgroup, trust relationships, functional levels, deprecated functional levels, namespace, sites, replication, schema, and Passport. This chapter will also delve into understanding group policies, group policy processing, Group Policy Management Console, computer policies, user and local policies.

Chapter 6: File and Print Services This chapter covers the file and print services. You will learn about local printers, network printers, printer pools, web printing, web management, driver deployment, file, folder, and share permissions vs. rights, auditing, and print job management.

Chapter 7: Popular Windows Network Services and Applications This chapter covers using Web services such as IIS, WWW, and FTP, installing from Server Manager, separate worker processes, adding components, sites, ports, SSL, and using certificates. You will also learn about server virtualization, including how to use snapshots and saved states, physical to virtual conversions, virtual to physical conversions, and nested virtualization.

Interactive Online Learning Tools

Studying the material in *Windows Server Administration Fundamentals* is an important part of self-learning, but we provide additional tools to help you prepare.

To start using these tools to jump-start your self-study, go to www.wiley.com/go/sybextestprep.

Lesson 1

Server Overview

Objective Domain Matrix

Technology Skill	Objective Domain Description	Objective Domain Number
Installing Windows Server 2016	Understand server installation options.	1.3
Introducing Server Roles	Identify application servers.	2.1
Comparing Physical Servers and Virtual Servers	Understand server virtualization.	2.5
Selecting Server Hardware	Identify major server hardware components.	5.1
Understanding Updates	Understand updates.	6.3

Key Terms

BIOS	server
clean installation	Server Core
disk cloning	server features
drives	server role
firmware	system preparation tool
motherboard	unattended installation
network connections	upgrade installation
Nano Server	virtual server
ports	Windows Activation
power supply	Windows Deployment Services (WDS)
processor	Windows Updates
RAM	

 Real World Scenario

Lesson 1 Case

You just got hired at the Acme Corporation. They have several Windows Server 2012 and Windows Server 2012 R2 Servers and a Windows Server 2016 Server. While talking to your management team, you determine that you need to upgrade all of the servers to Windows Server 2016 and you need to create a web farm consisting of 3 new web servers and a single backend SQL server, also running Windows Server 2016. Therefore, you need to figure out the best way to get to your goal.

Understanding What a Server Does

With today's computers, any computer on the network can provide services or request services depending on how the network is set up. A *server* is a computer that is a meant to be a dedicated service provider, and a client is a computer that requests services. A network that is made up of dedicated servers and clients is known as a client/server network. A server-based network is the best network for sharing resources and data, while providing centralized network security for those resources and data. Networks with Windows Server 2016 are usually client/server networks.

If you have been using Windows 7, Windows 8/8.1, or Windows 10 for a significant amount of time, you should realize that your computer is providing services and requesting services (although it most likely requesting services more than it is providing services). When you access a web page over the Internet, access your email, access a data file on another computer, or access a printer that is connected to the network, you are requesting services. While Windows servers are designed to provide a wide range of network services, Windows 7, Windows 8/8.1, and Windows 10 can provide printer and file sharing and web pages (although you are limited by the number of concurrent connections especially when compared to Windows servers and are not optimized for multi-user access). Therefore, while these versions of Windows are designed as clients, they can also provide services.

While computers with Windows Server 2016 are designed to provide services, they can also request services from other computers. For example, they can access a web server locally or over the Internet, access a software repository, or print to a network printer.

When determining the hardware and software needs, you need to look at the role that the computer needs to fill and the load the computer will be placed under. You can then start researching the hardware (including the number of computers, number of processors, amount of RAM, and amount of disk storage) and software requirements to reach those goals. You also need to look at disaster recovery including looking at the steps you will need to take if a server fails and you lose data.

Don't forget to plan your server for growth. Most servers should be designed for 3–5 years of service. So make sure you look at what your landscape may look at 3–5 years from deployment of the server. This will help you avoid purchasing and reinstalling the server several months later. It should also be noted that the bare basic of a server leaves little room for growth.

Introducing Server Roles

Before selecting the hardware and software components of a server, you must first understand what your server is supposed to do. The first step is to identify the server roles and network services that the server will need to provide. You also need to look at how many people will be accessing the server at once to help determine the load the server needs to fulfill.

Certification Ready?

Can you list and describe the basic server roles? 2.1

A *server role* is a primary duty that a server performs. You should note that a server could have multiple roles. Some of the more common server roles include:

- File services
- Print services
- Web services
- Remote access
- Application servers
- Email server
- Database server

A file server allows you to centrally locate files to be accessed by multiple people. Since the files are centrally located, it makes it easier for multiple users to access and find files (assuming they are organized well) and it is easier to back up these files since they are located in a single place. When using Microsoft Windows to provide file sharing, you will usually be using Server Message Block (SMB) to access Microsoft Shares or shared folders. Windows Servers can also provide NFS shares for Unix/Linux users.

Print services allow multiple users to access a centrally located printer. This allows you share an expensive printer that is fast or is a heavy-duty printer or supports advanced options such as color. Printers can be accessed as a network printer that is connected directly to the network or through a Microsoft Windows server (again using SMB).

Since the Internet has become more prevalent in today's business application, so has the use of web services. A web server will provide web services so that users can access web pages using their browser. These web services may be used to do research, provide leads for sales, allow customers to purchase goods and services, and provide customer support over the Internet. It can also be used to provide an easy method to access databases, run reports, track sales leads, provide customer support, and even help you with payroll and human resources. Since you are using your standard browser such as Internet Explorer, you will be using the Hypertext Transfer Protocol (HTTP) or HTTP Secure (HTTPS) protocols. Microsoft provides web services using Internet Information Services (IIS).

Remote access is a service that supports multiple inbound requests to connect to the server or network. It can provide terminal services so that multiple users can log on to a server remotely and access a desktop, start menu, and programs much like if they were sitting in front of the server. On the other hand, remote access can also provide network access over the Internet using a virtual private network (VPN), which allows a user to be at home yet have full access to their internal network resources such as email and data files.

Lastly, the application server role provides an integrated environment for deploying and running server-based business applications. In other words, the server will provide a network application. Different from accessing a file from a shared folder and your PC doing all of the work, the server will also do some of the processing.

When talking about server and server applications, you may hear the terms front end and back end. In client/server applications, the client part of the program is often called the front end, and the server part is called the back end. The front end is the interface that is provided to a user or another program. It may be accessed via a web page or a customized application that runs on the client PC. The back end will often contain a database that is used to store, organize, query and retrieve data.

One commonly used application server that is essential for most corporations is the mail server. The mail server is a server that stores and manages electronic messages (email) among users. If you are using Microsoft email products, you will be using Microsoft Exchange to act as your mail servers, and you would most likely access the email using Microsoft Outlook or a web browser.

Another example of an application server is if you have a sales tracking application or inventory control applications. You would access this type of server on your company network by using a customized program or using your browser. You will then request information or input some data, which will then be retrieved from or sent to the backend server running a database such as Microsoft SQL server.

When Windows Server 2016 is installed, an administrator has a very important decision to make. They need to decide which roles and features will be installed on the new server. Many administrators do not properly utilize their servers; they may overuse or underutilize them. Domain controllers can help an administrator authenticate users on the network. But once they have authenticated the users, their tasks have been completed and then are not very busy during the day. Domain controllers have some tasks that they must complete all day, but the server where they occupy is not as heavily used when compared to say a SQL Server or an Exchange mail server.

If a domain controller is being used as a virtual machine or if there are more than enough servers, then having a domain controller with no other applications on it (except DNS) may be acceptable. But if the servers are limited, then maybe consider putting other services or applications on the server. Remember, some applications work better on a member server than they do on domain controllers. So make sure to research an application to determine best practices.

Knowing the different roles and features that can be installed on a Windows Server 2016 machine can help an administrator to design, deploy, manage, and troubleshoot technologies in Windows Server 2016. Some of the available roles in Windows Server 2016 can be seen in Figure 1.1, which shows the Add Roles and Features Wizard in Server Manager.

FIGURE 1.1   Available roles in Windows Server 2016

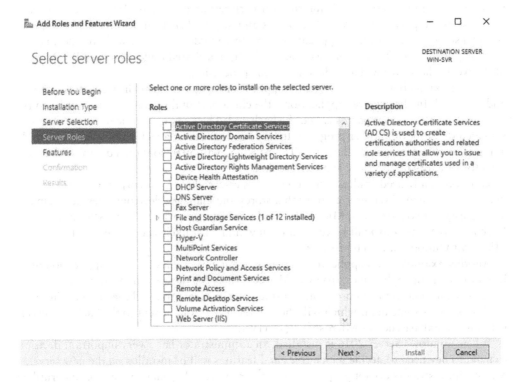

The following roles can be installed on a Windows Server 2016 machine:

Active Directory Certificate Services (AD CS)   The AD CS server role allows an administrator to build a public key infrastructure (PKI) and provide public key cryptography, digital certificates, and digital signature capabilities for an organization. AD CS provides a set of customizable services that allows an administrator to issue and manage PKI certificates. These certificates can be used in software security systems that employ public key technologies.

Active Directory Domain Services (AD DS)   The AD DS server role allows an administrator to create secure and manageable infrastructure for user and resource management and to provide support for directory-enabled applications, such as Microsoft Exchange Server.

Active Directory Federation Services (AD FS)   AD FS provides Internet-based clients with a secure identity access solution that works on Windows and non-Windows operating systems. AD FS gives users the ability to do a single sign-on (SSO) and access applications on other networks without needing a secondary password.

Active Directory Lightweight Directory Services (AD LDS)   AD LDS is a directory service that provides flexible support for directory-enabled applications, without the dependencies and domain-related restrictions of AD DS.

Active Directory Rights Management Services (AD RMS)   AD RMS is the server role that provides an administrator with management and development tools that work with industry security technologies including encryption, certificates, and authentication to help organizations create reliable information protection solutions.

Device Health Attestation   Helps protect a corporate network by verifying that client systems meet corporate policy. For example, an administrator can make sure that all computers connected to a network have their proper updates, antivirus, and proper configuration policies before connecting to the network.

Dynamic Host Configuration Protocol (DHCP)   An Internet standard that allows organizations to reduce the administrative overhead of configuring hosts on a TCP/IP-based network. Some of the features include DHCP failover, policy-based assignment, and the ability to use Windows PowerShell for DHCP Server.

Domain Name System (DNS)   DNS services are used in TCP/IP networks. DNS will convert a computer name or fully qualified domain name (FQDN) to an IP address. DNS also has the ability to do a reverse lookup and convert an IP address to a computer name. DNS allows an administrator to locate computers and services using their user-friendly names.

Fax Server   Allows an administrator to send and receive faxes. It also allows an administrator to manage fax resources such as jobs, settings, reports, and fax devices on a specific computer or on the network.

File and Storage Services   Allows an administrator to set up and manage one or more file servers. These servers can provide a central location on a network where an administrator can store files and then share those files with network users. If users require access to the same files and applications or if centralized backup and file management are important issues for an organization, then administrators should set up the network servers as file servers.

Host Guardian Service (HGS)   Allows an administrator to have a more secure environment for the organization's virtual machines. The HGS role provides the Attestation & Key Protection services that enable Guarded Hosts to run Shielded virtual machines.

Hyper-V   Allows administrators to create and manage a virtualized environment by taking advantage of the technology built into the Windows Server 2016 operating system. When an administrator installs the Hyper-V role, all required virtualization components are installed. Some of the required components include the Windows hypervisor, Virtual Machine Management Service, the virtualization WMI provider, the virtual machine bus (VMbus), the virtualization service provider (VSP), and the virtual infrastructure driver (VID).

MultiPoint Services   Allows multiple users, each with their own independent and familiar Windows experience, to simultaneously share one computer.

Network Controller   Provides the point of automation needed for continual configuration, monitoring, and diagnostics of virtual networks, physical networks, network services, network topology, address management, and so on within a datacenter.

Network Policy and Access Services (NPS)   Administrators use this server role to install and configure Network Policy Server (NPS), which helps safeguard the security of a network.

Print and Document Services   Allows an administrator to centralize print server and network printer tasks. This role also allows an administrator to receive scanned documents from network scanners and route the documents to a shared network resource, Windows SharePoint Services site, or email addresses. Print and Document Services also provides fax servers with the ability to send and receive faxes while also giving the administrator the ability to manage fax resources such as jobs, settings, reports, and fax devices on the fax server.

Remote Access   Provides connectivity through DirectAccess, VPN, and Web Application Proxies. DirectAccess provides an Always On and Always Managed experience. Remote Access provides VPN access including site-to-site connectivity. Web Application Proxies enable web-based applications from a corporate network to client devices outside of the corporate network. Remote Access also includes routing capabilities, including Network Address Translation (NAT).

Remote Desktop Services   Allows for faster desktop and application deployments to any device, improving remote user effectiveness while aiding to keep critical data secure. Remote Desktop Services allows for both a virtual desktop infrastructure (VDI) and session-based desktops, allowing users to connect from anywhere.

Volume Activation Services   Helps an organization benefit from using this service to deploy and manage volume licenses for a medium to large number of computers.

Web Server (IIS)   Allows an administrator to set up a secure, easy-to-manage, modular, and extensible platform for reliably hosting websites, services, and applications.

Windows Deployment Services   Allows an administrator to install a Windows operating system over the network. Administrators do not have to install each operating system directly from a CD or DVD.

Windows Server Essentials Experience   Allows an administrator to set up the IT infrastructure and provides a powerful functions such as PC backups to help protect corporate data and Remote Web Access that allows access to business information from anywhere in the world. Windows Server Essentials Experience also allows for easy connection to cloud-based applications and services.

Windows Server Update Services (WSUS)   Allows administrators to deploy application and operating system updates. By deploying WSUS, administrators have the ability to manage updates that are released through Microsoft Update to computers in their network. This feature is integrated with the operating system as a server role on a Windows Server 2016 system.

Configure Windows Server Security Settings

All Windows operating systems include security settings that an administrator can use to help harden computer security profiles. Microsoft publishes these security baselines and are based on Microsoft security recommendations. These are created from real-world security experience obtained through a partnership with commercial organizations and the US government.

These security baselines include recommended settings for Windows Firewall, Windows Defender, and other security settings. These are provided as Group Policy object (GPO) backups that an administrator can import into Active Directory Domain Services (AD DS) and then deploy them to domain-joined servers. Ad administrator can also use the Local Script tools to configure standalone (non-domain-joined) servers.

Back Up Information and Systems

An administrator should perform scheduled backups, including any applications and data stored on Windows Server. This will help protect against attacks on the server. An administrator should perform backups frequently so that they can easily restore to a point-in-time prior to an attack.

An administrator can perform backup's on-premises by using solutions such as System Center Data Protection Manager or cloud-based backups by using Microsoft Azure Backup Server. There are also a number of backup solutions available from Microsoft partners.

Management and Monitoring Using Operations Management Suite

Microsoft Operations Management Suite (OMS) is a cloud-based IT management solution that helps administrators manage and protect their on-premises and cloud infrastructure. OMS is a cloud-based service, and an administrator can manage their apps, services, and infrastructure with minimal cost. OMS is updated periodically with new features and can help reduce an organizations ongoing maintenance and upgrade costs.

OMS also works with on-premises System Center components to broaden an organizations existing management investments on the cloud. System Center and OMS work together to provide a full hybrid management experience.

OMS offers the following capabilities and features:

- Automation and control—this feature automates administrative processes with runbooks using Windows PowerShell. Runbooks can access apps, operating systems, or services that are managed using PowerShell. It also provides configuration management with Windows PowerShell Desired State Configuration (DSC), which can enforce an organization's configuration settings on-premises and in Azure automatically.

- Insight and analytics—this feature can collect, correlate, search, and act on logs and performance data generated by Windows operating systems and apps. It provides real-time insights for all of an organization's workloads and servers, on-premises and in Azure.

- Protection and recovery—this feature can back up recovery workloads and servers. Azure Backup protects app data for on-premises and cloud-based servers. Azure Site Recovery helps provide disaster recovery by coordinating replication, failover, and recovery of on-premises Hyper-V virtual machines.

- Security and compliance—this feature identifies, assesses, and mitigates security risks. To ensure the ongoing security of an on-premises and cloud workloads and servers, it uses:
  - Security and Audit solution—collects and analyzes security events
  - Antimalware solution—provides current malware protection status
  - System Updates solution—provides current software update status

Protect Privileged Identities

Privileged identities are accounts that have an elevated privilege, such as a user account that is a member of the Domain Admins, Enterprise Admins, or Local Administrators. These can also include accounts that have been granted privileges directly, such as being able to perform backups or other rights listed in the User Rights Assignment node in the Local Security Policy console.

Administrators need to protect these privileged identities from attackers. It's important to understand how identities can get compromised; then an administrator can try to plan on preventing attackers from accessing these accounts.

Privileged identities can get compromised when an organization doesn't have guidelines in place on how to protect them. Some examples how privileged identities can get compromised:

- An organization is using more privileged accounts than are necessary.
- Being signed in with elevated privileges all the time, which allows for unlimited duration, can make the account susceptible to attack and increases the odds that the account can be compromised.
- Social engineering research. Most credential attackers start out by researching an organization and then conducting social engineering.
- Leveraging accounts with elevated privileges. Attackers can gain access to accounts with elevated permissions. One of the more common methods of doing so is by using the Pass-the-Hash or Pass-the-Token attacks.

TABLE 1.1   How to Prevent Attackers from Gaining Access to Privileged Identities

Methods used for preventing an attacker from gaining access to privileged identities	How to mitigate
More privileges than are necessary	Implement Just Enough Administration (JEA) for all IT administrators who administer Windows Server and the apps and services running on Windows Server by using Windows PowerShell.
Signed in using elevated privileges all the time	Implement Just in Time Administration (JIT) for all users who require elevated privileges so that the elevated privileges can only be used for a limited amount of time.

Methods used for preventing an attacker from gaining access to privileged identities	How to mitigate
Compromising identity and Pass-The-Hash attacks	Implement Microsoft Advanced Threat Analytics (ATA) to help detect compromised identities in on-premises workloads and servers. ATA is an on-premises solution that can be used to manage physical and virtualized workloads.
Pass-The-Hash attacks	Implement Credential Guard to help protect credentials from attacks. Can also implement Remote Credential Guard to help protect credentials from attacks such as Pass-the-Hash or Pass-the-Token that can be performed on servers that host Remote Desktop connections.
Just Enough Administration (JEA)	JEA is a security technology that helps restrict IT administrative rights using Windows PowerShell remoting. JEA uses the built-in capabilities of the Windows PowerShell scripting environment and implements role-based access control (RBAC). An administrator can configure JEA as a Windows PowerShell session endpoint on any computer to manage that computer or remote computers.
	With JEA, an administrator connects using a regular, non-elevated user credentials. After JEA authorizes the account, the JEA runs the Windows PowerShell commands specified by using an elevated virtual account on the targeted computer. With this approach the user account is never actually signed in by using elevated credentials.
Just in Time Administration (JIT)	JIT Administration is a security best practice that allows an administrator to only use elevated identities when performing IT administration tasks.
	Microsoft provides JIT administration using the following:
	■ Local Administrator Password Solution (LAPS)— available as a free download to help manage local administrator password on Windows operating systems in your organization.
	■ Microsoft Identity Manager 2016—an on-premises identity and access management system that provides JIT administration.
Advanced Threat Analytics (ATA)	ATA is an on-premises product that helps detect identity compromise in an organization. ATA has the ability to capture and parse network traffic for authentication, authorization, and information gathering protocols. ATA uses this data to build a profile about users and other entities on a network so that it can detect anomalies and known attack patterns.

TABLE 1.1 How to Prevent Attackers from Gaining Access to Privileged Identities *(continued)*

Methods used for preventing an attacker from gaining access to privileged identities	How to mitigate
Credential Guard	Credential Guard uses virtualization-based security for encryption so that only privileged system processes can access them. It is used to help protect privileged identities by protecting the credentials on Windows Server 2016. Credential Guard uses: ▪ Virtualization-based security (required) ▪ Secure boot (required) ▪ TPM 2.0 either discrete or firmware (preferred—provides binding to hardware) The virtualization-based security requires: ▪ 64-bit CPU ▪ CPU virtualization extensions plus extended page tables ▪ Windows hypervisor
Remote Credential Guard	Remote Credential Guard helps protect credentials over a Remote Desktop connection by keeping the credentials on the device hosting the RDP connection and redirecting Kerberos requests back to the device that establishes the connection. If the server (or client) hosting the Remote Desktop connection is compromised, the credentials are not exposed because the credentials and credential derivatives are never sent to the device hosting the Remote Desktop connection. To use Remote Credential Guard, the Remote Desktop client and server must meet the following requirements: ▪ Must be joined to an Active Directory domain and be in the same domain or a domain with a trust relationship. ▪ Must use Kerberos authentication. ▪ Must be running at least Windows 10 version 1607 or Windows Server 2016. ▪ The Remote Desktop classic Windows app is required. The Remote Desktop Universal Windows Platform app doesn't support Remote Credential Guard. You can enable Remote Credential Guard by using a registry setting on the Remote Desktop server and Group Policy or a Remote Desktop Connection parameter on the Remote Desktop client.

Methods used for preventing an attacker from gaining access to privileged identities	How to mitigate
Harden the Windows Server	Windows Server 2016 includes built-in security mechanisms and powerful security tools that can be configured to further lock down the server.
Control Flow Guard	Control Flow Guard is built into Windows to help protect the operating system and applications from a class of memory corruption—based attacks.
Windows Defender	Windows Defender is included in the Windows operating system. It helps protect Windows devices against viruses, malware, spyware, and other threats. Windows Defender has been optimized for running on Windows Server and is enabled by default in Windows Server 2016.

The advanced security features include:

- Virus protection and removal

- Malware protection and removal

- Spyware protection and removal

- Boot-time protection

- Real-time protection

- Cloud-based protection

    - Network inspection and protection

    - Free automatic updates to antimalware definitions and Windows Defender itself

Can configure Windows Defender by using Group Policy, Windows PowerShell, Windows Management Instrumentation (WMI), or interactively through the Windows Defender user interface. The Windows Server security baselines also include Microsoft recommended settings for Windows Defender.

TABLE 1.1 How to Prevent Attackers from Gaining Access to Privileged Identities *(continued)*

Methods used for preventing an attacker from gaining access to privileged identities	How to mitigate
Device Guard	Device Guard provides the ability to specify which binaries are authorized to run on a server, including user mode and kernel mode binaries.
	Helps protect against the following threats:
	▪ Exposure to new malware for which no malware signature is yet known
	▪ Exposure to unsigned code as most malware is unsigned
	▪ Malware that gains access to the kernel and then captures sensitive information or damages the system
	Device Guard code integrity policies can be run in the following modes:
	▪ In audit mode, Device Guard will trigger an audit log event whenever a non-authorized binary is running but will not block the binary from running. The Device Guard logs are available in the following event log: Logs\Microsoft\Windows\CodeIntegrity\Operational.
	Audit mode allows an administrator to identify apps that are note wanted in the organization. Can create a code integrity policy file based on the captured audit information in the event log.
	▪ In enforcement mode, Device Guard will block any binary that should be denied. Should configure Device Guard for enforcement mode after a selected group of devices in audit mode has identified the apps to allow.
Secure Boot	Secure Boot is an industry standard that helps ensure that a device boots only software that is trusted by the device manufacturer. Secure Boot helps protect devices from rootkits and other low-level malware attacks by blocking unauthorized (non-signed) software.
	When a device starts, the device firmware checks the signature for each piece of boot software to ensure they are trusted. If all boot software signatures can be confirmed, the firmware starts the operating system.
	Need to ensure that Secure Boot is enabled in the device's firmware.

Methods used for preventing an attacker from gaining access to privileged identities	How to mitigate
Operations Management Suite (OMS)	An administrator can use OMS to help detect threats as well as identify devices that are not current on software updates and antimalware definitions.
Improve threat detection	Threat detection is an essential part of Windows Server security. The sooner a threat can be detected the quicker an administrator can react before an attacker can reach full control. Microsoft provides threat detection for servers using Windows Defender Advanced Thread Protection (ATP).

Selecting Server Hardware

When choosing what server to use and what hardware components make up the server, keep the following in mind. First, the server is designed to provide network services. Since a server is designed to be used by multiple users at the same time, the server is usually much more powerful than most client PCs. Remember that, if the server fails or becomes inaccessible, the problem will affect multiple people. Therefore, you need to choose hardware that is less prone to failure than a normal client PC and has some redundancy built in. You also need to make up plans so you know how to deal with these problems when they occur.

Certification Ready?

What subsystems affect server performance the most? 5.1

The primary subsystems that make up a server are:

- Processor
- Memory
- Storage
- Network

If any of these fails, the entire system can fail. In addition, if any one of these is asked to do more than what it was designed for, it can cause a bottleneck that may affect the performance of the entire system.

While you strive for a 100% up-time, it is next to impossible to get it over a long enough period of time. However, by anticipating the type of failure that could occur, adding additional servers, components, or technology that will make the system more fault tolerant, and making up good plans so that you can react quickly when a failure occurs, you can mediate much of this to reduce your chances of a failure and to reduce the effect of a failure. In addition, while you need to spend money to make a system more fault tolerant, just about every organization has a limit on how much money they can put toward a server or network service.

The subsystems just listed are not the only components that make up the server but are the primary ones that are often looked at when determining what a server can handle. Servers may also include sound cards, but normally do not need to provide sound to multiple users using the sound card. Instead, data will be sent over the network to an individual client, and the client sound card will produce the sound. The same could also be said for video. You are not going to have 20 monitors connected to a single computer providing graphics. Therefore, you do not normally require a high-performance video system for the server.

Processor

The computer, including servers, is built around one or more integrated chips called the *processor*. It is considered the brain of the computer since all of the instructions it performs are mathematical calculations and logical comparisons. Today's processors are mostly produced by Intel and AMD.

Today, the clock speed of the processor is usually expressed in gigahertz (GHz). A gigahertz is 1 billion (1,000,000,000) cycles per second. During each cycle, a circuit will react in a predictable way (bring in a value, perform a calculation, or perform a comparison). It is these reactions that make the computer do what it does. Of course, if a processor runs at a faster speed, it would be safe to assume it could do more in a quicker amount of time.

Over the last several years, though, speed is not the only factor that determines processor performance. Today, processors sold today are multi-core processors, which are like having two or more processing cores packaged as one. In addition, they use other technologies to keep the processor working at peak efficiency much like using an assembly line approach or trying to anticipate what it needs to do first so that it can keep the pipelines always working.

Having additional cores doesn't always mean a linear increase in performance. For example, having two cores doesn't always means that you get double the performance. In these cases, performance is limited by how well the software is optimized to use both cores.

Another factor is how much data a processor can process. Today's processors are 64-bit processors as compared to the older 32-bit processors. A 64-bit processor is a processor with a default word size of 64 bits and 64-bit external data bus. Most people don't realize that today's processors can already handle 64-bit calculations (remember every value, small and large numbers, and numbers with decimal points are broken down into 0s and 1s (bits)). Most processors internally can process 128, 256, and maybe larger numbers. But one of the main benefits of 64-bit processors is that they can process significantly more memory than 32-bit processors (4 GB with a 32-bit address bus and 64 GB with a 36-bit address bus). Technically a 64-bit processor can access up to 16.3 billion gigabytes (16 exabytes). The AMD64 architecture currently has a 52 bit limit on physical memory (which supports up to 4 petabytes or 4048 terabytes) and only supports a 48-bit virtual address space (256 terabytes). Usually, you will reach the limit of the motherboard or memory chips before you reach the limit of the processor.

With more data in memory, a 64-bit processor can work faster because it can access larger amounts of RAM instead of swapping data back and forth with the much slower disks. In addition, with the larger internal registrys, it can process larger numbers without breaking them into several smaller numbers, and it can even take several smaller numbers and do some mathematically calculation or comparison to these numbers at the same time. Today, just about every computer processor sold is a 64-bit processor.

Today's 64-bit processors include virtualization technology (VT), which enables a processor to act as if it were several processors working in parallel, to enable several operating systems to run at the same time in the same machine. As of this writing, to run Microsoft's Hyper-V, which is Microsoft's virtualization software, you need to have processors and BIOS that support virtualization technology.

If an operating system and programs are written to use the larger 64-bit calculations and use the additional accessible memory, the processing power of a computer can be significantly increased. Most programs designed for a computer running a 32-bit version of Windows will work on a computer running 64-bit versions of Windows. Notable exceptions are some antivirus programs and some hardware drivers. The biggest problem that you may encounter is finding 64-bit drivers for some of your older hardware devices.

RAM

RAM, which stands for random access memory, is the computer's short-term or temporary memory. It stores instructions and data that the processor accesses directly. If you have more RAM, you can load more instructions and data from the disks. In addition, having sufficient RAM can be one the largest factor in your overall computer performance. Unfortunately, if power is discontinued from the RAM such as what occurs when you shut off your PC, the contents of the RAM disappear. This is the reason you use disks for long-term storage.

Storage

Traditionally, hard *drives* are half electronic/half mechanical devices that store magnetic fields on rotating platters. Today, some hard drives, known as solid-state drives, are electronic devices with no mechanical components. Since solid-state drives do not contain mechanical components, they are much faster than half electronic/half mechanical devices. While most personal computers have only local storage consisting of internal hard drives, servers may connect to external storage through a network-attached storage (NAS) or storage area network (SAN).

Most systems today have some form of optical drive. Older systems will have compact disk drives, which use disks similar to a music CD player. Newer systems have either a DVD or Blu-Ray drive. In either case, the optical drives store information using laser light. Traditional, optical disks were considered as read-only devices, but many systems have burning capabilities that allow the user to write data to special optical disks.

Network Connections

The last primary component that makes up a server is the *network connection*. Without a network connection, the server will not be able to communicate with other servers and the clients. Most servers will include one or more network interface cards or NICs. Since servers are designed to support many network connections, you must have the available bandwidth from the server. Today, the minimum speed of today's server network cards are 1 Gbits/sec or faster.

The Motherboard

Another component that brings these four subsystems together is the *motherboard*. For the processor to communicate with the rest of the system, the processor plugs in or connects to a large circuit board called the motherboard or system board. The motherboard allows the processor to branch out and communicate with all of the other computer components. While everything is made around the processor, the motherboard is considered the nervous system of the PC. While the capabilities of the motherboard have been greatly expanded (most include sound and network connectivity), you can further expand the capabilities of the system by installing expansion cards, sometimes referred to as daughter boards. See Figure 1.2.

FIGURE 1.2   A motherboard connected to power supply and disk drives

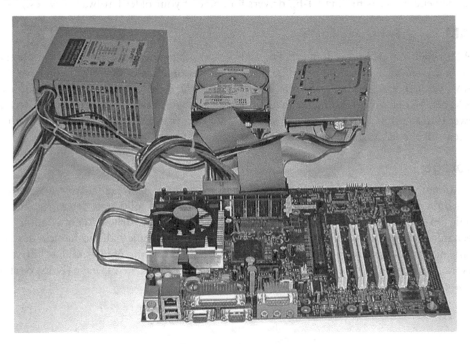

On the motherboard, you will find the processors, RAM, motherboard chipset, and the motherboard BIOS. The chipset would represent the nerve clusters that connect your various components including the keyboard, disk drives, and RAM. Depending on the design of the motherboard, one chipset will run faster than another chipset or have more redundant features. Of course, these types of systems usually cost more.

On the motherboard and expansion cards, you will find firmware. *Firmware* is software contained in read-only memory (ROM) chips. Different from RAM, ROM instructions are permanent and can't be changed or erased except with special software. So when you shut off your computer, those instructions remain so that when you turn your computer on again, it knows how to boot the system, test the system, and find a boot device such as your hard drive.

Instructions that control much of the computer's input/output functions, such as communicating with disks, RAM, and the monitor kept in the System ROM chips are known as the *BIOS* (basic input/output system). You can think of the BIOS as the instincts of the computer. By having instructions (software) written on the BIOS, the system already knows how to communicate with some basic components such as a keyboard and how to read some basic disks such as IDE drives. It also looks for additional ROM chips, which may be on the motherboard or on expansion cards that you add to the system. These additional ROM chips will have additional instructions to operate additional devices such as adding SCSI or RAID drives.

If you have not realized it by now, the instructions written on the BIOS is software. Different from the normal software you purchase at a store or order off the Internet, it is not written on a disk. Unfortunately like any software, the BIOS may need to have a bug fixed or may need to be expanded to support a new type of hardware that did not exist when the BIOS was written. Sometimes a newer BIOS version can lead to better system performance. To overcome some problems, you would have to check with your system or motherboard manufacturer to see if they have a new version of the BIOS that you can download and apply to your system. The process of updating your system ROM BIOS is called flashing the BIOS.

Unfortunately, flashing the BIOS is a delicate process. If the process gets interrupted partway while you are flashing the BIOS or you install the wrong version, your system may not become accessible, and you may need to replace your motherboard to overcome the problem.

Therefore, if it is your first time in flashing a system, you should do it a couple of times with someone who has done it before. In addition, you should enter your BIOS or CMOS Setup program and write down all of your current settings in case you have to restore your previous settings. Lastly, be sure to thoroughly review the system or motherboard manufacturer to determine what version of the BIOS your system has and which is the correct version to download and install. You will then download the BIOS image and some executable program to flash the BIOS.

To enter the BIOS or CMOS setup program, you would press a key or combination of keys early during the boot process before the operating system loads. Common keys are usually the Del key or F10 key. To find out which key or keys, you should look at the screen during boot up or access the server or motherboard manual.

WARNING   You want to make sure you don't have any mishaps such as power failures or someone tripping over the power cord while you are doing the upgrade. Remember if the process stops partway through, the system may become unusable.

Power Supplies and Cases

Before moving on, there should be a quick discussion on power supplies and cases. A case provides an enclosure that helps protect the components that are inside of the case. The case with the power supplies and additional fans are usually designed to provide a fair amount of airflow through the system to keep the system cool. Typically if you have items that are designed for performance, they can produce a good amount of heat, and too much heat is always bad for electronic and mechanical devices.

The *power supply* can be thought of as the blood of the computer. The computer runs on electricity. Without it, the computer will be just a box. Since power supplies are half electronic and half mechanical devices, they are considered high failure items when you compare then to pure electronic devices such as memory chips or processors. Mechanical devices tend to wear out over a period of time. Therefore, servers may have redundant power supplies. In addition, to resist power outages or even power fluctuations, the server or server room may be connected to one or more uninterruptable power supplies (UPSs) and/or power generators.

Ports

Servers are still computers. As with any computer, you still need to be able to add external devices to the server. *Ports* are plug sockets that enable an external device such as a printer, keyboard, mouse or external drive. These ports are usually identified by the shape of the plug socket, the number of pins, the number of rows of pins, and the orientation of the pins (male or female). The most popular ports are:

- Parallel port—2-row, 25-pin female D port. Considered a legacy port that used to connect printers.

- Serial port—2-row, 9 pin male D port. While considered a legacy port, is often used to connect to switches and routers to configure them. It can also be used to connect legacy keyboards, mice, and printers.

- VGA port—3-row, 15-pin female D connector. Used to connect a monitor to the computer.

- Universal Serial Bus (USB)—A popular device that can be used to connect keyboards, mice, printers, modems, and external disk drives.

- PS/2Mouse or Keyboard port—6-pin Mouse mini0DIN. Port used to connect a legacy mouse.

- RJ-45 Connector—Used to connect a 10Base-T/100Base-T/1000Base-T network cable.

- DVI-I—A high-quality video interface designed to replace VGA ports.

   See Figure 1.3.

FIGURE 1.3   Common ports (PS/2 keyboard and mouse ports, serial port, parallel port, 1394 port, several USB port, Ethernet port, DVI-I port, and VGA port)

Comparing Servers and Workstations

When you purchase any computer, you can usually choose between a mobile computer, a personal computer, a workstation, or a server. Mobile computers are not designed to be stand-alone servers. A personal computer and workstation are designed for a single user. The workstation usually contains components for faster performance over a standard inexpensive personal computer so that they can perform heavy graphics or extensive mathematical calculations. But again, a workstation is designed for only one person.

A server, on the other hand, has two goals. First since servers are designed to support many users, they often have an increased load compared to a single user computer. Second, since many users can rely on accessing a server, the server needs to be reliable. Therefore, servers often contain components that are fault-tolerant and reliable (such as redundant power supplies, redundant hard drives, and redundant network cards). Therefore, systems designated as servers contain additional circuitry to detect problems with the system including the system overheating, a fan has failed, and even if a system has been opened. Of course, the system being opened is more of a security feature than a fault-tolerant component.

While servers typically have high-performance items, they often do not have the newest and fastest items. Instead, the server will have components that perform well but that have been thoroughly tested and are considered reliable.

Comparing Physical Servers and Virtual Servers

Certification Ready?

What can virtual servers do for a corporation? 2.5

So far, the discussion has been focused mostly on physical servers. Over the last few years, virtualization has become more popular. Virtual machines or *virtual servers* technology enable multiple operating systems to run concurrently on a single machine. This allows for a separation of services so that changes on one virtual server will not affect the other virtual servers. In addition, it allows a better utilization of hardware since most hardware is sitting idle most of the time with nothing to do. Therefore, by placing several virtual servers on a powerful server, you can better utilize the hardware while keeping cost to a minimum. In addition, it can easily and quickly create Windows test environments in a safe, self-contained environment.

One leader of virtualization is VMware. To compete against VMware, Microsoft includes Hyper-V, which is a replacement to Microsoft's Virtual Server and Virtual PC.

Locating the Server

After you select and purchase the server and its components, you also need to figure out where it should go. The server room is the work area of the Information Technology (IT) department that contains the servers and most of the communication devices including switches and routers. The room should be secure, with only a handful of people allowed to have access to it. Of course, the room should be secure and locked when not in use and possibly include some type of biometric access that also provides a log of who enters the server room. The server room should also provide clean power and uninterruptable power and proper cooling. It should also contain equipment to perform proper backups.

When you purchase a server, you can choose from numerous sizes and form factors. Larger server rooms with lots of servers will typically contain servers that fit horizontally into a rack. Since these servers are the same width, you can stack 10–20 servers within a rack or server cage. The size of a piece of rack mounted equipment is frequently described as a number in "U". For example, one rack unit is often referred to as "1U", 2 rack units as "2U", and so on. One rack unit is 1.75 inches (44.45 mm) high.

Other servers stand upright and are usually not made to be stacked on top of each other. Of course, servers that stand upright typically take up more room than a stackable server, especially when you have multiple servers.

Selecting the Software

Software is the instructions that the hardware follows and makes the computer do what it does. It also provides us with an interface so that we can use, configure, and manage the computer. With a server, you would first choose the operating system, choose the roles that the operating system provides, and then install any additional software to make the server do what you want. Fortunately, Microsoft includes a wide range of network programs and servers included with their Windows Server products and also has a wide range of additional products to expand what a server can do.

Windows NT (first released in 1993) is a family of operating systems produced by Microsoft. Since then, Microsoft has built on top of the previous version and has released Windows 2000 Server, Windows Server 2003, Windows Server 2003 R2, Windows Server 2008, Windows Server 2008 R2, Windows Server 2012, Windows Server 2012 R2, and Windows Server 2016.

The newest client operating system released by Microsoft is Windows 10. In the past when a Microsoft client operating system was released, the server version was also released. Windows 7 is paired with Windows Server 2008 R2. Windows 8 is paired with Windows Server 2012, and Windows 8.1 is paired with Windows Server 2012 R2. However, Microsoft decided to release Microsoft Server 2016 almost a year after the release of Windows 10.

Windows Server 2016 builds on previous Windows servers operating systems, expanding existing technology and adding new features to enable IT professionals to increase the reliability and flexibility of their server infrastructures. New virtualization tools, Web resources, and management enhancements help save time, reduce costs, and provide a platform for a dynamic and efficiently managed data center and provide security enhancements. Powerful tools such as Internet Information Services (IIS) version 10, updated Server Manager and Hyper-V platforms, and Windows PowerShell version 5.0 combine to give customers greater control, increased efficiency, and the ability to react to front-line business needs faster than ever before. If you don't know what all of these means, hang on, we will eventually go over all of this.

Similar to previous Windows Servers operating systems, there are multiple editions of Windows 2016.

Windows Server 2016 Essentials Edition   This edition corresponds to the Windows Small Business Server from earlier versions of Windows Server, and it is designed for small businesses. It allows up to 25 users and 50 devices. It supports two processor cores and up to 64 gigabytes (GB) of random access memory (RAM). It does not support many of the features of Windows Server 2016, including virtualization.

Windows Server 2016 Standard Edition   This edition is designed for physical server environments with little or no virtualization. It provides many of the roles and features available for the Windows Server 2016 operating system, and it supports up to 64 processor sockets and up to 4 terabytes (TB) of RAM. It includes licenses for up to two virtual machines and supports Nano Server installation. Licensing is processor core based.

Windows Server 2016 Datacenter Edition   Because it includes unlimited Windows Server–based virtual machine licenses for unlimited Windows Server–based virtual machines that run on the same physical server, this edition is ideal for highly virtualized infrastructures, including private cloud and hybrid cloud environments. It provides all of the roles and features available for the Windows Server 2016 operating system, and it supports up to 64 processor sockets, up to 640 processor cores, and up to 4 TB of RAM. It also includes new features such as Storage Spaces Direct and Storage Replica, along with new Shielded Virtual Machines and features for software-defined data center scenarios. Licensing is processor core based.

Microsoft Hyper-V Server 2016   This edition acts as a stand-alone virtualization server for virtual machines. It includes all new features around virtualization in Windows Server 2016. Although it supports limited file server features, it does not support other Windows server roles. Although the host operating system has no licensing cost, the virtual machines must be licensed separately. It supports up to 64 processor sockets and up to 4 TB of RAM. It supports domain joining. Different from the Standard and Datacenter editions, Hyper-V Server edition does not have a GUI, but it does have a user interface that displays a menu of configuration tasks.

Windows Storage Server 2016 Workgroup Edition   This edition is meant as an entry-level unified storage appliance. It allows 50 users, one processor core, and 32 GB of RAM.

Windows Storage Server 2016 Standard Edition   This edition is meant as a unified storage appliance that supports up to 64 sockets but is licensed on a two-socket, incrementing basis. It supports up to 4 TB of RAM, and it includes two virtual machine licenses. It includes Domain Name System (DNS) and Dynamic Host Configuration Protocol (DHCP) server roles, but does not support others, including Active Directory Domain Services (AD DS), Active Directory Certificate Services (AD CS), and Active Directory Federation Services (AD FS). Licensing is processor core based.

For small data centers that consist of only a few servers, you should consider Windows Server 2016 Standard edition. For large data centers that will use powerful physical servers or blades, you should consider purchasing a Datacenter edition for each physical server or blade. However, both are licensed based on the number of cores within the physical processors.

Since 64-bit processors have become the industry standard for systems ranging from the most scalable servers to desktop PCs, Windows Server 2016 is only available in 64-bit version. Like earlier Windows server operating system, Windows Server 20016 will provide for 32-bit applications with Windows on Windows 64, or WOW64. Both 32-bit and 64-bit applications can run natively on x64 processors, with Windows Server managing the transitions—resulting in excellent performance for both. The end result is a platform that utilizes the existing wealth of 32-bit applications while also providing a smooth migration path to 64-bit computing.

Introducing Server Roles in Windows Server 2016

A server is designed to provide services. Therefore, Windows Server 2016 has organized the most common services into server roles, whereas a server role describes the function of the server. When you define a server role in Windows Server 2016 (see Table 1.2), you are installing and configure a set of software programs that allow a computer to perform a specific function for multiple users or other computers within a network.

TABLE 1.2   Available roles in Windows Server 2016

Role Name	Description
Active Directory Certificate Services	Provides service for creating and managing public key certificates used in software security systems that employing public key technologies to prove the identity of person, device, or service, which can be used by secure mail, secure wireless networks, virtual private networks (VPNs), Internet Protocol Security (IPSec), Encrypting File System (EFS), smart card logon, and others. For ease of use, the digital certificates interface with Microsoft's Active Directory.
Active Directory Domain Services	To transform a server into a domain controller to provide a directory service via Microsoft's Active Directory (AD), which stores information about users, computers, and other devices on the network. Active Directory helps administrators securely manage this information and facilitates resource sharing and collaboration between users. Active Directory is required for directory-enabled applications such as Microsoft Exchange Server (email server) and to apply other Windows Server technologies such as Group Policy.
Active Directory Federation Services	Active Directory Federation Services provides Web single sign-on (SSO) technologies to authenticate a user to multiple Web applications using a single user account.
Active Directory Lightweight Directory Services (ADLDS)	For applications that require a director for store application data as a data store without installing Active Directory domain services. Since this run as a non-operating-system service allows multiple instances of AD LDS to run concurrently on a single server, and each instance can be configured independently for servicing multiple applications.
Active Directory Rights Management Services (AD RMS)	Technology that works with Active Directory RMS enabled applications to help safeguard digital information from unauthorized use by specifying who can use the information and what they can do with it (open, modify, print, forward, and/or take other actions with the information).
Dynamic Host Configuration Protocol (DHCP) Server	Allows servers to assign, or lease, IP addresses to computers and other devices that are enabled as DHCP clients.
Domain Name System (DNS) Server	Provides naming service that associates names with numeric Internet addresses. This makes it possible for users to refer to network computers by using easy-to-remember names instead of a long series of numbers. Windows DNS services can be integrated with Dynamic Host Configuration Protocol (DHCP) services on Windows, eliminating the need to add DNS records as computers are added to the network.

TABLE 1.2   Available roles in Windows Server 2016 *(continued)*

Role Name	Description
Fax Server	Sends and receives faxes, and allows you to manage fax resources such as jobs, settings, reports, and fax devices on this computer or on the network.
File and Storage Services	Provides technologies for storage management, file replication, distributed namespace management, fast file searching, and streamlined client access to files.
Hyper-V	Provides the services that you can use to create and manage virtual machines (virtualized computer system that operates in an isolated execution environment which allows you to run multiple operating systems simultaneously) and their resources.
Network Policy and Access Services	Delivers a variety of methods (including using VPN servers, dial-up servers, routers, and 802.11 protected wireless access points) to provide users with local and remote network connectivity, to connect network segments, and to allow network administrators to centrally manage network access and client health policies.
Print and Document Services	Enables users to print to and manage centralized printers that are connected directly or indirectly to print servers.
Remote Access	Provides seamless connectivity through DirectAccess, Virtual Private Network (VPN), and Web Application Proxy.
Remote Desktop Services	Allows users to connect to a terminal server to remotely run programs, use network resources, and access the Windows desktop on that server.
Web Server (IIS)	Enables sharing of information on the Internet, an intranet, or an extranet via a unified Web platform that integrates Internet Information Server (IIS) 10 to provides web pages, File Transfer Protocol (FTP) services or newsgroups, ASP.NET, Windows Communication Foundation, and Windows SharePoint Services.
Windows Deployment Services	Used to install and configure Microsoft Windows operating systems remotely on computers with Pre-boot Execution Environment (PXE) boot ROMs.
Windows Server Update service	Allows network administrators to specify the Microsoft updates that should be installed and to create separate groups of computers for different sets of updates.

Introducing Server Features in Windows Server 2016

Windows Server 2016 Features are software programs that are not directly part of a role. Instead, they are often used to augment the functionality of one or more role or enhance the functionality of the entire server. The features that are included in Windows Server 2016 are shown in Table 1.3.

TABLE 1.3   Features available in Windows Server 2016

Feature Name	Description
.NET Framework 3.5 Features	Combines .NET Framework 2.0 Application Programming Interface (APIs) with new technologies to build applications with appealing user interfaces and provide various forms of security for those services.
NET Framework 4.6 Features	Provides a consistent programming model and APIs that are required for some programs to function.
Background Intelligent Transfer Service (BITS)	Short for Background Intelligence Service, allows a client computer to transfer files in the foreground or background asynchronously so that the responsiveness of other network applications are preserved.
BitLocker Drive Encryption	Helps protect data on disks by encrypting the entire volume.
Containers	Provides services and tools to create and manage Windows Server Containers and their resources. Containers are isolated, resource-controlled, and portable operating environments that can be moved from server to server as needed.
Failover Clustering	Allows multiple servers to work together to provide high availability of services and applications. If one server fails, a second server is available to take over its work.
Group Policy Management	A Microsoft Management Console snap-in that allows easy management of Active Directory Group Policies to secure or standardize a network environment.
LPR Port Monitor	Enables the computer to print to printers that are shared using a Line Printer Daemon (LPD) service. LPD service is commonly used by UNIX-based computers and printer-sharing devices.
Message Queuing	Provides guaranteed message delivery, efficient routing, security, and priority-based messaging between applications.

TABLE 1.3   Features available in Windows Server 2016 *(continued)*

Feature Name	Description
Multipath I/O	Along with the Microsoft Device Specific Module (DSM) or a third-party DSM, provides support for using multiple data paths to a storage device on Windows.
Network Load Balancing	Distributes traffic across several servers, using the TCP/IP networking protocol. NLP is particularly useful for ensuring that stateless application such as web servers running IIS are scalable by adding additional servers as the load increases.
Peer Name Resolution Protocol	Allows applications to register and resolve names on your computer so that other computers communicate with these applications.
Quality Windows Audio Video Experience	A networking platform for audio and video streaming applications on IP home networks.
Remote Assistance	Enables you or a support person to offer assistance to users with computer issues or questions.
Remote Differential Compression	Computes and transfers the differences between two objects over a network using minimal bandwidth.
Remote Server Administration Tools	Includes a MMC snap-in and a command-line tool to remotely manage roles and features.
RPC over HTTP Proxy	Relays RPC traffic from client applications over HTTP to the server as an alternative to clients accessing the server over a VPN connection.
Simple TCP/IP Services	Supports Character Generator, Daytime, Discard, Echo and Quote of the Day TCP/IP services.
SMTP Server	Supports the transfer of email messages between email systems. SMTP is short for Simple Mail Transfer Protocol.
SNMP Services	Includes the SNMP service and SNMP WMI provider. SNMP is short for Simple Network Management Protocol. SNMP is used in network management systems to monitor network-attached devices for conditions that warrant administrative attention.
Telnet Client	Uses the Telnet protocol to connect to a remote Telnet server and run applications on that server.
TFTP Client	Allows to read files or write files to a remote Trivial FTP (TFTP) server.

Feature Name	Description
Windows Defender	Helps protect your machine against malware.
Windows Internal Database	A relational data store that can be used only by Windows roles and features.
Windows PowerShell	A command-line shell and scripting language.
Windows Process Activation Service	Generalizes the IIS process model, removing the dependency on HTTP.
Windows Search Service	Allows you to back up and recover your operating system, applications, and data.
Windows Server Backup	Allows you to back up and recover your operating system, applications, and data.
Windows Server Migration Tools	Includes Windows PowerShell cmdlets that facilitate migration of server roles, operating system settings, files, and shares from other servers running Windows Server 2016 or earlier operating systems to Windows Server 2016.
WINS Server	WINS, short for Windows Internet Naming Service, provides a distributed database for registering and querying dynamic mappings of NetBIOS names for computers and groups used on your network.
Wireless LAN Service	Configure and starts the WLAN AutoConfig service, regardless of whether the computer has any wireless adapters.
XPS Viewer	Used to read, set permissions for, and digitally sign XPS documents.

Comparing Full Version Server Core and Nano Server

Starting with Windows Server 2008, you can install Windows in one of two modes: Windows Server 2016 with Desktop Experience or Windows Server 2016 Server Core, both of which are provided on the installation DVD. When you think of the Full Version, the full version is the normal version that you would expect of Windows with a fully functionally GUI interface.

Server Core installation provides a minimal environment with no File Explorer or Desktop shell for running specific server roles and no Start button. See Figure 1.4. Just about the only thing that you can see is a command prompt window to type in commands. Since the system has a minimal environment, the system runs more efficiently, focusing on what it needs to provide instead of processing fancy graphics for you to manage the system.

It also reduces the attack surface for those server roles because not all of the components that Windows has will be running that could be exploited by a hacker.

FIGURE 1.4 A server running Server Core

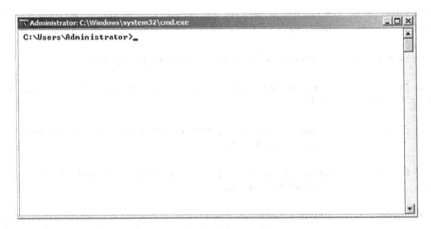

A Server Core machine can be configured for the following roles:

- Active Directory Lightweight Directory Services (ADLDS)
- DHCP Server
- DNS Server
- Domain controller/Active Directory Domain Services
- File Services (including DFSR and NFS)
- IIS 10
- web server (but does not include ASPNET, .Net Framework, IIS Management Console, IIS Legacy Snap-In and IIS FTP Management)
- Print Services
- Streaming Media Services
- Terminal Services including Easy Print, TS Remote Programs, and TS Gateway
- Windows Server Virtualization

A Server Core machine can be configured for the following features:

- Backup
- Bitlocker Drive Encryption
- Failover Clustering

- Multipath IO
- Network Load Balancing
- Removable Storage
- Simple Network Management Protocol (SNMP)
- Subsystem for UNIX-based applications
- Telnet client
- Windows Internet Name Service (WINS)

Nano Server is a new installation option that was introduced with Windows Server 2016. Nano Server is administered remotely and optimized for hosting in private clouds and data centers. The Nano Server runs from a VHD, either from within Hyper-V or you can boot directly from the VHD at startup. It has a smaller hardware footprint than Windows Server Core, it has no local sign-in capability, and it supports only 64-bit applications, tools, and agents.

Installing Windows Server 2016

Before you can start using, managing, or configuring an operating system, you will need to first install the operating system.

Certification Ready?

Can you list all of the methods to install Windows? 1.3

Although the hardware requirements to support Windows Server 2016 will depend on the servers that the server is hosting, the load on the server, and how responsive you want your server to be. However, Table 1.4 show the Windows Server 2016 on a physical machine:

- Processor: A 64-bit processor running 1.4 GHz
- RAM: 512 MB
- Free hard drive space: 32 GB

TABLE 1.4   System requirements for Windows Server 2016

Component	Requirement
Processor	Minimum: 1.4 GHz (x64 processor)
	Maximum number of physical sockets: 1 (Foundation) 4 (Web and Standard), 8 (Enterprise), 64 (Datacenter)
Memory	Minimum: 512 MB RAM
	Maximum: 24 TB
Disk Space Requirements	Minimum: 32 GB or greater
Display	Super VGA (1024 × 768) or higher resolution monitor
Other	DVD Drive, Keyboard and Microsoft Mouse (or compatible pointing device), network adapter, and Internet access

If you want to run the Desktop Experience, you should increase the requirements even more. Although Microsoft states that you would need an additional 4 GB of free disk space, you should consider two core processors running at 1.4 GHz, 2 GB of memory, and 50 GB free as the minimum if you desire fair performance. Then based on the server roles and applications the server will run, you will increase the requirements even further. You should also add additional disk space if you are to perform a network installation or for computers with more than 16 GB of RAM.

In addition, storage and network adapters must be PCI Express compliant. Ethernet adapters should be at least gigabit throughput. The graphics device and monitor should be capable of Super VGA (1024 × 768). If you need to install Windows Server 2016, you will also need a DVD drive.

The requirements for Nano Server will depend on the features and roles installed. The smallest Nano Server VHD will be approximately 440 MB. But after installing IIS or commonly used drivers, the VHD with IIS will be just over 500 MB.

 Remember, the amount of RAM and disk space is not the place to skimp. At the time this book was written, the requirements listed above were the current requirements. Make sure to check the Microsoft website for the most current information.

Nano Server Installation

Windows Server 2016 introduced a new type of server installation called Nano Server. Nano Server allows an administrator to remotely administer the server operating system. It was largely designed and created for private clouds and datacenters.

Nano Server is similar to Microsoft Windows Server Core, but the Nano Server operating system uses considerably less hard drive space, has no local logon or GUI capabilities, and only supports 64-bit applications and tools.

Installing Windows Server 2016 Nano Server

Since Nano Server takes up much less hard drive space and does not have many of the normal server components, it is faster when it comes to setups, reboots, and updates. Nano Server is available for Windows Server 2016 on both Standard and Datacenter editions.

When Microsoft created Nano Server, they had some very specific thoughts of how this version could be used, such as using Nano Server as a DNS server, an IIS server, an application server for cloud-based applications, or even a storage unit for file servers.

However, there are a few disadvantages of Nano Servers. A Nano Server cannot act as Domain Controller, Group Policy objects (GPOs) are not supported, and Nano Servers cannot be configured to use System Center Configuration Manager, System Center Data Protection Manager, NIC Teaming, or as proxy servers. Nano Servers also uses a version of Windows PowerShell that has many differences as a server using regular PowerShell.

At the time this book was written, Nano Server supports only the Current Branch for Business (CBB) licensing model.

When it comes to installing Nano Servers, there are some different options. There is no downloadable version of just Windows Server 2016 Nano Server. Nano Server is included on the Windows Server 2016 Standard or Datacenter physical media. Both server versions have a folder called NanoServer. The NanoServer folders contain a .wim image and a subfolder called Packages. The Packages subfolder is needed when an administrator wants to add server roles and features to the image.

However, if an administrator wants a simple way to create a Nano Server virtual hard drive (VHD), they can just download the Nano Server Image Builder. This software tool helps administrators easily create a Nano Server VHD that can then be used to boot a server with or use in Microsoft's Hyper-V server.

Creating a Nano Server VHD

1. Download the Nano Server Image Builder from Microsoft's website at `https://www.microsoft.com/en-us/download/details.aspx?id=54065` by clicking the Download button.

2. A file named `NanoServerImageBuilder.msi` will be created. Double-click the file. If an Open File Security Warning dialog box appears, click the Run button.

3. The Nano Server Image Builder Setup wizard will begin. Click Next at the introduction screen.

4. At the Licensing screen, click the I Accept The Terms check box and then click Next.

5. At the Destination Folder screen, choose where to install the Nano Server Image Builder files. Click Next.

6. At the Ready To Install screen, click the Install button. If a User Account Control box appears, click the Yes button.

7. Once the Installation is complete, click the Finish button.

8. Open Windows Explorer and navigate to the destination folder chosen from step 5. Double-click the `NanoServerImageBuilder.exe` file. If a UAC dialog box appears, click Yes.

9. In order for the Image Builder to work, an administrator must also download the Windows ADK kit from Microsoft. This can be found at `https://developer.microsoft.com/en-us/windows/hardware/windows-assessment-deployment-kit`. Click the version you want to download.

10. The administrator will be asked if they want to run or save the file. This option is up to the administrator. Some will save the file to the same destination folder as the Nano Server Image Builder. Once downloaded, double-click the `adksetup.exe` file (if saved). If a dialog box appears, click Run.

11. Specify the destination of where to place the Windows ADK files to install and click Next.

12. At the Windows Kit Privacy screen, you can choose either option. By choosing Yes, the administrator will be asked to participate in Microsoft's feedback program. This is up to the administrator; for this exercise, I chose No. Click Next.

13. At the License Agreement screen, click Accept.

14. At the Features screen, accept the defaults and click Install. If a UAC screen appears, click Yes.

15. After the installation is complete, click the Close button.

16. Double-click the `NanoServerImageBuilder.exe` file. When the UAC screen appears, click Yes.

17. Now the administrator has the ability to create a Nano Server image or a bootable USB. For this exercise, you are going to create an image. So click the top choice, Create A New Nano Server Image. See Figure 1.5.

18. At the Before You Begin screen, click Next.

19. At the Select Installation Media screen, point the folder for the Windows Server 2016 installation files where the NanoServer Folder resides. Click Next.

20. At the License Agreement screen, click the box that states "I have read and agree to the terms." Then click Next.

21. At the Deployment Type screen, choose how to create the virtual machine image. Assign a name and set the size and specify a directory to copy the image creation log files. Click Next.

22. At the Basic Installation screen, click Next.

23. At the Select Optional Packages screen, choose any other options to install such as DNS, IIS, etc. Then click Next.

FIGURE 1.5   Nano Server image choice

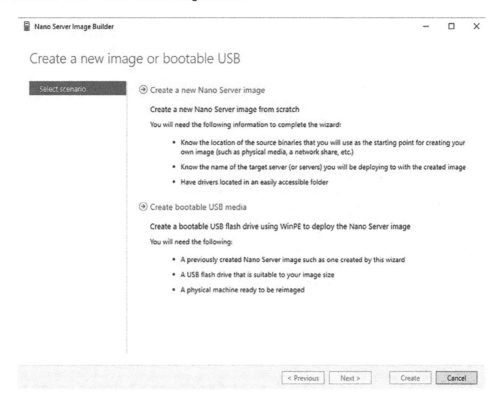

24. At the Drivers screen, add any drivers needed for the installation and click Next.

25. Next the Destination screen will appear. Enter the name of the computer and the administrator's password. Make sure the Time Zone is correct and click Next.

26. At this time, choose whether to join a domain or not. For this exercise, you are not going to join a domain. Just click Next.

27. Leave the default network settings and click Next.

28. At the Advanced Configuration Screen, choose the top option, Create a Basic Nano Server Image. See Figure 1.6.

29. Once the link is clicked, will see a Confirmation screen. Click the Create button.

30. Once the image is complete, click the Close button.

31. Open Windows Explorer and go to the folder where the VHD was created. Ensure that the VHD file has been created. The administrator can now run this VHD in Microsoft Hyper-V.

FIGURE 1.6   Advanced Configuration screen

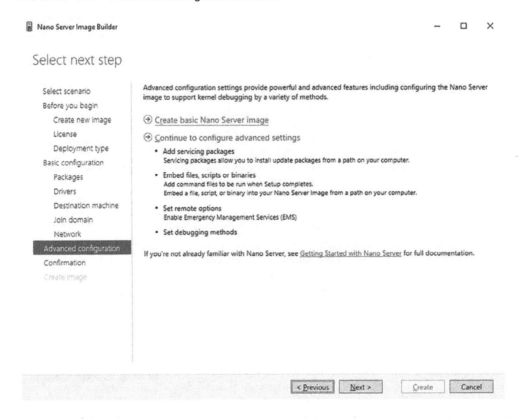

Interactive Installs

Advantages to using unattended installations as a method for automating Windows Server 2016 include:

- Can be configured to provide an automated query response while still allowing users to selectively provide specified input during the installation.

- Can be expanded to include installation instructions for applications, additional language support, service packs, and device drivers.

- Can be used to install clean copies of Windows Server 2016 or upgrade an existing operating system to Windows Server 2016.

- Saves time and money since users do not have to interactively respond to each installation query.

- Windows Server 2016 physical media does not need to be distributed to all the computers on which it will be installed.

Disadvantages of using unattended installation as a method for automating Windows Server 2016 include:

- An administrator does not physically walk through the installation of Windows Server 2016 on the client machine. If there are any problems, it will be unknown until the end user has issues.

- Require more initial setup than a standard installation of Windows Server 2016.

- Someone must have access to each client computer and must initiate the unattended installation process on the client side.

VHD/VHDX Installation Source

In addition to virtual networks, administrators need to administer virtual hard disks that are attached to the virtual machines. A virtual hard disk in Hyper-V, apart from a pass-through disk, is a VHD or VHDX file that simulates a hard drive on the virtual machine.

Windows Server 2016 Hyper-V has a feature called Shared Virtual Hard Disk. This allows an administrator to cluster virtual machines by using shared virtual hard disk (VHDX) files. Shared virtual hard disks allow an administrator to build a high availability infrastructure, which is key if setting up either a private cloud deployment or a cloud-hosted environment for managing large workloads. Shared virtual hard disks allow two or more virtual machines to access the same virtual hard disk (VHDX) file.

Native Boot allows an administrator to create a virtual hard disk (VHDX), install Windows to it, and then boot it up, either on the computer side-by-side with the existing installation or as a new device. A native-boot VHDX can be used as the running operating system on designated hardware without any other parent operating system. This differs from a scenario where a VHDX is connected to a virtual machine on a computer that has a parent operating system.

Windows disk-management tools such as the DiskPart tool and the Disk Management Microsoft Management Console (Diskmgmt.msc) can be used to create a VHDX file. A supported Windows image (.wim) file can be applied to a VHD, and the VHDX can be copied to multiple systems. The Windows boot manager can be configured to boot directly into the VHD.

The VHDX can also be connected to a virtual machine for use with the Hyper-V Role in Windows Server.

VHDXs can be applied to computers or devices that have no other installations of Windows, without a virtual machine or hypervisor. A hypervisor is a layer of software under the operating system that runs virtual computers. This allows for more flexibility in workload distribution because a single set of tools can be used to manage the images for virtual machines and designated hardware.

An administrator can also deploy the VHDX to a computer that already has Windows installed on it and use a boot menu to select between the existing version of Windows or the version on the VHD.

Prerequisites for VHD/VHDX are:

- An administrator machine with the Windows Assessment and Deployment Kit (Windows ADK) tools installed.
- A generalized Windows image (.WIM file).
- A bootable Windows PE drive.
- A destination computer or device on which to install the VHDX. This device requires 30 GB or more of free disk space. Can install the VHDX to a device already running other operating system installations, or as the only operating system on a device.

Understanding Virtual Memory and Paging File

If a computer lacking RAM and needs to run a program or perform an operation, Windows can use virtual memory to compensate. Virtual memory combines a computer's RAM with temporary space on the hard disk. When RAM runs low, virtual memory moves data from RAM to space called a paging file. By default, the paging file is stored as C:\pagefile.sys.

Unfortunately, if something needs to be accessed from the virtual memory on disk, it is significantly slower than accessing it directly from RAM.

Managing the Paging File

To manage the paging file in Windows Server 2016, perform the following:

1. Right-click Computer and select Properties.
2. In the left pane, click Advanced System Settings. If prompted for an administrator password or confirmation, type the password or provide confirmation.
3. On the Advanced tab, under Performance, click Settings.
4. Click the Advanced tab, and then, under virtual memory, click Change.
5. Clear the "Automatically manage paging file size for all drives" check box.
6. Under Drive {Volume Label}, click the drive that contains the paging file to change.
7. Click the Custom Size radio button, type a new size in megabytes in the Initial Size (MB) or Maximum Size (MB) box, click Set, and then click OK.

Increasing the size of the paging files usually doesn't require a restart for the changes to take effect; however, if an administrator decreases the size, then the computer will need to be restarted. It is recommended that an administrator doesn't disable or delete the paging file.

The default paging file size is equal to 1.5 times the total RAM. However, this default configuration may not be optimal in all situations, such as with servers that contain large databases. Therefore, unless an administrator has an application that uses a larger paging file, the administrator should consider adding more RAM to the system. In addition, if there are multiple physical drives, the administrator can move the paging file from the boot volume to another volume.

Performing Clean Installations

A *clean installation* is installing the software from scratch on a new drive or on a newly reformatted drive. Many people find that doing a clean install of an operating system is the best way to go because you are starting fresh. The disadvantage is that the system and all of its software needs to be reinstalled, patched, and configured and data copied over, something that may take hours or even days.

To boot from a DVD drive, you insert the DVD into your DVD/Blu-ray drive and turn on the computer. If the system does not boot from the DVD, you might need to configure the BIOS Setup program to boot from the DVD/Blu-ray drive, and you might need to configure the boot order so that the DVD/Blu-ray drive booting will occur before any other boot drives.

Install Windows Server 2016 with Desktop Experience

To install Windows Server 2016 with Desktop Experience, perform the following steps.

1. Insert the Windows Server 2016 disc into the DVD drive and turn on the computer. Press any key to boot from the DVD (if necessary).

2. The computer switches to the Windows graphical interface and the Windows Setup page appears, as shown in Figure 1.7. Using the drop-down lists provided, select the appropriate language to install, the time and currency format, and the keyboard or input method. Then, click Next.

FIGURE 1.7   The Windows Setup page

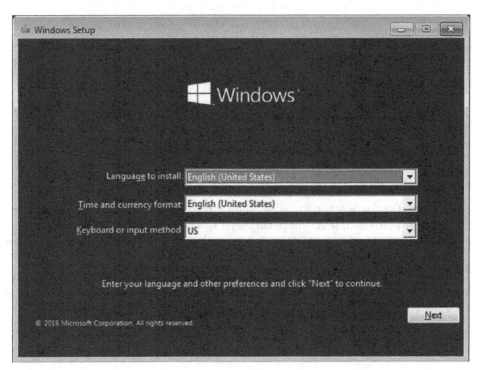

3. On the Windows Server 2016 Install Now page, click Install now.

4. When the Activate Windows page appears, in the text box, type the Windows Server 2016 activation key and then click Next.

5. On the Select the Operating System to Install page (as shown in Figure 1.8), select Windows Server 2016 Datacenter (Desktop Experience). Click Next.

FIGURE 1.8 Selecting which operating system to install

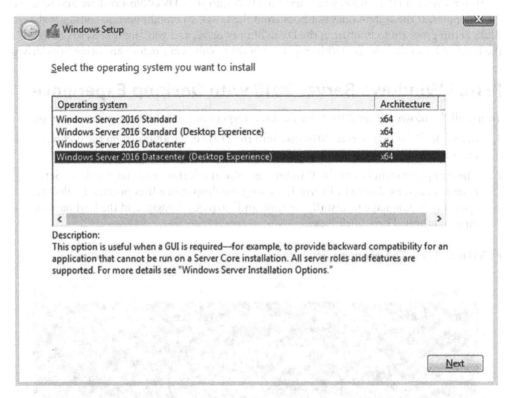

6. On the License Terms page, select the "I accept the license terms" option and then click Next.

7. Click the Custom: Install Windows Only (Advanced) option.

8. The Where Do You Want to Install Windows? page appears, as shown in Figure 1.9. From the list provided, select the partition on which you want to install Windows Server 2016, or select an area of unallocated disk space where the Setup program can create a new partition. Then click Next.

9. After several minutes, during which the Setup program installs Windows Server 2016, the computer reboots. When the Customize Settings page appears, in the Password and Reenter Password text boxes, type **Pa$$w0rd**. Click Finish.

FIGURE 1.9   The Where Do You Want to Install Windows? page

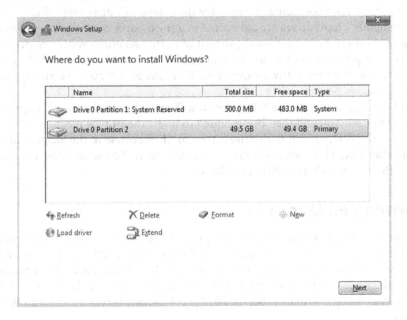

The Where Do You Want to Install Windows? page enables you to create, manage, and delete the partitions on your disks. It also allows you to load specialized storage drivers.

Clicking the Drive options (advanced) button on the page causes four additional buttons to appear. These buttons have the following functions:

- Delete removes an existing partition from a disk, permanently erasing all its data. You might want to delete partitions to consolidate unallocated disk space, enabling you to create a new, larger partition.

- Extend enables you to make an existing partition larger, as long as unallocated space is available immediately following the selected partition on the disk.

- Format enables you to format an existing partition on a disk, thereby erasing all its data. You do not need to format any new partitions you create for the install, but you might want to format an existing partition to eliminate unwanted files before installing Windows Server 2016 on it.

- New creates a new partition of a user-specified size in the selected area of unallocated space.

In some cases, it might be necessary to install a driver supplied by a hardware manufacturer before the disks (for example, RAID drivers) in the computer appear in the Setup program. During the Windows Server 2016 installation procedure, the Setup program enables you to select the partition or area of unallocated disk space where you want to install the operating system. The Where Do You Want to Install Windows? page lists the partitions on all the computer's disk drives that the Setup program can detect with its default drivers. In most cases, all the computer's drives should appear in the list; if they do not, it is probably because Windows does not include a driver for the computer's drive controller.

If the computer's hard drives are connected to a third-party controller, rather than the one integrated into most motherboards, the list of partitions might appear empty, and you might need to supply a driver for the Setup program to see the drives. Check the controller manufacturer's website for a driver supporting Windows Server 2016, or another recent version of Windows Server.

To load the disk driver, on the Where Do You Want to Install Windows? page, click the Load driver button. You will then be prompted to insert the storage medium that contains the drivers (CD, DVD, or USB flash drive). You can then browse to the location of the driver and click OK. Then, select the driver and click Next. You would then continue with the rest of the Windows Server 2016 installation.

Performing an Upgrade

If you want to upgrade or move an older server operating system to Windows Server 2016, you can use existing hardware and upgrade to Windows Server 2016 or you can install Windows Server 2016 on new hardware and migrate the roles, features, settings, and data from the older servers to the new server. You can upgrade from Windows Server 2008 R2 with Service Pack 1, Windows Server 2012, or Windows Server 2012 R2 to Windows Server 2016.

If you have a 64-bit computer running Windows Server 2008 R2, Windows Server 2012, or Windows Server 2012 R2, you can upgrade it to Windows Server 2016 based on the following paths:

- Windows Server 2008 R2 Standard (with Service Pack 1) or Windows Server 2008 R2 Enterprise (with Service Pack 1) to Windows Server 2016 Standard or Windows Server 2016 Datacenter

- Windows Server 2008 R2 Datacenter (with Service Pack 1) to Windows Server 2016 Datacenter

- Windows Web Server 2008 R2 (with Service Pack 1) to Windows Server 2016 Standard

- Windows Server 2008 R2 Datacenter (with Service Pack 1) to Windows Server 2016 Datacenter

- Windows Server 2008 R2 Enterprise (with Service Pack 1) to Windows Server 2016 Standard or Windows Server 2016 Datacenter

- Windows Server 2008 R2 Standard (with Service Pack 1) to Windows Server 2016 Standard or Windows Server 2016 Datacenter

- Windows Web Server 2008 R2 (with Service Pack 1) to Windows Server 2016 Standard

- Windows Server 2012 Datacenter or Windows Server 2012 R2 Datacenter to Windows Server 2016 Datacenter

- Windows Server 2012 Standard or Windows Server 2012 R2 Standard to Windows Server 2016 Standard or Windows Server 2016 Datacenter

If you want to run Windows Server 2016 on a new machine or you are not using one of the previous upgrade paths, you must perform a migration.

 You cannot perform an upgrade that includes one language to another with a different language.

When you want to upgrade to Windows Server 2016, you should follow these guidelines:

- Verify that the current server will support Windows Server 2016. In addition, make sure you have the appropriate drivers before installation.
- Update your antivirus program, run it, and then disable it. After you install Windows, remember to re-enable the antivirus program, or install new antivirus software that works with Windows Server 2016.
- Back up your files. You can back up files to an external hard disk, a DVD or CD, or a network folder.
- Connect to the Internet. Make sure your Internet connection is working so that you can get the latest installation updates. These updates include security updates and hardware driver updates that can help with installation. If you don't have an Internet connection, you can still upgrade or install Windows.

If your system is a production system, verify and/or test all applications to make sure they are compatible with Windows Server 2016.

Upgrading to Windows Server 2016

To upgrade a server to Windows Server 2016, perform the following steps.

1. Log on to a server running Windows Server 2012 R2 as **adatum\administrator** with the password of **Pa$$w0rd**.
2. Insert the Windows Server 2016 installation disc into the DVD drive. Then open the DVD drive, and double-click the Setup program. The Windows Setup window opens.
3. On the Get Important Updates page, the Download And Install Updates (Recommended) option is already selected. Click Next.
4. On the Product Key page, in the Enter Product key text box, type the product key and then click Next.
5. Select the desired Windows version, Windows Server 2016 or Windows Server 2016 (Desktop Experience). Click Next.
6. On the License Terms page, click the Accept button.
7. On the Choose What to Keep page, you can select Keep Personal Files and Apps, or Nothing. The Keep Personal Files And Apps option will be grayed out if you are installing an edition of Windows that is different from the one you're currently using. Click Next. If you are prompted to indicate whether you want to continue using this selection, click the Yes button.

8. On the Ready To Install page, click the Install button.

After several minutes, during which the Setup program upgrades Windows Server 2012 or Windows Server 2012 R2 to Windows Server 2016 and restarts the computer several times, the system finalizes the installation and the Windows sign-on screen appears.

In the past, Microsoft has provided tools to check your system to see if it is ready for the operating system. Today, you would use the Microsoft Assessment and Planning (MAP) Toolkit, which is designed to give you essential infrastructure knowledge for planning your migration to Windows Server 2016. The MAP Toolkit takes inventory of your current server environment, determines hardware and device compatibility and readiness, and then generates actionable reports of recommended upgrades for migration. Power savings benefits are calculated with MAP's Power Savings Assessment tool, enabling you to quickly determine potential savings with Windows Server 2016 prior to deployment.

Download

The Microsoft Assessment and Planning (MAP) Toolkit is located at: `https://www` `.microsoft.com/en-us/download/details.aspx?id=7826`.

Migrating Roles and Features to Windows Server 2016

Once an administrator decides which roles and features are going to be installed, then they can either install those roles and features from scratch or migrate them from a previous version of Windows server.

Windows Server 2016 includes a set of migration tools that administrators can use to ease the process of migrating server roles, features, operating system settings, and data. Administrators can migrate this data from an existing server that is running Windows Server 2008 R2, Windows Server 2012, Windows Server 2012 R2, or Windows Server 2016 to a computer that is running Windows Server 2016.

Using the Windows Server Migration Tools to migrate roles, role services, and features can streamline the deployment of new servers. An administrator can migrate roles and features on any server, including Server Core, installation option of Windows Server 2016, and virtual servers. By using Windows Server Migration Tools, an administrator can reduce migration downtime, increase the accuracy of the migration process, and help eliminate conflicts that could otherwise occur during the migration process.

One advantage of using the migration tools is that most support cross-architecture migrations (x86-based to x64-based computing platforms), migrations between physical and virtual environments, and migrations between both the full and Server Core installation options of the Windows Server operating system.

To use the Windows Server Migration Tools, the feature must be installed on both the source and destination computers. Windows Server Migration Tools installation and preparation can be divided into the following stages:

1. Installing Windows Server Migration Tools on destination servers that run Windows Server 2016.

2. Creating deployment folders on destination servers that run Windows Server 2016 for copying to source servers.

3. Copying deployment folders from destination servers to source servers.

4. Registering Windows Server Migration Tools on source servers.

To use Windows Server Migration Tools, you must be a member of the Administrators group on both the source and destination servers to install, remove, or set up the tools. Administrators can install Windows Server Migration Tools 2016 by using either the Add Roles Or Features Wizard in Server Manager or Windows PowerShell deployment cmdlets for Server Manager.

To install Windows Server Migration Tools on a Server Core installation of Windows Server 2016 using Windows PowerShell, complete the following steps:

1. Open a Windows PowerShell session by typing **powershell.exe** in the current command prompt session and then pressing Enter.

2. In the Windows PowerShell session, install Windows Server Migration Tools by using the `Windows PowerShell Install-WindowsFeature` cmdlet for Server Manager. In the Windows PowerShell session, type the following, and then press Enter. (Omit the `ComputerName` parameter if you are installing the Windows Server Migration Tools on the local server.)

```
Install-WindowsFeature Migration –ComputerName computer_name
```

Disk Cloning and System Preparation Tool

One way to install Windows Server 2016 is to use *disk cloning* software such as Norton Ghost to create an image file, which is a sector-by-sector copy stored in a large file. To use the disk cloning software, you use the installation disk to install Windows onto a master computer (also called reference computer), update and patch the computer, customize Windows, and install any additional software. You then use the cloning software to copy the contents of a hard drive to a file. You use the disk cloning software to copy the contents of the image to a target computer.

If you create a cloned copy of Windows and apply the cloned copy to multiple computers, each copy of Windows cloned to a target computer using the same image has the same parameters, including the same computer name and security identifier (SID). Unfortunately, for these computers to operate properly without conflict on a network, these parameters have to be unique.

To overcome this problem, you run the System Preparation Tool (Sysprep), which removes the security identifiers and all other user-specific or computer-specific information from the computer before you run the disk cloning software to make the cloned disk image. When you copy the cloned image to the disk image, a small wizard runs that enables you to specify the computer name and other computer-specific information. The SID and other information is re-created automatically. The Sysprep utility is located in the c:\Windows\ System32\sysprep or the c:\Windows\SysWOW64\sysprep folder.

Most of the time, you will execute the following command:

```
Sysprep.exe /oobe /generalize
```

See Figure 1.10.

FIGURE 1.10   Running the Sysprep.exe command

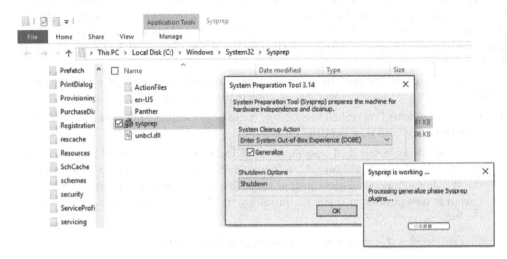

The /generalize will prepare the Windows installation to be imaged. If this option is specified, all unique system information is removed from the Windows installation. The security ID (SID) resets, any system restore points are cleared, and event logs are deleted. The next time the computer starts, a specialize configuration pass runs. A new security ID (SID) is created, and the clock for Windows activation resets, if the clock has not already been reset three times.

The /oobe (oobe stands for Out of the Box Experience) will restart the computer into Windows Welcome mode. Windows Welcome enables end users to customize their Windows operating system, create user accounts, name the computer, and other tasks. Any settings in the oobe system configuration pass in an answer file are processed immediately before Windows Welcome starts.

Performing an Unattended Installation

An *unattended installation* is an installation that requires little interaction to install. To perform an unattended installation of Windows you would use an answer file. An answer file is an XML file that stores the answers for a series of graphical user interface (GUI) dialog boxes. The answer file for Windows Setup is commonly called autounattend.xml. Since the answer file is an XML file, you can use any text editor such as Notepad to create and modify the answer file.

A sample answer file can be found at https://social.technet.microsoft.com/wiki/ contents/articles/36609.windows-server-2016-unattended-installation.aspx. However, you will find it much easier if you use the Windows System Image Manager (SIM) to create the answer file. It can also be used to validate the answer file.

To install Windows SIM, you first need to download and install Windows Automated Installation Kit (AIK) for Windows 10 from the Microsoft website (https://developer .microsoft.com/en-us/windows/hardware/windows-assessment-deployment-kit). To start Windows SIM, you then click the Start button, select Microsoft Windows AIK, and select Windows System Image Manager (see Figure 1.11).

FIGURE 1.11   Windows System Image Manager

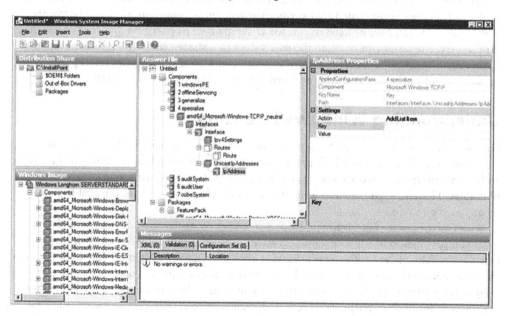

After you create an answer file called autounattend.xml, you place the file to removable media, such as a USB flash device, CD/DVD drive, or floppy disk. You then insert the removable media into the destination computer and boot the destination computer from DVD. Setup automatically searches for autounattend.xml and performs the installation with the parameters specified without any interaction from you.

Using Windows Deployment Services

Windows Deployment Services (WDS) is a technology from Microsoft for network-based installation of Windows operating system including Windows 7, Windows 8/8.1, Windows 10, Windows Server 2012 R2, and Windows Server 2016. The deployment of

Windows can be fully automated and customized through the use of unattended installation scripting files.

The Windows installation files can be distributed within a Windows Imaging Format (WIM) file. WIM is the file-based imaging format that Windows Server uses for rapid installation on a new computer. WIM files store copies (known as images) of the operating systems, such as Windows PE, Windows 10, or Windows Server 2016. Maintaining an operating system in a WIM file is easy because you can add and remove drivers, updates, and Windows components offline, without ever starting the operating system.

Windows Deployment Services uses the WIM files to install Windows. If set up properly, you need to boot a computer with Windows PE or perform a PXE boot. Windows Preinstallation Environment (Windows PE) is a minimal Win32 operating system with limited services, built on the Windows kernel. It is used to prepare a computer for Windows installation, to copy disk images from a network file server, and to initiate Windows Setup.

You then connect to the WDS server and install Windows from a configured image. A configuration script is executed that verifies the computer's configuration and hardware requirements. It can also be used to run the Diskpart tool to partition and format the disk. If necessary, the script can back up the user's data to a shared folder on another computer. Eventually, the script connects to a shared folder containing the Windows Setup files and runs the Windows Setup program to install the operating system fully unattended.

Understanding Windows Licensing

One of the biggest costs to any IT department is the cost of software. When you add the client copies of Windows and Office, the cost of the server operating system and the cost of additional enterprise software such as Exchange or SQL, it can easily add up to thousands of dollars. Therefore, you need to look at your available options to get the best price for what you need to do.

A software license is given to you from a software company including Microsoft that gives you permission to use a specific software package and usually comes with many restrictions. Most licenses from corporations such as Microsoft are more like a lease rather than purchasing the actual software. The typical restriction limits you to use only one copy of the software per license and prohibit you to distribute or copy the license in any way (except for backup purposes). Licenses for enterprise-class server software (such as Microsoft Exchange or Microsoft SQL) could also require a Client Access License (CAL) for each user that is to access the server software.

The least inexpensive license to obtain is the OEM (Original Equipment Manufacturer) license, which can only be purchased with a new computer from a system builder such as HP or IBM. Unfortunately, these licenses are tied to a specific machine and cannot be transferred later to a new machine. The OEM is usually responsible for technical support on the software that you bought.

The retail license (usually purchased from your office or computer store or over the Internet) allows you move it from one machine to another. Of course, retail software usually costs more than OEM software. Another disadvantage of using retail software from Microsoft you need to enter a key code and activate the software. Another disadvantage is that if you move the software to another computer or you make semi-significant changes such as adding RAM or a new hard drive, you may need to re-activate the software.

Lastly, Microsoft has several volume licensing programs available to organize their licenses and stay up to date with the newest software at a discounted price. The Open license is intended for businesses with at least 5 PCs and Select License and Enterprise Agreement Plans are licensing programs intended for corporations with at least 250 PCs. Each of these programs may have additional benefits such as free take-home licenses and training.

Volume licensing can be further broken down into Multiple Activation Key (MAK) and Key Management Services (KMS). With MAK, each key has to be registered and activated individually, while Key Management Services (KMS) uses a KMS server to automatically connect to Microsoft's license warehouse and activate the key.

Understanding Windows Activation

Activation helps verify that your copy of Windows is genuine and that it has not been used on more computers than the Microsoft Software Terms allow. Windows Server 2016 requires product activation, which validates each Windows Server 2016 license through an online activation service at Microsoft by phone, through KMS, or through Active Directory Domain Services, in order to be fully functional. During the activation step, you install the proper license key for Windows.

 There are no activation grace periods. If you do not activate Windows Server 2016, you cannot use the personalization settings or customize the operating system.

 As part of the planning, you must ensure that you have the correct number of licenses for your Windows operating systems, including Windows Server 2016. Windows Server 2016 is licensed by physical processor core, not by server. You can purchase additional licenses for two physical processor cores at a time.

You can activate Windows in two ways: manually or automatically. With manual activation, you must enter the product key and activate over the Internet to the special clearinghouse website, or over the phone by using a retail product key or a *multiple activation key (MAK)*. To activate over the Internet, you open Settings, click Update & Security, and click Activate, as shown in Figure 1.12. When you use a MAK, you can activate multiple computers, up to a set activation limit.

FIGURE 1.12   Activating Windows

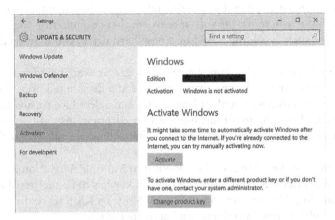

You can also use *Original Equipment Manufacturer (OEM) keys* with computers. Manufacturers provide OEM keys, which are typically tied to specific computers. OEM keys are usually distributed with systems running Windows 7 or higher but can also be found on systems running Windows Server operating systems.

If you have many clients and servers, consider setting up a Volume Activation Services server. When you install the Volume Activation Services server role, you can choose Key Management Service or Active Directory–Based Activation. After adding the Volume Activation Services role, you can use the Volume Activation Tools GUI to configure activation. When you use Volume Activation Services, each activated computer must contact the KMS server periodically to renew its activation status. To report on activated licenses, you can use the Volume Activation Management Tool (VAMT), which is part of the Windows Assessment and Deployment Kit (ADK).

Configuring Update Settings

Windows Update provides your Windows 10 and Windows 2016 users with a way to keep their computers current by checking a designated server. The server provides software that patches security issues, installs updates that make Windows and your applications more stable, fixes issues with existing Windows programs, and provides new features. The server can be hosted by Microsoft, or it can be set up and managed in your organization by running the Windows Server Update Services (WSUS) or System Center 2016 Configuration Manager.

When you first install Windows Server 2016, you can choose how you want Windows Update to function. On a Windows Server 2016 computer, you can open Settings and click Update & Security to open the Windows Update page (see Figure 1.13).

FIGURE 1.13   The Windows Update page

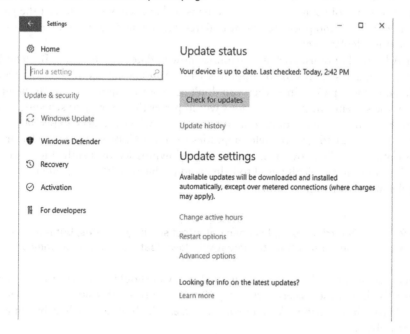

By clicking Advanced options, you can configure for Automatic Updates, give updates for other Microsoft products when Windows is updated, defer upgrades, and view update history (as shown in Figure 1.14).

FIGURE 1.14   The Windows Update Advanced Options page

For corporations, you can also use Windows Server Update Services (WSUS) or System Center 2016 Configuration Manager to keep your systems updated. Smaller organizations might use WSUS or cloud-based services such as Microsoft Intune to keep systems up to date. The advantage of using one of these systems is that it allows you to test the patch, schedule the updates, and prioritize client updates. Once you determine a patch is safe, you can enable it for deployment.

Under Advanced options, you can customize how updates are installed. By default, the "Choose how updates are installed" option is set to Automatic (recommended), which means Windows will pick a time when you don't use your computer to install the updates and reboot the system. Most organizations would prefer the "Notify to schedule restart" option so that Windows will not reboot your computer when you least expect it.

Windows Server 2016 lets you defer upgrades to your PC. By selecting the Defer upgrades option, new Windows features won't be downloaded or installed for several months. This option is typically used to help avoid problems with an update that might cause problems within your organization.

Deferring upgrades does not affect security updates, but it does prevent you from getting the latest Windows features as soon as they are available.

If Windows Update fails to retrieve any updates, you should check your proxy settings in Internet Explorer to see whether the program can get through your proxy server (if any) or firewall. You should also make sure you can access the Internet, such as by going to the Microsoft website.

You can view your update history by opening the Advanced Options and selecting View your update history. On the Update History page, each update, including the KB article number, the version, and the date installed, is shown. If you click Successfully Installed On *<date>* for a specific update, it will give a short description of the update.

At the top of the View Your Update History page, you can click Uninstall Updates to open the Control Panel Installed Updates page, as shown in Figure 1.15. To uninstall or roll back an update, right-click the desired update and choose Uninstall. You will then be prompted to uninstall the update. When you click Yes, the update will be uninstalled.

FIGURE 1.15   The Control Panel Installed Updates page

Skill Summary

In this lesson you learned:

- A server is a computer that is a meant to be a dedicated service provider, and a client is a computer that requests services.

- Before selecting the hardware and software components of a server, you should identify the server roles and network services that the server will need to provide and how many people will be accessing the server at once to help determine the load the server needs to fulfill.

- The primary subsystems that make up a server are processor, memory, storage, and network.

- The computer, including servers, is built around one or more integrated chips called the processor. It is considered the brain of the computer since all of the instructions it performs are mathematical calculations and logical comparisons.

- A 64-bit processor is a processor with a default word size of 64 bits and 64-bit external data bus, which allows you to access much more RAM than a 32-bit processor.

- The amount of RAM can be one the largest factor in your overall computer performance.

- For the processor to communicate with the rest of the system, the processor plugs in or connects to a large circuit board called the motherboard or system board. The motherboard allows the processor to branch out and communicate with all of the other computer components.

- Instructions that control much of the computer's input/output functions, such as communicating with disks, RAM, and the monitor kept in the System ROM chips are known as the BIOS (basic input/output system).

- The process of updating your system ROM BIOS is called flashing the BIOS.

- While a server needs to have solid performance, the server needs to be reliable.

- Virtual machines technologies enable multiple operating systems to run concurrently on a single machine.

- Windows Server 2016 has organized the most common services into server roles. A server role describes the function of the server.

- Windows Server 2016 Features are software programs that are not directly part of a role, or they can support or augment the functionality of one or more roles or enhance the functionality of the entire server.

- Server Core installation provides a minimal environment with no Windows Explorer shell for running specific server roles and no Start button.

- Before installing software, you should look at the system requirements as a starting point to make sure your server meets those requirements.

- A clean installation is installing the software from scratch on a new drive or on newly reformatted drive. Many people find that doing a clean install of an operating system is the best way to go because you are starting fresh.

- In some instances, you will want to take a current system and upgrade from an older version of Windows to Windows Server 2016.

- One way to install Windows Server 2016 is to use disk cloning software such as Norton Ghost to create an image file, which is a sector-by-sector copy stored in a large file.

- If you clone a computer, you need to run the System Preparation Tool (Sysprep), which removes the security identifiers and all other user-specific or computer-specific information from the computer before you run the disk cloning software to make the cloned disk image.

- An Answer file is an XML file that stores the answers for a series of graphical user interface (GUI) dialog boxes, which is used to automatically install Windows.

- Windows Deployment Services (WDS) is a technology from Microsoft for network-based installation of Windows operating system including Windows 7, Windows 8/8.1, Windows 10, Windows Server 2012 R2, and Windows Server 2016. The deployment of Windows can be fully automated and customized through the use of unattended installation scripting files.

- Microsoft product activation is an anti-piracy technology designed to verify that software products are legitimately licensed.

- After installing Windows, check to see if Microsoft has any fixes, patches, service packs, and device drivers, and apply them to the Windows system.

Knowledge Assessment

Fill in the Blank

1. A _____ is a primary duty that a server performs.

2. The computer including servers is built around one or more integrated chips called the _____.

3. A _____ processor can typically process more data at the same time and can access much more memory than a 32-bit processor.

4. Making sure you have sufficient _____ is one of the biggest factors in performance even more than disk and processor.

5. For the processor to communicate with the rest of the system, the processor plugs in or connects to a large circuit board called the _____.

6. Firmware is software contained in _____ chips.

7. Instructions that control much of the computer's input/output functions, such as communicating with disks, RAM, and the monitor kept in the System ROM chips are known as the _____.

8. The process of update your system ROM BIOS is called _____ the BIOS.

9. _____ installation provides a minimal environment with no Windows Explorer shell for running specific server roles and no Start button.

10. A(n) _____ is an XML file that stores the answers for a series of graphical user interface (GUI) dialog boxes.

Multiple Choice

1. What technology provided by Microsoft is used to perform network-based installation of Windows operating systems including Windows 7, Windows 8/8.1, Windows 10, and Windows Server 2016?

    A. IAS

    B. Server Core

    C. SIM

    D. WDS

2.   What does the name of the answer file on a USB drive have to be to perform an automatic installation?

   A.   `autounattend.xml`

   B.   `auto.xml`

   C.   `auto.txt`

   D.   `automatic.xml`

3.   What is the program you should you use to create or validate an answer file used to install Windows?

   A.   IAS

   B.   Server Core

   C.   SIM

   D.   WDS

4.   What is the maximum amount of memory that Windows Server 2016 Standard Edition?

   A.   2 GB

   B.   4 GB

   C.   1 TB

   D.   24 TB

   E.   64 TB

5.   How many days grace period do you have where you will have to activate Windows Server 2016?

   A.   3 days.

   B.   10 days.

   C.   15 days.

   D.   30 days.

   E.   There is no grace period.

6.   Which of the following is not a primary subsystem found in a server?

   A.   Processor

   B.   Memory

   C.   Sound

   D.   Storage

7.   What type of installation do you use that starts from scratch?

   A.   A clean upgrade

   B.   A clean installation

   C.   A formatting installation

   D.   A backup installation

8. What command would you use to prepare a Windows installation for imaging that will remove the SID and computer name?

   A. Sys

   B. Sysprep

   C. SIDPrep

   D. WDSPrep

9. What does Microsoft use to fight pirated copies of Windows?

   A. WDS

   B. IAS

   C. Sysprep

   D. Activation

10. Which edition of Windows Server 2016 gives you the most access to processors and memory?

   A. Foundation

   B. Standard

   C. Enterprise

   D. Datacenter

True/False

1. If you have a power outage while you are flashing the BIOS, you can just restart the process when the power is restored.

2. Windows Server 2016 can be only on 64-bit processors.

3. The lowest edition of Windows Server 2016 is the Standard edition.

4. When you clone a server with Windows Server 2016, you just need to blank the computer name and administrator password.

5. The standard protocol to share files on Windows Server 2016 is SMB

Competency Assessment

Scenario 1-1: Server Analysis

You are designing a new network for the Acme Corporation. You expect to have a lot of sales over the Internet. How many servers do you think you will need, what hardware requirements should you use, and what role would you assign to each server? Hint: when you purchase something over the Internet, what type of server do you access to purchase something? Then what type of server do you think you will need in the background that will keep track of those sales?

Scenario 1-2: Identify Ports

Look at the back of your computer and draw a diagram that shows all of the ports and the purpose of the port.

Proficiency Assessment

Scenario 1-3: Installing Windows Server 2016

Go to Microsoft's website and find and download the evaluation copy of Windows Server 2016. Burn the image to a DVD. Then boot a computer and install Windows Server 2016 following the steps listed in the Clean Installation section. When configuring your disk, only use half of the disk for your C drive.

Scenario 1-4: Using Windows Updates

Use the Windows Update program to patch Windows.

 **Real World Scenario**

Workplace Ready: Selecting the Right Server

If you are new to server administration, trying to determine the right server can be quite challenging. So what can you do?

First, you will need to do a lot of reading including looking for the minimum requirements and always go beyond the minimum. If it says it needs 2 GB of memory, plan for at least 4 GB. If it needs a single processor running at 2 GHz, plan for dual processors running at 2.4 GHz. If it is the specification for the operating system, always double them as a minimum. In addition, when you are researching look for load recommendations or load specifications or guidelines.

Next, if you have a similar server, you should at its current load and try to compare to the predicted load to see if it is different. You can also look at processor, memory, disk, and network performance.

You should also ask people who use the server about perceived performance to see if it is adequate or if it should be increased. You should then verify the performance by using the network application in the same way and measure how long it takes for a task to be done.

Lesson 2

Managing Windows Server 2016

Objective Domain Matrix

Technology Skill	Objective Domain Description	Objective Domain Number
Managing devices and device drivers	Understand device drivers.	1.1
Managing Services	Understand services.	1.2
Using the Control Panel	Understand remote access.	2.3

Key Terms

Administrative Tools	registry
Computer Management console	Remote Assistance
Control Panel	Remote Desktop
device drivers	Server Management console
device manager	secure desktop
domain	services
Initial Configuration Tasks	signed driver
Microsoft Management Console	workgroup
Plug and Play (PnP)	

 Real World Scenario

Lesson 2 Case

You just installed several computers for the Acme Corporation. Now, you have to get each server connected to the network and add each computer to the domain. You then need to install each of the network services that each server is going to host.

Configuring Windows Server 2016

Windows Server 2016 is a robust and flexible system that is made to work on and support a wide range of hardware. Although it was designed for larger computers, it can work on laptops and desktop computers. In addition, it can also be executed as a virtual machine.

Because Windows Server 2016 contains a graphical user interface, the primary tools to configure Windows are Windows Server 2016 Settings and Control Panel, which are also graphical tools.

Configuring and Customizing the Start Menu, Desktop, Taskbar, and Notification Settings

The *desktop* is the main screen that you see when you first start the computer and log on to Windows. Like the top of an actual desktop, it is where you perform your work by opening and running one or more applications. It also includes the Recycle Bin, which is used to recover files that have been previously deleted.

At the bottom of the desktop, you will find the *taskbar*, which shows you the programs that are running and allows you to navigate between those programs. On the taskbar, the Start button is shown at the lower-left corner. When you click the Start button, you open the Windows Server 2016 Start menu (as shown in Figure 2.1), which is a blend of the Windows 7 Start menu and the Windows 8 Start screen.

FIGURE 2.1   Viewing the Windows Server 2016 desktop with the Start menu open

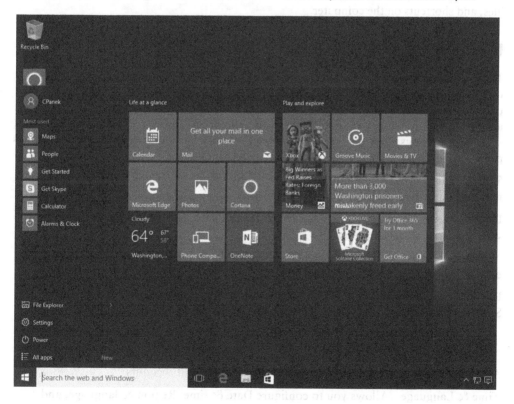

The left side of the Windows Server 2016 Start menu shows the most used programs and provides you with access to File Explorer, Settings, Power, and All apps. When you click All programs, all installed programs are shown in alphabetical order. When you right-click an installed application, you can choose Pin to Start or Pin to taskbar.

When you *pin* a program, the icon for that program displays on the taskbar even when the program isn't running. This provides you with quick access to your frequently used programs. Shortcuts for Task View, Microsoft Edge, File Explorer, and Store appear there by default. You can unpin programs from the taskbar as well. You'll learn about shortcuts later in this lesson.

The right side of the Windows Server 2016 Start menu displays tiles, which are larger than the icons found on the Windows desktop. Unlike the static icons, tiles can contain dynamic content provided by the software they represent. For example, the tile for a web browser can contain a thumbnail of the currently open website, while the Messaging tile can display part of your latest incoming email. Tiles in Windows Server 2016 that contain this type of dynamic content are called *live tiles*.

The tiles on the Start menu are configurable in a number of ways. You can move the tiles around, change their size, change their groupings, and control whether they display live content. It is also possible to remove seldom-used tiles and add new tiles for applications, files, and shortcuts on the computer.

Using Windows Server 2016 Settings

The *Windows Server 2016 Settings* is a modern interface for common configuration settings that would have been found in Control Panel on older versions of Windows. In addition, you will find additional settings such as touch screen, tablet, and privacy settings that are geared toward phones and tablets that you will not find in Control Panel.

To open settings, click the Start button and then click Settings, which opens the Settings page (see Figure 2.2). These settings are organized as follows:

System   Allows you to configure the display, notifications & actions, apps and features, multitasking, tablet mode, power & sleep options, and default apps

Devices   Provides quick access to hardware devices, such as printers, which you can use with the currently selected app

Network & Internet   Keeps track of Wi-Fi connections and allows you to configure VPN, dial-up connections, Ethernet connections, and proxy settings

Personalization   Provides settings for the background, colors, lock screen, themes, and Start menu

Apps   Allows you to uninstall, change defaults and other features related to installed applications

Accounts   Allows you to change the profile picture and add accounts

Time & Language   Allows you to configure Date & time, Region & language, and Speech

Ease Of Access   Provides settings for Narrator, Magnifier, high contrast, closed captions, keyboard, and mouse settings

FIGURE 2.2   Accessing Windows Server 2016 Settings

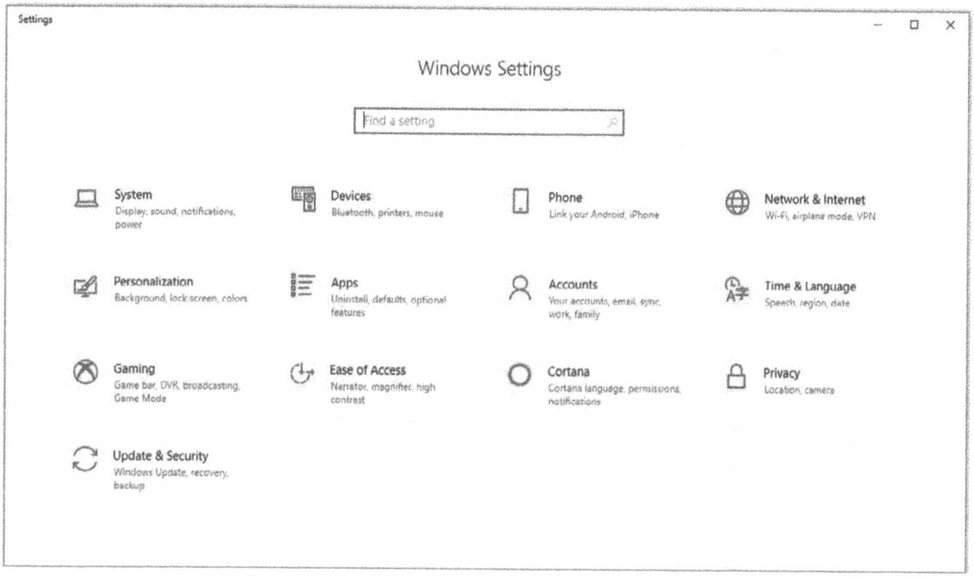

Cortana   Allows you to modify Cortana's language, permissions and how you will be notified

Privacy   Allows you to configure camera, microphone, speech, account information, contacts, calendar, messaging, and application radios control for Wi-Fi/Bluetooth connection

Update and security: Allows you to configure Windows Update, activate Windows, perform backups and recoveries, and configure Windows Defender

Using Control Panel

With previous versions of Windows, *Control Panel* was a primary graphical utility to configure the Windows environment and hardware devices. It can be accessed in Windows Server 2016 by right-clicking the Start button and choosing Control Panel. See Figure 2.3.

Each category includes a top-level link, and under each top-level link are several of the most frequently performed tasks for the category.

As with current and previous versions of Windows, you can change from the default Category view to Classic view (a large icon view or a small icon view). Icon view is an alternative view that provides the look and functionality of Control Panel in Windows 2000 and earlier versions of Windows, where all options are displayed as applets or icons.

FIGURE 2.3 Opening Control Panel

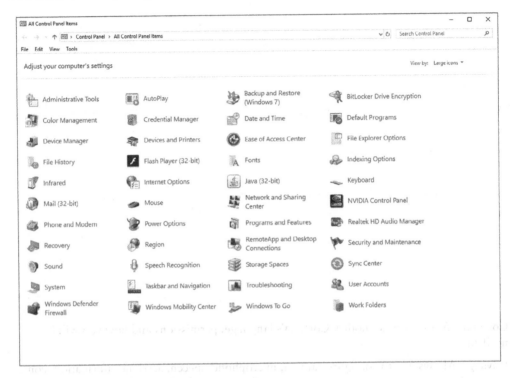

Configuring System Settings

Some of the most important configuration settings for a user are the system settings within Control Panel. These include gathering generation information about your system, changing the computer name, adding the computer to a domain, accessing the device manager, configuring remote settings, configuring startup and recovery options, and configuring overall performance settings.

To access the system settings, you can do one of the following:

- In Control Panel, in Category view, click System and Security and then click System or click View amount of RAM and processor speed.

- In Control Panel, in Classic view, double-click the System applet.

- Right-click Computer and choose Properties.

- Right-click the Start button and choose System.

In Windows, there are often several ways to perform a task.

At the top of the screen, your Windows edition and system type are shown. If Windows comes in 64-bit, it will show 64-bit Operating System in the middle of the screen. Toward the bottom of the screen, you will see the computer name and domain (if any) if Windows is activated and the Product ID. See Figure 2.4.

FIGURE 2.4   Displaying System settings

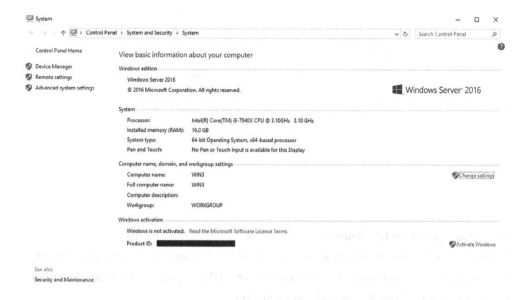

To help identify computers, you should name each computer with a meaningful name. This can be done within the System settings within Control Panel. You can also add a computer to a domain or workgroup.

Every computer must have a unique computer name assigned to a network. If two computers have the same name, one or both of the computers will have trouble communicating on the network. To change the computer name, open System from Control Panel. Then click the Change Settings option in the Computer name, domain, and workgroup settings. In the System Properties dialog box, with the Computer Name tab selected, click the Change button. See Figure 2.5. Any changes to the computer name or workgroup/domain name will require a reboot.

FIGURE 2.5   Displaying System Properties

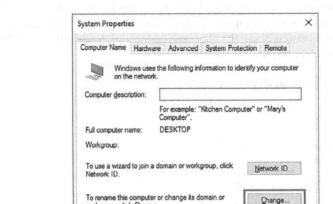

Add a Computer to the Domain

To add a computer running Windows Server 2016 to the domain, perform the following steps:

1. On a computer that is running Windows Server 2016, log on as a local administrator.

2. Right-click the Start button and choose System.

3. When the Control Panel System page opens, in the "Computer name, domain, and workgroup settings" option, click the Change Settings option.

4. When the System Properties dialog box opens, the Computer Name tab is already selected. Click the Change button.

5. When the Computer Name/Domain Changes dialog box opens, select the Domain option. Then type in the name of the domain, such as **Adatum.com,** and click OK.

6. When the Windows Security dialog box opens, log on as **administrator** with the password of **Pa$$w0rd,** and click OK.

7. When you receive a welcome to the domain message, click OK.

8. When you are prompted to restart your computer to apply these changes, click OK.

9. Back at the System Properties dialog box, click Close.

10. When you are prompted to restart your computer to apply these changes, click Restart Now.

The *Remote Desktop Protocol (RDP)* is a proprietary protocol that was developed by Microsoft to connect to another computer over a network connection using the same graphical interface that you would use if you were sitting in front of the physical server. RDP uses TCP port 3389. Typically, you would access computers remotely using the *Remote Desktop Connection (RDC)*, which would allow you to connect to a Remote Desktop Session Host or to a Remote Application.

To enable either or both of these technologies, open the System Properties (open Control Panel, click System and Security, click Security, and then click Remote settings), as shown in Figure 2.6. By default, the Remote Assistance feature is not installed on Windows Server 2016. By default, Remote Desktop is installed, but it is not enabled.

FIGURE 2.6 Enabling Remote Desktop

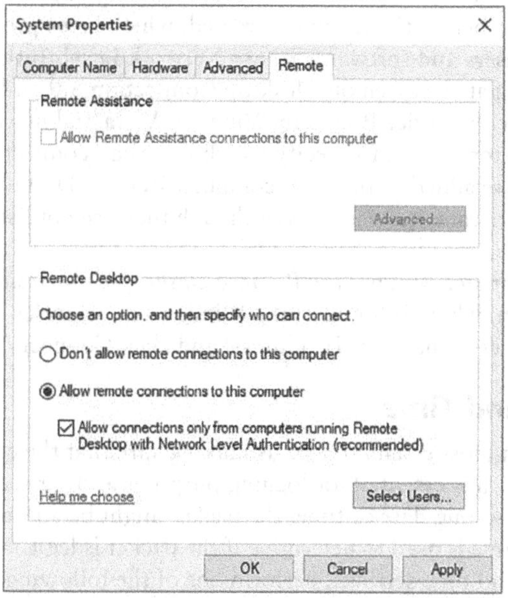

Install the Remote Assistance Feature

To install the Remote Assistance feature, perform the following steps:

1. Open Server Manager.

2. At the top of the Server Manager console, click Manage ➤ Add Roles and Features. The Add Roles and Feature Wizard opens.

3. On the Before You Begin page, click Next.

4. Select Role-Based Or Feature-Based Installation and then click Next.

5. On the Select Destination Server page, select the server that you are installing to and click Next.

6. On the Select Server Roles page, click Next.

7. On the Select Features page, select the Remote Assistance feature and click Next.

8. On the Confirm Installation Selections page, click Install.

9. When the installation is complete, click Close.

Click the Advanced button in the Remote Assistance section to specify the maximum amount of time an invitation can remain open (the default is 6 hours) and whether the computer can be controlled remotely or not. You can also specify whether you can create invitations that can only be used from computers running Windows Vista or later, which will encrypt the IP address, which, in turn, cannot be read by Windows XP.

For Remote Desktop, the "Allow connections only from computers running Remote Desktop with Network Level Authentication (recommended)" option is used to require the user to be authenticated before the session is created, which helps protect the remote computer from malicious users and software. To use Network Level Authentication, the client computer must be using at least Remote Desktop Connection 6.0 and operating systems such as Windows XP with Service Pack 3 or Windows Vista and newer.

The Select Users button is used to specify which users can connect to the system using the RDP. These users are added to the local computer Remote Desktop Users group. The Administrators group already has access even though they are not listed in the Remote Desktop Users list.

To connect to a computer, you use the *Remote Desktop Connections (RDC)*, which is the mstsc.exe program, which is found in the Windows Accessories folder. When the program opens, specify a server name or IP address, and click Connect.

Changing Date and Time

One of your easiest but most essential tasks is making sure that the computer has the correct date and time, which is essential for logging purposes and for security. If a secure packet is sent with the wrong date or time, the packet might be automatically denied because the date and time is used to determine if the packet is legit.

To access the date and time settings, perform one of the following steps:

- In Category view in Control Panel, click Clock, Language, and Region and then click Set the time and date.

- In Icon view, double-click Date and Time.

- If the date and time is shown in the notification area, double-click the date and time.

To set the clock:

1. Click the Date and Time tab and then click "Change date and time."

2. Double-click the hour, minutes, or seconds and then click the arrows to increase or decrease the value.

3. Click OK.

To change the time zone, click "Change time zone" and then click your current time zone in the drop-down list. Then click OK.

If you are part of a domain, the computer should be synchronized with the domain controllers. When you have a computer that is not part of a domain, you can synchronize with an Internet time server by clicking the Internet Time tab and then selecting the check box next to "Synchronize with an Internet time server." Then select a time server and click OK.

Configuring and Optimizing User Account Control (UAC)

User Account Control (UAC) is a technology used with Windows 10 and Windows Server 2016 to enhance system security by detecting and preventing unauthorized changes to the system. Some applications might not run properly using a standard user credential if the application needs to access restricted files or registry locations.

Certification Ready?

Which security mechanism is used to notify you when a program makes changes to the system?

With UAC, when a user logs on to Windows Server 2016, the system issues a token, which indicates the user's access level. Standard users receive a standard user token, and members of the Administrators group receive two tokens, a standard user token and an administrator token. Normally, both types of users use the standard user token. However, if you need to perform an administrative task, UAC prompts indicate that a change needs to be made. If you are an administrator, click Yes to continue. If you are not an administrator, you must log on with an Administrator account. If malicious code tries to access your system and make changes without your knowledge, the UAC prompts notify you, and you can stop the program from making those changes.

In Windows 10 and Windows Server 2016, the number of operating system applications and tasks that require elevated permission is fewer when compared with older versions of Windows. The default UAC setting allows a standard user to perform the following tasks without receiving a UAC prompt:

- View Windows settings
- Pair Bluetooth devices with the computer
- Reset the network adapter and perform other network diagnostic and repair tasks
- Establish a local area network (LAN) connection or wireless connection

- Modify display settings
- Play and burn CD/DVD media
- Change the desktop background for the current user
- Open Date and Time in Control Panel and change the time zone
- Use Remote Desktop to connect to another computer
- Change the user's own password
- Configure battery power options
- Configure accessibility options
- Restore a user's backup files
- Set up computer synchronization

UAC will prompt you and require elevation to an Administrator account for the following tasks:

- Install and uninstall applications
- Install a driver for a device
- Install Windows updates
- Install an ActiveX control
- Open Windows Firewall in Control Panel
- Change a user's account type
- Configure Remote Desktop access
- Add or remove a user account
- Copy or move files into the Program Files directory or the Windows directory
- Schedule automated tasks
- Restore system backup files
- Configure Automatic Updates
- Browse to another user's directory

In Windows Server 2016, four UAC settings are available through Control Panel:

Always notify me   The user is always prompted when changes are made to the computer and the desktop is dimmed.

Notify me only when apps try to make changes to my computer (default)   When a program makes a change, a prompt appears, and the desktop dims. Otherwise, the user is not prompted.

Notify me only when apps try to make changes to my computer (do not dim my desktop)   When a program makes a change, a prompt appears, and the desktop does not dim.

Never notify me   UAC is off.

To configure UAC through Control Panel, use the following procedure.

Review UAC Settings

To review UAC settings, log on to Windows Server 2016 using an account with administrator privileges and then perform the following steps:

1. Right-click the Start button, and click Control Panel.

2. In the Control Panel, search for UAC, and click Change User Account Control settings. Alternatively, you can click System and Security ➤ Change User Account Control Settings. The User Account Control Settings dialog box opens, as shown in Figure 2.7

FIGURE 2.7   Reviewing UAC settings

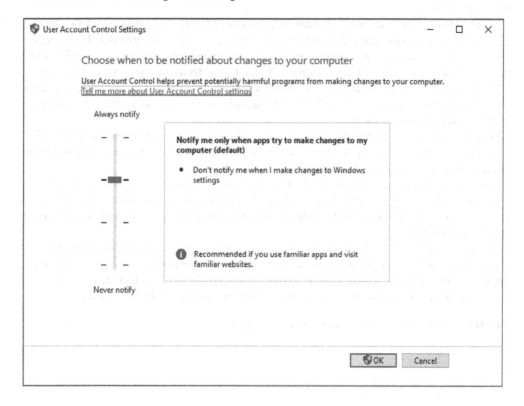

3. Read the current setting and then drag the slider up and down to each setting to review its description:

   ▪ Always notify me

   ▪ Notify me only when apps try to make changes to my computer (default)

   ▪ Notify me only when apps try to make changes to my computer (do not dim my desktop)

   ▪ Never notify me

4. In the User Account Control Settings dialog box, click Cancel.

Networking with Windows Server 2016

When accessing computers on a network, you typically communicate by using their host names. If you are accessing a website, you enter a friendly name such as www.microsoft.com. Every device that connects to your network or the Internet must have an Internet Protocol (IP) address. You also need a way to associate these names to their assigned IP address.

Internet Protocol (IP) is the key protocol in the TCP/IP suite. It is responsible for adding addressing information to the packets for the sender and the receiver, as well as adding data to help route and deliver the packet. Windows Server 2016 uses TCP/IP as its default networking protocol.

Transmission Control Protocol/Internet Protocol (TCP/IP) is a set of protocols that allows computers to exchange data within a network and between networks. These protocols (or rules) manage the content, format, timing, sequencing, and error control of the messages that are exchanged between the devices. Every device that communicates over TCP/IP must have a unique IP address. Windows Server 2016 uses a dual-layer architecture that enables it to implement both IPv4 and IPv6 address schemes. Both share the common TCP Transport layer protocol.

Before configuring TCP/IP on your network, take time to plan the implementation. For example, how big do you expect your network to be? How will your network be designed from a physical and logical standpoint?

Network settings can be configured either manually or automatically using DHCP. Using manual settings can introduce configuration issues that could affect communications. Using a centralized approach to IP address management requires you to have a solid understanding of DHCP.

In Windows Server 2016, the *Network and Sharing Center* (as shown in Figure 2.8) is the primary tool that can view, create, and modify local area network (LAN), wireless local area network (WLAN), virtual private network (VPN), dial-up, and Broadband connections. It can also be used to configure connections and advanced sharing settings.

FIGURE 2.8   Using the Network and Sharing Center

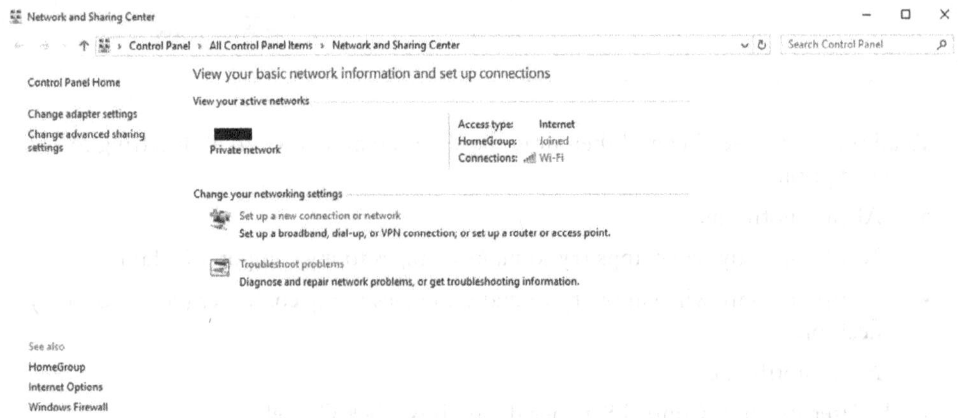

Configuring TCP/IP on a Windows Server 2016 computer can be done manually or automatically. Setting up TCP/IP manually involves configuring it to use a static IP address. This involves entering an IP address, a subnet mask, and (if you need to access computers outside of the local network segment) a default gateway address. To resolve friendly names to IP addresses, you also need to configure at least one IP address for a DNS on your network.

Define a Static IPv4 Address

To define a static IPv4 address, perform the following steps:

1. On LON-SVR1, on the taskbar, right-click the network status icon and choose Open Network And Sharing Center.
2. Click Change Adapter Settings.
3. Right-click a network adapter, such as Ethernet, and choose Properties.
4. When the Ethernet Properties dialog box opens, as shown in Figure 2.9, click Internet Protocol Version 4 (TCP/IPv4) and then click Properties.

FIGURE 2.9   Configuring the properties of an Ethernet adapter

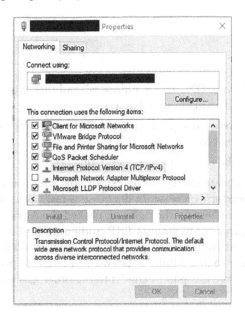

5. Select "Use the following IP address" and then type the IPv4 address, subnet mask, and default gateway you want to use, as shown in Figure 2.10.

FIGURE 2.10 Entering a static IPv4 address

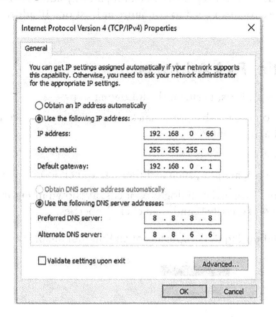

6. Select "Use the following DNS server addresses" and then type an IP address for a preferred DNS server and an alternate DNS server.

7. Click OK to accept your settings and to close the Internet Protocol Version 4 (TCP/IPv4) Properties dialog box.

8. Click Close to close the Ethernet Properties dialog box.

If you selected the Validate settings upon exit option after configuring IP settings, Windows Server 2016 performs a network diagnostics test to check your settings for any problems and offers to help fix them. If you clicked the Advanced button, you could make additional configurations to your TCP/IP configuration. For example, in Windows Server 2016, you can configure multiple gateways. When you do this, a metric is used to determine which gateway to use. Multiple gateways are used to provide fault tolerance so if one router goes down, the computer defaults to the other gateway. You can configure additional gateways and DNS settings in the Advanced TCP/IP Settings dialog box (see Figure 2.11).

FIGURE 2.11   Reviewing advanced TCP/IP setting options

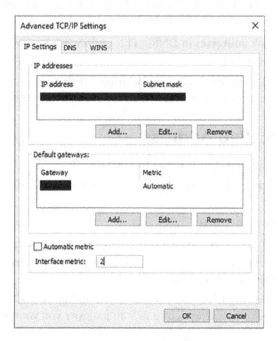

DNS server addresses, in order of use   You can specify multiple DNS servers to use for name resolution. The order listed determines the sequence in which your client attempts to resolve host names. If the first server does not respond to a name resolution request, the client contacts the next one in the list.

Append primary and connection specific DNS suffixes   This is selected by default. If you attempt to access a computer named FileServer1, and the parent name is contoso.com, the name resolves to FileServer1.contoso.com. If the FQDN does not exist in the domain, the query fails. The parent name used (contoso.com) is configured on the System Properties/ Computer Name tab.

Append parent suffixes of the primary DNS suffix   This is selected by default. It works as follows: If the computer FS2 is in the eastcoast.contoso.com domain, DNS attempts to resolve the name to FS2.eastcoast.contoso.com. If this doesn't work, it tries FS2.contoso.com.

Append these DNS suffixes (in order)   Use this option when you want to specify DNS suffixes to use other than resolving names through your parent domain.

DNS suffix for this connection   This setting overrides DNS names that are already configured for this connection. This is typically configured through the System Properties/Computer Name tab by clicking the More button.

Register this connection's addresses in DNS   This option, selected by default, automatically enters the FQDN in DNS records.

Use this connection's DNS suffix in DNS registration   If this option is selected, all IP addresses for this connection are registered in DNS at the parent domain.

Define a Static IPv6 Address

To define a static IPv6 address, perform the following steps.

1. On the taskbar, right-click the network status icon and choose Open Network And Sharing Center.
2. Click Change Adapter Settings.
3. Right-click a network adapter, such as Ethernet, and choose Properties.
4. When the Ethernet Properties dialog box opens, click Internet Protocol Version 6 (TCP/IPv6) and then click Properties.
5. Select "Use the following IPv6 address" (as shown in Figure 2.12) and then type the IPv6 address, subnet prefix length, and default gateway you want to use.

FIGURE 2.12   Entering a static IPv6 address

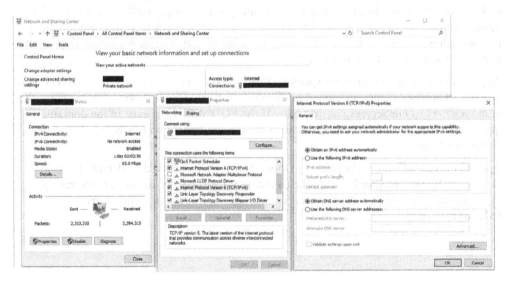

6. Select "Use the following DNS server addresses" and then type an IP address for a preferred DNS server and an alternate DNS server.

7. Click OK to accept your settings and to close the Internet Protocol Version 6 (TCP/IPv6) Properties dialog box.

8. Click Close to close the Ethernet Properties dialog box.

Before moving on to the next section, you should understand how proxy settings can affect your access to the network or the Internet. A proxy server is a server that is used to translate between public and private networks using Network Address Translation (NAT). It is usually placed on the edge of a corporate network. With NAT, you can have a single public address and multiple private addresses. A proxy server hides the internal addresses and allows you to have a multitude of private addresses.

When you purchase a wireless router for your house, you connect your cable or DSL modem to the wireless router, which will be assigned a public external address. You can then connect multiple computers or hosts inside your house, which are assigned private addresses. The router will then translate between the public address and the private addresses.

Usually when you go to the Internet within a corporation, you need to specify the address and port of the proxy server. If not, while you may be able to access internal resources, you will not be able to access resources on the Internet.

To change the proxy settings for Internet Explorer (which is also used for other applications), you can do one of the following:

- Start Internet Explorer. Then select the Connections tab and click the LAN settings button.

- While in Category view in the Control Panel, click Network and Internet and then click Internet Options. Then select the Connections tab and click the LAN settings button.

- While in Icon view, double-click Internet Options. Then select the Connections tab and click the LAN settings button.

Most corporations should have servers that automatically configures the proxy settings when you have automatically detect settings enabled. However, if you need to use a different proxy server, you will need to deselect "Automatically detect settings" and select the "Use a proxy server for your LAN" option. You will then specify an address and port number for your proxy server. Common ports are 80, 8080, and 3128. Since you don't want to go through the proxy server for your internal servers, you would usually select the Bypass proxy server for local address box. See Figure 2.13.

FIGURE 2.13   Proxy Settings in Internet Explorer

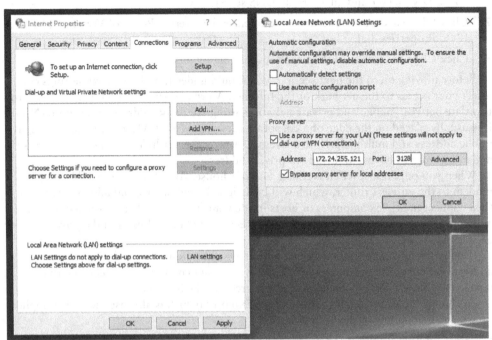

Managing Devices and Device Drivers

Since a computer running Windows Server 2016 can have a wide array of devices, it can sometimes be a challenge to make all devices operate correctly, especially since servers often have non-standard hardware that may require you to manually install or update drivers.

Certification Ready

How do you manage device drivers in Windows? 1.1

Device drivers are programs that control a device. You can think of them as translator between the device and the operating system and programs that use the device. Programmers write code that access generic commands such as sending sound, and the device driver will translate those generic commands to specific commands understood by the device such as a specific sound card. While Windows Server 2016 includes many drivers (built-in or included on the installation DVD), some drivers will come with the device or you will have to go to the manufacturer's website to download them. Since these drivers are software, there may be times where you may need to go to the manufacturer's website to retrieve newer drivers (although sometimes older drivers work better than newer drivers) or download them through Microsoft's updates.

To prevent you from constantly inserting the Windows Server 2016 installation DVD, Windows Server includes a driver store with an extensive library of device drivers. Drivers will be located in the C:\Windows\System32\DriverStore. In the DriverStore folder, you will find subfolders with located driver information such as en-US for US English and will have hundreds of different drivers. When you add a hardware device, Windows can check the Driver Store for the correct driver.

Understanding Plug and Play Devices

For years, Windows has benefited from *Plug and Play* (PnP) where you install or connect a device, the device is automatically recognized, it is automatically configured, and the appropriate driver is installed. Today, this technology has been expanded beyond expansion cards to include other technologies.

Way back in 1983, Intel and Microsoft released Plug and Play. As a computer technician, this made life a lot easier because you did not have to worry about setting DIP switches or jumpers on the card. Today, if you use Plug and Play hardware combined with a Plug and Play operating system such as Windows, you can plug in the hardware, and Windows will search for an appropriate device driver and automatically configure it to work without interfering with other devices. If Windows does not have a driver available on the device after detection, Windows will prompt you to provide a media or path to the driver. Eventually, the driver will be added to the driver store. Today, Plug and Play has been expanded beyond expansion cards to include USB, IEEE 1394 (also known as FireWire), and SCSI devices.

Today, most devices are Plug and Play. Therefore, you add or connect a new device, and Windows will automatically recognize the device and load the appropriate drivers. When a driver cannot be found, it may ask if you want to connect to the Internet in an attempt to find one or to specify the location of one such as on a disk. You can also open the Control Panel, click Hardware, and select "Add a device" under the Devices and Printers section. It will then search for any devices that are not currently recognized by Windows.

As part of the configuration process, Windows assigns the following system resources to the device you are installing so that the device can operate at the same time as other expansion cards:

- Interrupt request (IRQ) line numbers – The device sends a signal to get the attention of the processor when it's ready to accept or send information. Each device must be assigned a unique IRQ number.

- Direct memory access (DMA) channels – Memory access that does not involve the processor.

- Input/output (I/O) port addresses – A channel through which data is transferred between a device and the processor. The port appears to the processor as one or more memory addresses that it can use or send or receive data.

- Memory address ranges – A portion of computer memory that can be allocated to a device and used by a program or the operating system. Devices are usually allocated a range of memory addresses.

Understanding Signed Drivers

Windows was designed to work with a large array of devices. Unfortunately, in the past, there were times when a device was added and a driver was loaded, the driver caused problems with Windows. As a result, Microsoft started using signed drivers to help fight faulty drivers. While signed drivers will not fix a faulty driver, it makes sure the publisher of the driver is identified, the driver has not been altered, and the driver has been thoroughly tested to be reliable and will not cause a security problem.

A *signed driver* is a device driver that includes a digital signature, which is an electronic security mark that can indicate the publisher of the software and information that can show if a driver has been altered. When it is signed by Microsoft, the driver has been thoroughly tested to make sure that the driver will not cause problems with the system's reliability and not cause a security problem.

Drivers that are included on the Windows installation DVD or downloaded from the Microsoft's update website are digitally signed. A driver that lacks a valid digital signature, or was altered after it was signed, cannot be installed on 64-bit versions of Windows. If you have problems with a device driver, you should only download drivers from Microsoft's update website or the manufacturer's website.

 You cannot install a driver that lacks a valid digital signature or that has been altered after it was signed on Windows Server 2016.

Using Devices and Printers

Starting with Windows Server 2008 and Windows Vista, Windows includes the Devices and Printers to quickly allow users to see all the devices connected to the computer and to configure and troubleshoot these devices. IT will also allow you to view information about the make, model, and manufacturer and give you detailed information about the sync capabilities of a mobile phone or other mobile devices.

Devices and Printers folder gives you a quick view of devices connected to your computer that you can connect or disconnect from your computer through a port or network connection. Therefore, this would include mobile devices such as music players and digital cameras, USB devices, and network devices. See Figure 2.14. It does not include items installed inside your computer such as internal disk drives, expansion cards, and RAM, and it will not display legacy devices such as keyboards and mice connected through a PS/2 or serial port.

To open the Devices and Printers, open the Control and click "View devices and printers" under Hardware while in Category view or double-click Devices and Printers in Icon view. You can also open Devices and Printers by clicking the Start button and clicking Devices and Printers.

FIGURE 2.14   Devices and Printers

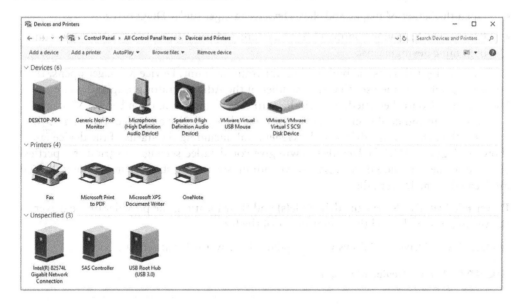

When you right-click a device icon in the Devices and Printers folder, you can select from a list of tasks that vary depending on the capabilities of the device. For example, you might be able to see what's printing on a network printer, view files stored on a USB flash drive, or open a program from the device manufacturer. For mobile devices that support the new Device Stage feature in Windows, you can also open advanced, device-specific features in Windows from the right-click menu, such as the ability to sync with a mobile phone or change ringtones.

Using Device Manager

Device Manager provides you with a graphical view of the hardware (internal and external) that is installed your computer and gives you a way to manage and configure your devices. With Device Manager, you can determine whether a device is recognized by Windows and if the device is working properly. You can also enable, disable, or uninstall the device, roll back the previous version of the driver, identify the device driver including its version, and change hardware configuration settings.

To open the Device Manager, you can do one of the following:

- Open the Control Panel in Category view, click Hardware, and click Device Manager.
- Open the Control Panel in Icon view and double-click Device Manager.
- Open the System Properties and click Device Manager.

- Open the Computer Management console and click Device Manager.

- Open the Server Manager and click Device Manager under Diagnostics.

- Execute the following command from a command prompt, Start Search box or Run box: mmc devmgmt.msc

If you are logged on as the built-in Administrator account, Device Manager opens. If you are logged on as the user that is a member of the Administrator group and you have User Account Control enabled, you will have to click Continue to open Device Manager.

If you locate and double-click a device or right-click a device and select Properties, you can view the details of the driver in the General tab including the status of the device (as shown in Figure 2.15). The Details tab will give you detailed settings of various properties assigned to the hardware device. As a server administrator, most of the items you will need are located at the Driver tab:

Driver File Details   Shows the driver file(s) and their location, the provider of the driver, the version of the file, and the digital signer of the file.

Update Device Drivers   Allows you to update the driver software for a device.

FIGURE 2.15   Device Manager

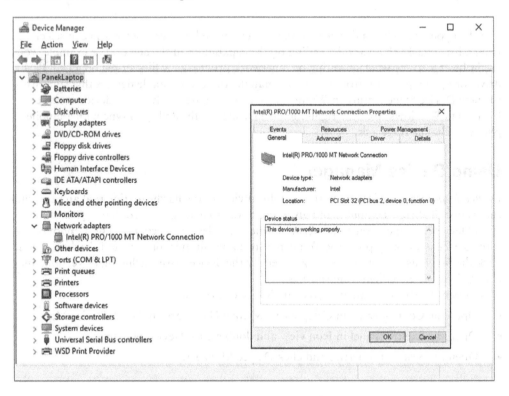

Roll Back Drivers Use to roll back a driver if problems exist when you update a device driver. If there's no previous version of the driver installed for the selected device, the Roll Back Driver button will be unavailable.

Disable/Enable Devices Instead of uninstalling the driver, you can use the Device Manager to disable the device.

Uninstall a Device Used to remove the driver software from the computer.

Additional tabs such as Advanced, Resources (Memory Range, I/O Range, IRQ and DMA), and Power Management may be shown depending on the type of device. See Figure 2.16. If there is conflict for your resources, you can try to use Device Manager to change the memory range, I/O range, IRQ, or DMA of the device). In addition, if you right-click a device in Device Manager, you can update driver software, disable the device, uninstall the device, or scan for hardware changes.

FIGURE 2.16 Device Properties

When you use the Device Manager that comes with Windows 10 and Windows Server 2016, you should note the following:

- A down black arrow indicates a disabled device. A disabled device is a device that is physically present in the computer and is consuming resources, but does not have a driver loaded.

- A black exclamation point (!) on a yellow triangle indicates the device is in a problem state.

- You also need to look to see if any devices are listed under Other devices or has a generic name such as Ethernet Controller or PCI Simple Communications Controller, which indicates that the proper driver is not loaded.

With Device Manager, an administrator can disable any device in the computer, using any of the following:

- By selecting the device and choosing Disable from the Action menu.
- By right-clicking the device and choosing Disable from the shortcut menu.
- By opening the device's Properties dialog box and on the Driver tab, clicking the Disable button.

Disabling a device does not affect the hardware in any way or uninstall the device driver; it just renders the device inoperative until it is enabled again. An administrator cannot disable devices that are necessary for the system to function, such as the processor, and some devices that are in use. Some events require that the system be restarted before they can be disabled.

 Disabling a device releases the hardware resources it was using back to the operating system. If the computer is restarted with the device disabled, then Windows may reassign those hardware resources to other devices. If an administrator re-enables the device, the computer may allocate different hardware resources than it had originally.

When an administrator updates a driver using Device Manager, they can point to a location on a computer where they have already saved the new driver, or they can run a search on the computer and the Internet. To update a device driver, use the following procedure.

Update a Device Driver

Log on to the computer using an account with Administrator privileges, and perform the following steps:

1. Open Device Manager and locate the device to be updated.
2. Double-click the device to update so that its Properties dialog box appears.
3. Click the Driver tab.
4. Click the Update Driver button. The "How do you want to search for driver software?" page appears.
5. Click "Browse my computer for driver software" to specify a location for the driver or to select from a list of installed drivers. Click "Search automatically for updated driver software" to initiate a search for a driver.
6. Click Next when the driver is located to install. The "Windows Has Successfully Updated Your Driver Software" page appears.
7. Click Close.
8. Close the Device Manager window.

When updating a device driver, the operating system does not discard the old driver completely. It is not uncommon for new drivers to cause issues, and many users find that they would prefer to go back to the older version.

This is possible with the Roll Back feature, which an administrator will initiate by clicking the Roll Back Driver button on the Driver tab of the device's Properties dialog box. This procedure uninstalls the current driver and reinstalls the previous version, returning the device to its state before the update was performed.

There is always the possibility of a problem that, depending on the devices involved, could be trivial or catastrophic. For a peripheral device, such as a printer, a hardware misconfiguration or faulty driver would probably just cause the new device to malfunction. However, if the device involved is a graphics adapter, a bad driver could prevent the system from functioning.

 Before installing new drivers, you should make sure you have a good backup.

Troubleshooting Problem Devices

To troubleshoot hardware or driver problems, consider some of the following techniques:

- Open the Properties dialog box for the device and check the Device Status box on the General tab. If the device is malfunctioning, this tab informs the administrator of its status and enables them to launch a troubleshooter.

- Open the Device Manager and delete the device entirely. Then restart the system and allow the system to detect and install the device again. This process will cause Windows to reallocate hardware resources to the device, which could resolve the problem if it was caused by a hardware resource conflict.

- If the device or driver malfunction prevents the system from running properly, the administrator can start the computer in Safe Mode by pressing the F8 key as the system starts. Safe Mode loads the operating system with a minimal set of generic device drivers, bypassing the troublesome ones, so the administrator can uninstall or troubleshoot them, as needed.

Device Manager also displays all of the devices installed on a computer. If a device is experiencing issues, then Device Manager uses symbols to provide information about the particular error condition.

The symbols are:

- Blue question mark inside white circle: The driver is installed, but may not provide full functionality.

- Red "X": The device is installed on the computer and is consuming resources, the protected mode driver is not loaded, or the device was installed improperly.

- Yellow warning symbol with black exclamation point: The device is in a problem state; the device might be functioning. A problem code will be displayed with the device.

- Blue "I" on white field: Use automatic settings was not selected for the device or the resource was manually selected; does not indicate a problem or disabled state.
- Problem code: This is the code that explains the problem with the device.
- White circle with down arrow: The device was disabled by an administrator or user.

Managing Through Group Policies

One asset of the Windows operating system is that it offers users a great deal of power and flexibility. From installing new software to adding device drivers, users can make many changes to their workstation configurations. However, this level of flexibility could be a likely issue. For example, an inexperienced user may accidentally change settings, causing problems that may require hours to correct. This is where Group Policies come in handy.

Group policies are a collection of rules that an administrator can apply to objects within Active Directory. Specifically, Group Policy settings are assigned at the site, domain, and OU levels, and they can apply to user accounts and computer accounts. For example, a system administrator can use group policies to configure the following settings:

- Restricting users from installing new programs
- Disallowing the use of the Control Panel
- Limiting choices for display and Desktop settings

Using Microsoft Management Console and Administrative Tools

The *Microsoft Management Console* (MMC) is one of the primary administrative tools used to manage Windows and many of the network services provided by Windows. It provides a standard method to create, save, and open the various administrative tools provided by Windows. When you open Administrative Tools, most of these programs are an MMC.

To start an empty MMC, go to the command prompt, Start Search box, or Run box, and type **mmc** or **mmc.exe**. Every MMC has a console tree that displays the hierarchical organization of snap-ins or pluggable modules) and extensions (a snap-in that requires a parent snap-in). By adding and deleting snap-ins and extensions, users can customize the console or access tools that are not located in Administrative Tools. You can add snap-ins to an MMC by opening the File menu and selecting Add/Remove Snap-ins. See Figure 2.17.

FIGURE 2.17 Adding snap-ins to a blank MMC

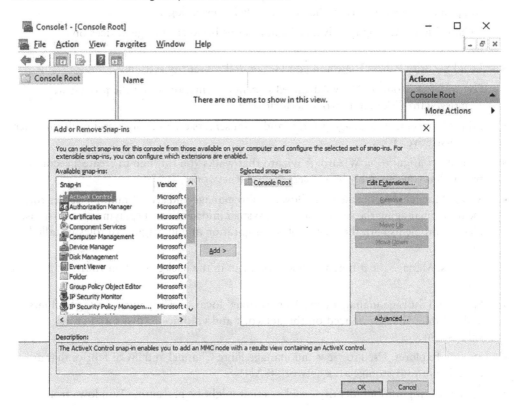

Administrative Tools is a folder in the Control Panel that contains tools for system administrators and advanced users. To access the Administrative Tools, open the Control Panel, open Administrative Tools by clicking Start, Control Panel, System and Security while in Category View or double-click the Administrative Tools applet while in Icon view. There is also a quick link on Windows Servers that can be accessed by clicking the Start button.

Some common administrative tools in this folder include the following:

- Component Services: Configure and administer Component Object Model (COM) components. Component Services is designed for use by developers and administrators.

- Computer Management: Manage local or remote computers by using a single, consolidated desktop tool. Using Computer Management, you can perform many tasks, such as monitoring system events, configuring hard disks, and managing system performance.

- Data Sources (ODBC): Use Open Database Connectivity (ODBC) to move data from one type of database (a data source) to another.

- Event Viewer: View information about significant events, such as a program starting or stopping, or a security error, that are recorded in event logs.
- iSCSI Initiator: Configure advanced connections between storage devices on a network.
- Local Security Policy: View and edit Group Policy security settings.
- Performance Monitor: View Advanced system information about the processor, memory, hard disk and network performance.
- Print Management: Manage printers and print servers on a network and perform other administrative tasks.
- Security configuration Wizard: A wizard that walks you through to create a security policy that you can apply to any server on the network.
- Server Manager: A console that allows you to manage and secure multiple server roles including managing the server's identity, system information, displaying server status, identify problems with the server role configuration and managing all roles installed on the server.
- Services: Manage the different services that run in the background on your computer.
- Share and Storage management: A centralized location for you to manage folders and volumes that are shared on the network and volumes in disks and storage subsystems.
- Storage Explorer: Used to view and manage Fibre Channel and iSCSI fabrics that are available in your storage area network (SAN)
- System Configuration: Identify problems that might be preventing Windows from running correctly.
- Task Scheduler: Schedule programs or other tasks to run automatically.
- Windows Firewall with Advanced Security: Configure advanced firewall settings on both this computer and remote computers on your network.
- Windows Memory Diagnostics: Check your computer's memory to see whether it is functioning properly.
- Windows PowerShell Modules: A task-based command-line shell and scripting language designed especially for system administration.
- Windows Server Backup: Use to back up and restore the server.

When you use these tools, you might assume that they are used only to manage the local computer. However, many of them can be used to manage remote computer as well. For example, you can use the Computer Management and Server Management console to connect to and manage other computers, assuming you have administrative rights to the computer.

Using Computer Management Console and Server Management Console

The Computer Management Console and Server Management console are two of the primary tools to manage a Windows server and include the most commonly used MMC snap-ins.

The *Computer Management Console* includes multiple snap-ins including Task Scheduler, Event Viewer, Shared Folders, Local Users and Groups, Performance, Device Management, Routing and Remote Access, Services, and WMI Control. See Figure 2.18. If you are using Windows 10, you can access the Computer Management console through the Administrative tools or by right-clicking Computer/My Computer and clicking Manage. If you are running Windows Server 2016, you can only access it from the Administrative Tools folder.

FIGURE 2.18   Computer Management Console

If you right-click Computer on a computer running Windows Server 2016, you will open the *Server Management console* instead. The Server Manager allows you to install Windows server Roles and Features, view the Event Viewer logs, access performance monitoring tools, Device Manager, Task Scheduler, Windows Firewall with Advanced Security,

Services, Local Users and Groups, Windows Server Backup, and Disk management. See Figure 2.19.

FIGURE 2.19   Server Manager Console

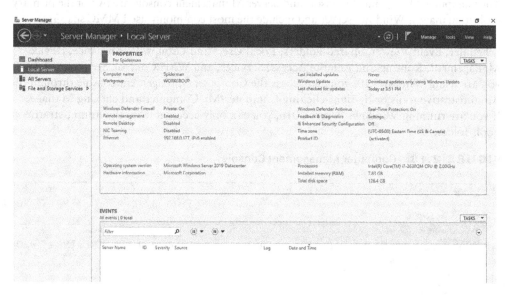

    Local Users and Groups will not appear on domain controllers.

The Remote Server Administration Tools pack is a feature available with Windows Server 2016 that enables remote management of Windows Server 2016, Windows Server 2012 R2, and Windows Server 2012 from a computer running Windows Server 2016, by allowing you to open and run management tools and snap-ins to manage roles, role services, or features on a remote computer.

The Remote Server Administration Tools include tools for the following roles:

- Active Directory Certificate Services Tools

- Active Directory Domain Services (AD DS) and Active Directory Lightweight Directory Services (AD LDS) Tools

- Active Directory Rights Management Services (AD RMS) Tools

- DHCP Server Tools

- DNS Server Tools

- Fax Server Tools

- File Services Tools

- Hyper-V Tools
- Network Policy and Access Services Tools
- Print and Document Services Tools
- Remote Desktop Services Tools
- Web Server (IIS) Tools
- Windows Deployment Services Tools

   The Remote Server Administration Tools include tools for the following features:

- BitLocker Drive Encryption Administration Utilities
- BITS Server Extensions Tools
- Failover Clustering Tools
- Network Load Balancing Tools
- SMTP Server Tools
- WINS Server Tools

Installing Programs, Roles, and Features

By default, most of the roles and features that are available for Windows Server 2016 must be installed or enabled before you can use them. This is to reduce the surface attack that hackers or malicious software could utilize. When managing servers, if you don't need a service or program running, you should not have installed or enabled.

Managing Programs

Windows Server 2016 includes many roles and features to provide a wide range of network services. However, you will often have to install programs. Some of these programs such as SQL Server or Exchange come from Microsoft, while many others do not. Therefore, you will need to know how to install and uninstall these applications.

   If you need to install a program in Windows such as an anti-virus software package, Microsoft Exchange, Microsoft SQL Server, or any other program that does not come with Windows Server, you usually insert the disk, usually a CD or DVD, into the drive and the installation program will automatically start. Other programs, you may need to run a command, download and install using your browser, or double-click an executable file such as file with an .exe or msi extension.

   Most Windows programs allow you to uninstall a program from your computer if you no longer use it or if you want to free up space on your hard disk. For Windows Server 2016, you can use Programs and Features to uninstall programs or to change a program's configuration by adding or removing certain options.

Uninstall or Change a Program

To uninstall a program or change a program in Windows Server 2016, perform the following:

1. Open the Control Panel.

2. If you are in Category View, click Programs and click Programs and Features. If you are in Icon view, double-click Programs and Features.

3. Select a program, and then click Uninstall. See Figure 2.20.

FIGURE 2.20   Programs and Features

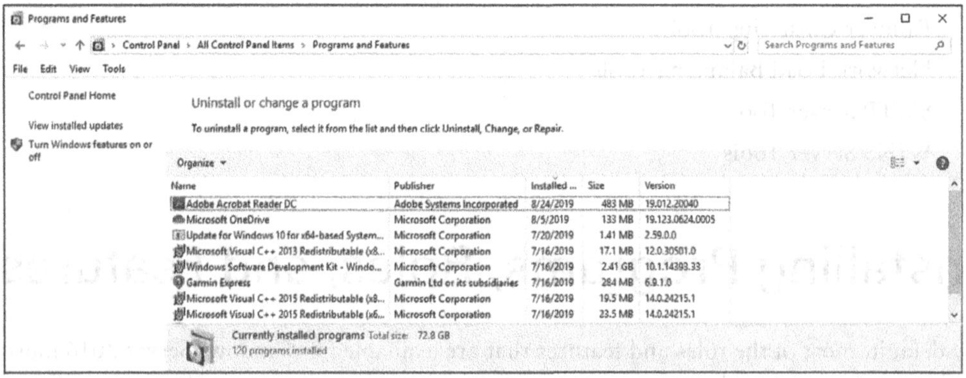

If the program you want to uninstall isn't listed, it might not have been written for Windows. You should check the documentation for the software.

Some programs include the option to repair the program in addition to uninstalling it, but many simply offer the option to uninstall. To change the program, click Change or Repair. If you are prompted for an administrator password or confirmation, type the password or provide confirmation.

Managing Roles and Features

A *server role* is a set of software programs that perform a specific function as a network service for multiple users. *Role services* are made up of one or more role services that provide the functionality of the server role. A *feature* is a software program that is not directly part of a server role, but can support or augment the functionality of a server role. To add, remove, or manage server roles and features, you use Server Manager.

Although you could install and configure all server roles and features, it is never recommended for several reasons. First, it would consume a large amount of resources. Second, by not running all roles and features, you are minimizing your security footprint by only using the necessary role services.

Install Windows Server 2016 Server Roles and Features

To install Windows Server 2016 server roles and features, perform the following steps:

1. Log on to LON-SVR1 as **adatum\administrator** with the password of **Pa$$w0rd**.

2. On LON-SVR1, to open Server Manager, click Start and then click the Server Manager tile.

3. When Server Manager opens, open the Manage menu and click Add Roles and Features.

4. When the Add Roles And Features Wizard opens, on the Before You Begin page, click Next.

5. On the Select Installation Type page, "Role-based or feature-based installation" is already selected. Click Next.

6. On the Server Selection page, select the desired server. Most of the time, the local server will already be selected. Click Next.

7. On the Select Server Roles page (as shown in Figure 2.21), select the desired server role. If the server role is already installed, expand the server role to select specific role services. If you are prompted to add or remove any features, click the Add Features button. Click Next.

FIGURE 2.21   Selecting server roles

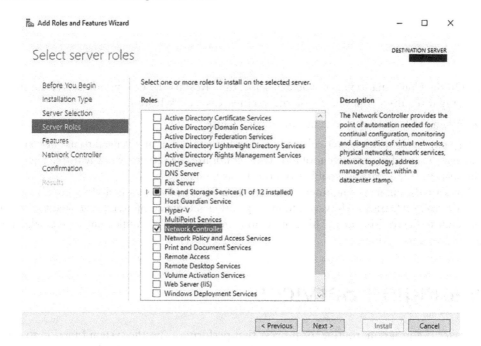

8. On the Select Features page (as shown in Figure 2.22), select the appropriate features and then click Next.

FIGURE 2.22   Selecting server features

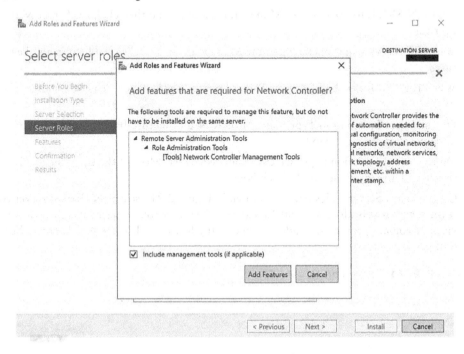

9. On the Confirmation page, you can select the "Restart the destination server automatically if required" option, if desired. In either case, click Install.

10. When the feature or role is installed, click Close.

Depending on which server role or feature you install, you might need to use Server Manager or an administrative tool to further configure the server role or feature. The administrative tools are accessible from the Tools menu.

You can also manage computers remotely with Server Manager, including installing server roles and features. However, to manage other remote computers, you need to add the computer to Server Manager. This can be done by opening the Manage menu and selecting the Add Servers option.

Managing Services

A *service* is a program, routine, or process that performs a specific system function to support other programs or to provide a network service. A service runs in the system background without a user interface. Some examples would include Web serving, event logging and file serving.

Certification Ready?

How does a service run in Windows? 1.2

To manage the services, use the Services console located under the Administrative Tools. The Services snap-in is also included in the Computer Management console. You can also execute the mmc services.mmc from a command prompt, Start Search box, or Run box. See Figure 2.23.

FIGURE 2.23   The Services console

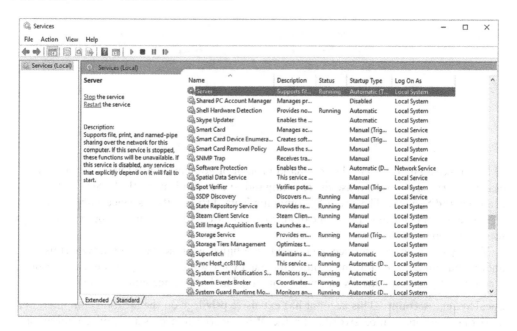

To start, stop, pause, resume, or restart services, right-click the service and click the desired option. On the left of the service name is a description. To configure a service, right-click the service and click the Properties option or double-click the service. See Figure 2.24. On the General tab, under the start-up type pull down option, set the following:

- Automatic—Specifies that the service should start automatically when the system starts.

- Automatic (Delayed Start)—Specifies that the service should start automatically after the services marked as automatic have started (which approximately 2 minutes).

- Manual—Specifies that a user or a dependent service can start the service. Services with manual start-up do not start automatically when the system starts.

- Disable—Prevents the service from being started by the system, a user, or any dependent service.

FIGURE 2.24 Managing an individual service

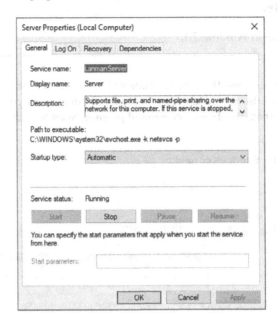

If you like doing things at the command prompt or you have a need use a script to start or stop a service, you would use the *sc* command to communicate with the Service Control Manager and Services. The *sc config* command is used to modify a service entry in the registry and Service Database. You can also use the net start and net stop commands to start and stop services.

When you configure a service, you need to configure what account the service runs under. You can use the built-in accounts included with Windows, or you can use a service account that you create locally or on the domain. The built-in accounts include:

Local System Account   This account has extensive privilege on the location computer, but it does not have its own password or profile. When it tries to access a remote computer, it presents the computer's credentials (computername$).

Local Service Account   Click This Account and then type **NT AUTHORITY\LocalService**. This account is a built-in account. (It's already created in the operating system.) It can run services in the background but has limited access to resources and objects, which helps protect the system if individual services are compromised. No password is required.

Network Service Account   Click This Account and then type **NT AUTHORITY\ NetworkService**. This account is similar to the Local Service account, but is geared toward networking services. Like the Local Service account, the Network Service account can run services in the background, but it helps protect the computer from compromise.

Another Account   Click This Account, click Browse, browse for a different user account, select it, and then click OK. Type the password for the user account you selected and then click OK.

You should always take care when changing the Startup parameters for a service including the Startup Type and Log On As settings since these changes might prevent key services from running correctly. In addition, Microsoft recommends that you do not change the Allow service to interact with desktop settings since this will allow the service to access any information displayed on the interactive user's desktop. A malicious user could then take control of the service or attack it from the interactive desktop. If you specify an account that does not have permission to log on as a service, the Services snap-in automatically grants the appropriate permissions to that account on the computer that you are managing. If you use a local or domain account, make sure that the account uses a password that does not expire and that you use a strong password.

As a general rule, you should use the account with minimum rights and permissions for the service to operate. In addition, you should use different service accounts for different services. So if you install Exchange and SQL on a box, you should have a service account for Exchange and a different service account for SQL. Of course, for you to put SQL and Exchange on the same box should only occur with small businesses with a handful of employees.

If you enable or disable a service and a problem occurs, you can try to start the service manually and see what happens. You can also check in the Event Viewer for more information on some of the errors. If the system does not boot because of the enabled or disables service, you should try to start the computer in Safe mode, which will only start the core services needed to operate, only load the necessary drivers to operate and load in 640×480 screen resolution with minimum number of colors. By using Safe mode, you should have an opportunity to fix the problem.

If you are new to Windows, particularly in administering and configuring Windows, you should take some time, click each service, and read the description of each service. You will learn that many service names are very descriptive. For now, let's cover two specific services:

- Server—Supports file, print and named-piped sharing over the network. If the Services service is not started, you will not be able to access shared folders including administrative shares such as C$ and IPC$.

- Workstation—Creates and maintains client network connections to remove servers using the SMB protocol. Without this service, you will not be able to access shared folders on other computers.

In case a service fails, an administrator can set up service recovery options as follows:

1. On the right-hand side of the Services window, right-click the service to set up recovery options for.

2. In the context menu, select Properties.

3. From the opened window, click the Recovery tab.

4. Select the computer's response if the service fails by specifying First Failure, Second Failure, and Subsequent failures actions, as in Figure 2.25.

FIGURE 2.25 Service recovery options

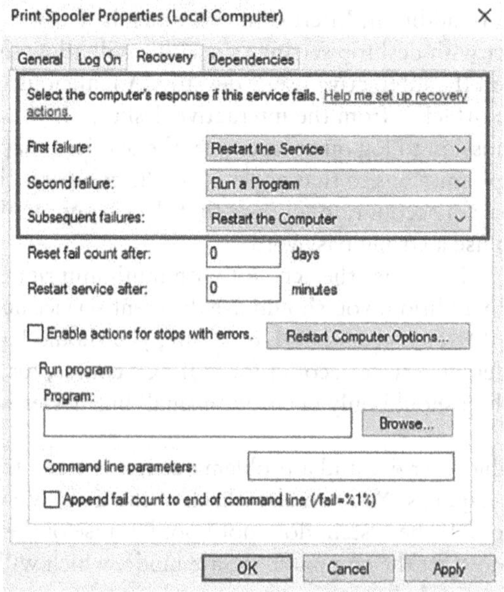

Print Spooler Properties (Local Computer)   ✕

General | Log On | Recovery | Dependencies

Select the computer's response if this service fails. Help me set up recovery actions.

First failure: Restart the Service   ˅

Second failure: Run a Program   ˅

Subsequent failures: Restart the Computer   ˅

Reset fail count after: [0]   days

Restart service after: [0]   minutes

☐ Enable actions for stops with errors.   [Restart Computer Options...]

Run program

Program:

[   ] [Browse...]

Command line parameters: [   ]

☐ Append fail count to end of command line (/fail=%1%)

[OK]   [Cancel]   [Apply]

5. Click OK.

Setting Up Services to Run with Dependencies

Setting up services to run with dependencies can be done using an elevated command prompt using the sc command. The syntax is:

```
sc config [service name] depend= <Dependencies(separated by / (forward slash))>
```

There is a space *after* the equals sign, and there is *not* one before it.

depend= parameter will *overwrite* existing dependencies list, not append.

To remove all dependencies:

sc config [service name] depend=

To list current dependencies:

sc qc [service name]

Windows Services are one of the most important cores of the Windows operating system. They work in the background. Different services can depend on each other and may not work without each other. These types of services are called dependencies and act as counterparts for each other. See Figure 2.26.

FIGURE 2.26   Services

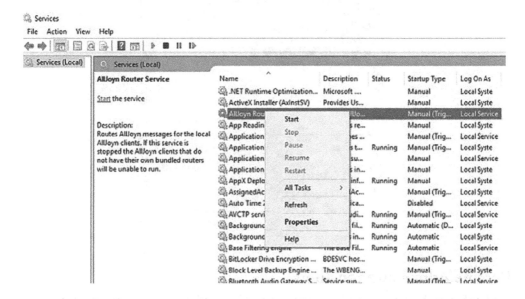

Find Dependencies of a Windows Service

If you find that there is an issue with a service, either manually or through an error message, an administrator needs to check the list of Windows Services to see if something is disabled or stopped. Sometimes components fail to start themselves or get disabled because of unknown reasons. This makes other services stop too.

To check the list of dependencies of a service, follow the steps here:

1. Open Windows Services and go to the services list, and select one of the services.

2. Right-click and select Properties.

3. This will open another window that has details about that service. Switch to Dependencies tab. See Figure 2.27.

FIGURE 2.27   Dependencies tab

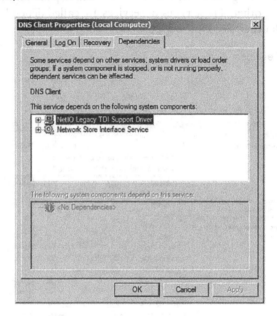

Remote Administration Tools

Remote Server Administration Tools (RSAT) enables administrators to remotely manage roles and features in Windows Server from a computer that is running Windows 10, Windows 8.1, Windows 8, Windows 7, or Windows Vista.

You cannot install RSAT on computers that are running Home or Standard editions of Windows. You can install RSAT only on Professional or Enterprise editions of the Windows client operating system.

In the RSAT releases for Windows 10, Windows 8.1, and Windows 8, tools are enabled by default.

To install RSAT, use the Add Features Wizard as shown in Figure 2.28. Table 2.1 shows the RSAT for Windows 10 Platform and Tools Support Matrix.

FIGURE 2.28   Add Features Wizard

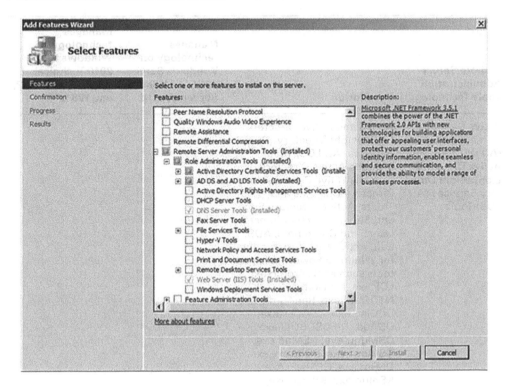

TABLE 2.1   RSAT for Windows 10 Platform and Tools Support Matrix

Remote Server Administration Tools Technology	Description	Manages technology on Windows Server 2012 and Windows Server 2012 R2	Manages technology on Windows Server 2016 Technical Preview, WS12 R2, and WS12
Active Directory Certificate Services (AD CS) Tools	AD CS Tools includes the Certification Authority, Certificate Templates, Enterprise PKI, and Online Responder Management snap-ins.	✓	✓

TABLE 2.1   RSAT for Windows 10 Platform and Tools Support Matrix *(continued)*

Remote Server Administration Tools Technology	Description	Manages technology on Windows Server 2012 and Windows Server 2012 R2	Manages technology on Windows Server 2016 Technical Preview, WS12 R2, and WS12
Active Directory Domain Services (AD DS) Tools and Active Directory Lightweight Directory Services (AD LDS) Tools	AD DS and Active Directory Lightweight Directory Services (AD LDS) Tools includes Active Directory Administrative Center, Active Directory Domains and Trusts, Active Directory Sites and Services, Active Directory Users and Computers, ADSI Edit, Active Directory module for Windows PowerShell; plus tools such as DCPromo.exe, LDP.exe, NetDom.exe, NTDSUtil.exe, RepAdmin.exe, DCDiag.exe, DSACLs.exe, DSAdd.exe,DSDBUtil.exe, DSMgmt.exe, DSMod.exe, DSMove.exe, DSQuery.exe, DSRm.exe, GPFixup.exe, KSetup.exe, KtPass.exe, NlTest.exe, NSLookup.exe, W32tm.exe.		✓
Best Practices Analyzer	Best Practices Analyzer cmdlets for Windows PowerShell	✓	✓
BitLocker Drive Encryption Administration Utilities	Manage-bde, Windows PowerShell cmdlets for BitLocker, BitLocker Recovery Password Viewer for Active Directory	✓	✓
DHCP Server Tools	DHCP Server Tools includes the DHCP Management Console, the DHCP Server cmdlet module for Windows PowerShell, and the Netsh command line tool.	✓	✓
DirectAccess, Routing and Remote Access	Routing and Remote Access management console, Connection Manager Administration Kit console, Remote Access provider for Windows PowerShell, Web Application Proxy	✓	✓

Remote Server Administration Tools Technology	Description	Manages technology on Windows Server 2012 and Windows Server 2012 R2	Manages technology on Windows Server 2016 Technical Preview, WS12 R2, and WS12
DNS Server Tools	DNS Server Tools include the DNS Manager snap-in, the DNS module for Windows PowerShell, and the Ddnscmd. exe command line tool.	✓	✓
Failover Clustering Tools	Failover Clustering Tools include Failover Cluster Manager, Failover Clusters (Windows PowerShell cmdlets), MSClus, Cluster. exe, Cluster-Aware Updating management console, Cluster-Aware Updating cmdlets for Windows PowerShell	✓	✓
File Services Tools	File Services Tools include the following: Share and Storage Management Tools, Distributed File System Tools, File Server Resource Manager Tools, Services for NFS Administration Tools, iSCSI management cmdlets for Windows PowerShell; Work Folders Management Tools - Distributed File System Tools include the DFS Management snap-in, and the Dfsradmin.exe, Dfsrdiag.exe, Dfscmd.exe, Dfsdiag.exe, and Dfsutil.exe command line tools and PowerShell modules for DFSN and DFSR - File Server Resource Manager Tools include the File Server Resource Manager snap-in, and the Dirquota.exe, Filescrn.exe, and Storrept.exe command line tools.	✓	✓ The Share and Storage Management snap-in is deprecated after the release of Windows Server 2016.
Group Policy Management Tools	Group Policy Management Tools include Group Policy Management Console, Group Policy Management Editor, and Group Policy Starter GPO Editor.	✓	✓

TABLE 2.1 RSAT for Windows 10 Platform and Tools Support Matrix *(continued)*

Remote Server Administration Tools Technology	Description	Manages technology on Windows Server 2012 and Windows Server 2012 R2	Manages technology on Windows Server 2016 Technical Preview, WS12 R2, and WS12
Hyper-V Tools	Hyper-V Tools include the Hyper-V Manager snap-in and the Virtual Machine Connection remote access tool.		Hyper-V in Windows 10 can manage Hyper-V in Windows Server 2012 R2 and Windows Server 2012.
IP Address Management (IPAM) Management Tools	IP Address Management client console	✓	✓
		IPAM tools in Remote Server Administration Tools for Windows 10 cannot be used to manage IPAM running on Windows Server 2012 R2 and Windows Server 2012.	IPAM tools in Remote Server Administration Tools for Windows 10 cannot be used to manage IPAM running on Windows Server 2012 R2 and Windows Server 2012.
Network Adapter Teaming, or NIC Teaming	NIC Teaming management console	✓	✓
Network Controller	Network Controller PowerShell module	Not available	✓
Network Load Balancing Tools	Network Load Balancing Tools include the Network Load Balancing Manager, Network Load Balancing Windows PowerShell cmdlets, and the NLB.exe and WLBS.exe command line tools.	✓	✓

Remote Server Administration Tools Technology	Description	Manages technology on Windows Server 2012 and Windows Server 2012 R2	Manages technology on Windows Server 2016 Technical Preview, WS12 R2, and WS12
Remote Desktop Services Tools	Remote Desktop Services Tools include the Remote Desktop snap-ins, RD Gateway Manager, tsgateway.msc, RD Licensing Manager, licmgr. exe, RD Licensing Diagnoser, lsdiag.msc. Use Server Manager to administer all other RDS role services except RD Gateway and RD Licensing.	✓	✓
Server for NIS Tools	Server for NIS Tools includes an extension to the Active Directory Users and Computers snap-in, and the Ypclear. exe command line tool	These tools are not available in RSAT for Windows 10 and later releases.	
Server Manager	Server Manager includes the Server Manager console. Remote management with Server Manager is available in Windows Server 2016 Technical Preview, Windows Server 2012 R2, and Windows Server 2012.	✓	✓
SMTP Server Tools	SMTP Server Tools include the Simple Mail Transfer Protocol (SMTP) snap-in.	These tools are not available in RSAT for Windows 8 and later releases.	
Storage Explorer Tools	Storage Explorer Tools include the Storage Explorer snap-in.	These tools are not available in RSAT for Windows 8 and later releases.	

TABLE 2.1   RSAT for Windows 10 Platform and Tools Support Matrix *(continued)*

Remote Server Administration Tools Technology	Description	Manages technology on Windows Server 2012 and Windows Server 2012 R2	Manages technology on Windows Server 2016 Technical Preview, WS12 R2, and WS12
Storage Manager for Storage Area Networks (SANs) Tools	Storage Manager for SANs Tools include the Storage Manager for SANs snap-in and the Provisionstorage.exe command line tool.	These tools are not available in RSAT for Windows 8 and later releases.	
Volume Activation	Manage Volume Activation, vmw.exe	✓	✓
Windows System Resource Manager Tools	Windows System Resource Manager Tools include the Windows System Resource Manager snap-in and the Wsrmc.exe command line tool.	✓ WSRM has been deprecated in Windows Server 2012 R2, and tools for managing WSRM are not available in Remote Server Administration Tools for Windows 8.1 and later releases of RSAT.	
Windows Server Update Services Tools	Windows Server Update Services Tools include the Windows Server Update Services snap-in, WSUS.msc, and PowerShell cmdlets.	C✓	✓

Remote Desktop Services

Before Windows Server 2008, Remote Desktop Services was called Terminal Services. Remote Desktop Services allows users to:

- Connect to virtual desktops
- Connect to RemoteApp programs
- Connect to session-based desktops
- Access remote connections from within a corporate network or from the Internet

Remote Desktop Services allows for faster desktop and application deployments to any device, improving remote user effectiveness while helping to keep critical data secure. Remote Desktop Services allows for both a *virtual desktop infrastructure (VDI)* and session-based desktops, allowing users to connect from anywhere.

Multipoint Services

Multipoint Services allows multiple users, each with their own independent and familiar Windows experience, to simultaneously share one computer.

There are several ways users can access their sessions. One way is by remoting into the server using the remote desktop apps with any device. Another way is through physical stations that stations attached to the Multipoint server:

The components of a Multipoint Services system include the following:

- Multipoint Services system software, which supports multiple monitors, keyboards, mouse devices, and other devices on the computer.

- The Multipoint Manager application, which allows for monitoring and taking actions on Multipoint Services stations.

- Maintenance and management tools.

- The Multipoint Dashboard application, which allows an administrator to complete daily tasks, such as communicating with other users.

Remote Desktop Gateway

Remote Desktop Gateway (RD Gateway) grants users on public networks access to Windows desktops and applications hosted in Microsoft Azure's cloud services.

The RD Gateway component uses Secure Sockets Layer (SSL) to encrypt the communications channel between clients and the server. The RD Gateway virtual machine must be accessible through a public IP address that allows inbound TCP connections to port 443 and inbound UDP connections to port 3391. This lets users connect through the internet using the HTTPS communications transport protocol and the UDP protocol.

The digital certificates installed on both the server and client must match in order to work. The name of the certificate must match the FQDN used to access RD Gateway, whether the FQDN is the public IP address' externally facing DNS name or the CNAME DNS record pointing to the public IP address.

For fewer users, the RD Web Access and RD Gateway roles can be combined onto a single virtual machine to help reduce cost.

A Remote Desktop Gateway is often used to allow remote desktop clients to connect from the internet to servers behind the Remote Desktop Gateway located on the corporate network.

Here is a summary of the steps needed to configure a Remote Desktop Gateway on Windows Server 2016:

1. Join the Windows 2016 server to the Active Directory domain.

2. Add the Remote Desktop Services role.

3. Create a Connection Authorization Policy; this states which groups are allowed access to the RD Gateway.

4. Create a Resource Authorization Policy; this states which servers are allowed access by which groups.

5. Purchase an SSL Certificate from a public Certificate Authority.

6. Apply the SSL Certificate to the Remote Desktop Gateway.

7. Accept the default RD Gateway TCP port (443) or change it to another port number.

8. Test the Remote Desktop Connection to a server behind the RD Gateway directly from the RD Gateway server. This ensures that there is connectivity from the RD Gateway to the servers that clients will be connected to.

9. Modify Firewall Rules to allow the RD Gateway port to the RD Gateway server.

10. Test the Remote Desktop Connection to a server behind the RD Gateway from the internet.

Virtual Private Networks (VPN)

Virtual private networks (VPNs) provide remote access to private networks across public connections.

A VPN extends a private network across a public network and enables users to send and receive data across shared or public networks as if their computing devices were directly connected to the private network. Applications running across a VPN may benefit from the functionality, security, and management of the private network.

To ensure security, the private network connection is established using an encrypted layered tunneling protocol and VPN users use authentication methods, including passwords or certificates, to gain access to the VPN.

Windows Server 2016's VPN support includes the following features:

- Can set up account lockout policies for dial-up and VPN users.

- Extensible Authentication Protocol (EAP) allows Microsoft or third parties to write modules that implement new authentication methods and retrofit them to servers. One example is the EAP-TLS module, which implements access control based on smart cards and certificates for VPN and dial-up users.

How VPNs Work

The VPN client supposes that the VPN server is connected to the Internet already. Here's the VPN connection process:

1. The client establishes a connection to the Internet. Dial-up networking or another connection method can be used. The client must be able to send packets to the Internet.

2. The client sends a VPN connection request to the server. The exact format of the request varies, depending on the protocol that the VPN is using (PPTP, L2TP, or SSTP).

3. The client authenticates with the server. The exact process varies according to the VPN protocol being used. If the client can't provide valid credentials, the connection is terminated.

4. The client and server negotiate parameters for the VPN session. This negotiation allows the two ends to agree on an encryption algorithm and strength.

5. The client and server go through the PPP negotiation process because both L2TP and PPTP depend on the lower-level PPP.

Application Virtualization (App-V)

Application virtualization helps prevent conflicts between applications on the same PC. It helps to isolate the application running environment from the operating system installation requirements by creating application-specific copies of all shared resources, and it helps reduce application-to-application incompatibility and testing needs. An example of an application virtualization tool is Microsoft Application Virtualization (App-V).

App-V can make applications available to end user computers without having to install the applications directly onto those computers. This is possible through a process known as sequencing the application. This enables applications to run in their own self-contained virtual environment on the client computer. The sequenced applications are isolated from each other. This eliminates application conflicts, but the applications can still interact with the client computer.

The App-V client is the feature that lets the end user interact with applications after they have been published to the computer. The client manages the virtual environment in which the virtualized applications run on each computer. After the client has been installed on a computer, the applications must be made available to the computer through a process known as publishing, which enables the end user to run the virtual applications. The publishing process copies the virtual application icons and shortcuts to the computer—typically on the Windows desktop or on the Start menu—but, also copies the package definition and file type association information to the computer. Publishing also makes the application package content available to the end user's computer.

The virtual application package content can be copied onto one or more Application Virtualization servers so that it can be streamed down to the clients on demand and cached locally. File servers and Web servers can also be used as streaming servers, or the content can be copied directly to the end user's computer. Table 2.2 shows the Microsoft Application Virtualization (App-V) System Features.

TABLE 2.2   Microsoft Application Virtualization (App-V) System Features

Feature	Function	Additional Information
Microsoft Application Virtualization Management Server	Responsible for streaming the package content and publishing the shortcuts and file type associations to the Application Virtualization client.	The Application Virtualization Management Server supports active upgrade, License Management, and a database that can be used for reporting.

TABLE 2.2   Microsoft Application Virtualization (App-V) System Features *(continued)*

Feature	Function	Additional Information
Content folder	Indicates the location of the Application Virtualization packages for streaming.	This folder can be located on a share on or off the Application Virtualization Management Server.
Microsoft Application Virtualization Management Console	This console is an MMC 3.0 snap-in management tool used for Microsoft Application Virtualization Server administration.	This tool can be installed on the Microsoft Application Virtualization server or located on a separate workstation that has Microsoft Management Console (MMC) 3.0 and Microsoft .NET Framework 2.0 installed.
Microsoft Application Virtualization Management Web Service	Responsible for communicating any read and write requests to the Application Virtualization data store.	The Management Web Service can be installed on the Microsoft Application Virtualization Management server or on a separate computer that has Microsoft Internet Information Services (IIS) installed.
Microsoft Application Virtualization Data Store	The App-V SQL Server database responsible for storing all information related to the Application Virtualization infrastructure.	This information includes all application records, application assignments, and which groups have responsibility for managing the Application Virtualization environment.
Microsoft Application Virtualization Streaming Server	Responsible for hosting the Application Virtualization packages for streaming to clients in a branch office, where the link back to the Application Virtualization Management Server is considered a wide area networks (WAN) connection.	This server contains streaming functionality only and provides neither the Application Virtualization Management Console nor the Application Virtualization Management Web Service.
Microsoft Application Virtualization Sequencer	The sequencer is used to monitor and capture the installation of applications to create virtual application packages.	The output consists of the application's icons, an .osd file that contains package definition information, a package manifest file, and the .sft file that contains the application program's content files.
Microsoft Application Virtualization Client	The Application Virtualization Desktop Client and the Application Virtualization Client for Remote Desktop Services provide and manage the virtual environment for the virtualized applications.	The Microsoft Application Virtualization client manages the package streaming into cache, publishing refresh, transport, and all interaction with the Application Virtualization servers.

Licensing

License Remote Desktop Services deployments with client access licenses (CALs).

Each user and device that connects to a Remote Desktop Session host needs a client access licenses (CAL). Administrators use RD Licensing to install, issue, and track RDS CALs.

When a user or a device connects to an RD Session Host server, the RD Session Host server determines if an RDS CAL is needed. The RD Session Host server then requests an RDS CAL from the Remote Desktop license server. If an appropriate RDS CAL is available from a license server, the RDS CAL is issued to the client, and the client is able to connect to the RD Session Host server and from there to the desktop or apps they're trying to use.

There are two types of CALs:

- Per Device
- Per User

The following table outlines the differences between the two types of CALs:

Per Device	Per User
CALs are physically assigned to each device.	CALs are assigned to a user in Active Directory.
CALs are tracked by the license server.	CALs are tracked by the license server.
CALs can be tracked regardless of Active Directory membership.	CALs cannot be tracked within a workgroup.
Can revoke up to 20% of CALs.	Cannot revoke any CALs.
Temporary CALs are valid for 52–89 days.	Temporary CALs are not available.
CALs cannot be over allocated.	CALs can be over allocated (in breach of the Remote Desktop licensing agreement).

When the Per Device model is used, a temporary license is issued the first time a device connects to the RD Session Host. The second time that device connects, as long as the license server is activated and there are available CALs, the license server issues a permanent RDS Per Device CAL.

When the Per User model is used, licensing is not enforced, and each user is granted a license to connect to an RD Session Host from any number of devices. The license server issues licenses from the available CAL pool or the Over-Used CAL pool. It is the administrator's responsibility to ensure that all of the users have a valid license and zero Over-Used CALs—otherwise, the administrator is in violation of the Remote Desktop Services license terms.

To ensure compliance with the Remote Desktop Services license terms, an administrator should track the number of RDS Per User CALs used and to make sure there are enough Per User CALs installed on the license server for all of the users.

Administrators can use the Remote Desktop Licensing Manager to track and generate reports on RDS Per User CALs.

The Remote Desktop Services license server issues client access licenses (CALs) to users and devices when they access the RD Session Host. An administrator can activate the license server by using the Remote Desktop Licensing Manager.

Install the RD Licensing Role

To install the RD Licensing Role perform the following:

1. Using an administrator account, sign into the server that will be used as the license server.
2. In Server Manager, click Roles Summary, and then click Add Roles. Click Next on the first page of the roles wizard.
3. Select Remote Desktop Services, and then click Next, and then Next on the Remote Desktop Services page.
4. Select Remote Desktop Licensing, and then click Next.
5. Configure the domain - select Configure a discovery scope for this license server, click This domain, and then click Next.
6. Click Install.

Activate the License Server

To activate the License Server perform the following:

1. Open the Remote Desktop Licensing Manager: click Start ➤ Administrative Tools ➤ Remote Desktop Services ➤ Remote Desktop Licensing Manager.
2. Right-click the license server, and then click Activate Server.
3. Click Next on the Welcome page.
4. For the connection method, select Automatic connection (recommended), and then click Next.
5. Enter the company information (name, the company name, geographic region), and then click Next.
6. Optionally enter any other company information (for example, email and company addresses), and then click Next.
7. Make sure that Start Install Licenses Wizard now is not selected, and then click Next.

Multiple Ports - Ports and Protocols

This table is sorted by port number instead of by service name.

Port	Protocol	Application protocol	System service name
n/a	GRE	GRE (IP protocol 47)	Routing and Remote Access
n/a	ESP	IPsec ESP (IP protocol 50)	Routing and Remote Access

Port	Protocol	Application protocol	System service name
n/a	AH	IPsec AH (IP protocol 51)	Routing and Remote Access
7	TCP	Echo	Simple TCP/IP Services
7	UDP	Echo	Simple TCP/IP Services
9	TCP	Discard	Simple TCP/IP Services
9	UDP	Discard	Simple TCP/IP Services
13	TCP	Daytime	Simple TCP/IP Services
13	UDP	Daytime	Simple TCP/IP Services
17	TCP	Quotd	Simple TCP/IP Services
17	UDP	Quotd	Simple TCP/IP Services
19	TCP	Chargen	Simple TCP/IP Services
19	UDP	Chargen	Simple TCP/IP Services
20	TCP	FTP default data	FTP Publishing Service
21	TCP	FTP control	FTP Publishing Service
21	TCP	FTP control	Application Layer Gateway Service
23	TCP	Telnet	Telnet
25	TCP	SMTP	Simple Mail Transfer Protocol
25	TCP	SMTP	Exchange Server
42	TCP	WINS Replication	Windows Internet Name Service
42	UDP	WINS Replication	Windows Internet Name Service
53	TCP	DNS	DNS Server
53	UDP	DNS	DNS Server
53	TCP	DNS	Internet Connection Firewall/Internet Connection Sharing

Port	Protocol	Application protocol	System service name
53	UDP	DNS	Internet Connection Firewall/Internet Connection Sharing
67	UDP	DHCP Server	DHCP Server
67	UDP	DHCP Server	Internet Connection Firewall/Internet Connection Sharing
69	UDP	TFTP	Trivial FTP Daemon Service
80	TCP	HTTP	Windows Media Services
80	TCP	HTTP	WinRM 1.1 and earlier
80	TCP	HTTP	World Wide Web Publishing Service
80	TCP	HTTP	SharePoint Portal Server
88	TCP	Kerberos	Kerberos Key Distribution Center
88	UDP	Kerberos	Kerberos Key Distribution Center
102	TCP	X.400	Microsoft Exchange MTA Stacks
110	TCP	POP3	Microsoft POP3 Service
110	TCP	POP3	Exchange Server
119	TCP	NNTP	Network News Transfer Protocol
123	UDP	NTP	Windows Time
123	UDP	SNTP	Windows Time
135	TCP	RPC	Message Queuing
135	TCP	RPC	Remote Procedure Call
135	TCP	RPC	Exchange Server
135	TCP	RPC	Certificate Services
135	TCP	RPC	Cluster Service

Port	Protocol	Application protocol	System service name
135	TCP	RPC	Distributed File System Namespaces
135	TCP	RPC	Distributed Link Tracking
135	TCP	RPC	Distributed Transaction Coordinator
135	TCP	RPC	Distributed File Replication Service
135	TCP	RPC	Fax Service
135	TCP	RPC	Microsoft Exchange Server
135	TCP	RPC	File Replication Service
135	TCP	RPC	Group Policy
135	TCP	RPC	Local Security Authority
135	TCP	RPC	Remote Storage Notification
135	TCP	RPC	Remote Storage
135	TCP	RPC	Systems Management Server 2.0
135	TCP	RPC	Terminal Services Licensing
135	TCP	RPC	Terminal Services Session Directory
137	UDP	NetBIOS Name Resolution	Computer Browser
137	UDP	NetBIOS Name Resolution	Server
137	UDP	NetBIOS Name Resolution	Windows Internet Name Service
137	UDP	NetBIOS Name Resolution	Net Logon
137	UDP	NetBIOS Name Resolution	Systems Management Server 2.0
138	UDP	NetBIOS Datagram Service	Computer Browser

Port	Protocol	Application protocol	System service name
138	UDP	NetBIOS Datagram Service	Server
138	UDP	NetBIOS Datagram Service	Net Logon
138	UDP	NetBIOS Datagram Service	Distributed File System
138	UDP	NetBIOS Datagram Service	Systems Management Server 2.0
138	UDP	NetBIOS Datagram Service	License Logging Service
139	TCP	NetBIOS Session Service	Computer Browser
139	TCP	NetBIOS Session Service	Fax Service
139	TCP	NetBIOS Session Service	Performance Logs and Alerts
139	TCP	NetBIOS Session Service	Print Spooler
139	TCP	NetBIOS Session Service	Server
139	TCP	NetBIOS Session Service	Net Logon
139	TCP	NetBIOS Session Service	Remote Procedure Call Locator
139	TCP	NetBIOS Session Service	Distributed File System Namespaces
139	TCP	NetBIOS Session Service	Systems Management Server 2.0
139	TCP	NetBIOS Session Service	License Logging Service
143	TCP	IMAP	Exchange Server
161	UDP	SNMP	SNMP Service
162	UDP	SNMP Traps Outgoing	SNMP Trap Service
389	TCP	LDAP Server	Local Security Authority
389	UDP	DC Locator	Local Security Authority
389	TCP	LDAP Server	Distributed File System Namespaces
389	UDP	DC Locator	Distributed File System Namespaces
389	UDP	DC Locator	Netlogon

Port	Protocol	Application protocol	System service name
389	UDP	DC Locator	Kerberos Key Distribution Center
389	TCP	LDAP Server	Distributed File System Replication
389	UDP	DC Locator	Distributed File System Replication
443	TCP	HTTPS	HTTP SSL
443	TCP	HTTPS	World Wide Web Publishing Service
443	TCP	HTTPS	SharePoint Portal Server
443	TCP	RPC over HTTPS	Exchange Server 2003
443	TCP	HTTPS	WinRM 1.1 and earlier
445	TCP	SMB	Fax Service
445	TCP	SMB	Print Spooler
445	TCP	SMB	Server
445	TCP	SMB	Remote Procedure Call Locator
445	TCP	SMB	Distributed File System Namespaces
445	TCP	SMB	Distributed File System Replication
445	TCP	SMB	License Logging Service
445	TCP	SMB	Net Logon
464	UDP	Kerberos Password V5	Kerberos Key Distribution Center
464	TCP	Kerberos Password V5	Kerberos Key Distribution Center
500	UDP	IPsec ISAKMP	Local Security Authority
515	TCP	LPD	TCP/IP Print Server
554	TCP	RTSP	Windows Media Services

Port	Protocol	Application protocol	System service name
563	TCP	NNTP over SSL	Network News Transfer Protocol
593	TCP	RPC over HTTPS endpoint mapper	Remote Procedure Call
593	TCP	RPC over HTTPS	Exchange Server
636	TCP	LDAP SSL	Local Security Authority
636	UDP	LDAP SSL	Local Security Authority
647	TCP	DHCP Failover	DHCP Failover
9389	TCP	Active Directory Web Services (ADWS)	Active Directory Web Services (ADWS)
9389	TCP	Active Directory Web Services (ADWS)	Active Directory Management Gateway Service
993	TCP	IMAP over SSL	Exchange Server
995	TCP	POP3 over SSL	Exchange Server
1067	TCP	Installation Bootstrap Service	Installation Bootstrap protocol server
1068	TCP	Installation Bootstrap Service	Installation Bootstrap protocol client
1270	TCP	MOM-Encrypted	Microsoft Operations Manager 2000
1433	TCP	SQL over TCP	Microsoft SQL Server
1433	TCP	SQL over TCP	MSSQL$UDDI
1434	UDP	SQL Probe	Microsoft SQL Server
1434	UDP	SQL Probe	MSSQL$UDDI
1645	UDP	Legacy RADIUS	Internet Authentication Service
1646	UDP	Legacy RADIUS	Internet Authentication Service
1701	UDP	L2TP	Routing and Remote Access

Port	Protocol	Application protocol	System service name
1723	TCP	PPTP	Routing and Remote Access
1755	TCP	MMS	Windows Media Services
1755	UDP	MMS	Windows Media Services
1801	TCP	MSMQ	Message Queuing
1801	UDP	MSMQ	Message Queuing
1812	UDP	RADIUS Authentication	Internet Authentication Service
1813	UDP	RADIUS Accounting	Internet Authentication Service
1900	UDP	SSDP	SSDP Discovery Service
2101	TCP	MSMQ-DCs	Message Queuing
2103	TCP	MSMQ-RPC	Message Queuing
2105	TCP	MSMQ-RPC	Message Queuing
2107	TCP	MSMQ-Mgmt	Message Queuing
2393	TCP	OLAP Services 7.0	SQL Server: Downlevel OLAP Client Support
2394	TCP	OLAP Services 7.0	SQL Server: Downlevel OLAP Client Support
2460	UDP	MS Theater	Windows Media Services
2535	UDP	MADCAP	DHCP Server
2701	TCP	SMS Remote Control (control)	SMS Remote Control Agent
2701	UDP	SMS Remote Control (control)	SMS Remote Control Agent
2702	TCP	SMS Remote Control (data)	SMS Remote Control Agent
2702	UDP	SMS Remote Control (data)	SMS Remote Control Agent
2703	TCP	SMS Remote Chat	SMS Remote Control Agent

Port	Protocol	Application protocol	System service name
2703	UPD	SMS Remote Chat	SMS Remote Control Agent
2704	TCP	SMS Remote File Transfer	SMS Remote Control Agent
2704	UDP	SMS Remote File Transfer	SMS Remote Control Agent
2725	TCP	SQL Analysis Services	SQL Server Analysis Services
2869	TCP	UPNP	UPnP Device Host
2869	TCP	SSDP event notification	SSDP Discovery Service
3268	TCP	Global Catalog	Local Security Authority
3269	TCP	Global Catalog	Local Security Authority
3343	UDP	Cluster Services	Cluster Service
3389	TCP	Terminal Services	NetMeeting Remote Desktop Sharing
3389	TCP	Terminal Services	Terminal Services
3527	UDP	MSMQ-Ping	Message Queuing
4011	UDP	BINL	Remote Installation
4500	UDP	NAT-T	Local Security Authority
5000	TCP	SSDP legacy event notification	SSDP Discovery Service
5004	UDP	RTP	Windows Media Services
5005	UDP	RTCP	Windows Media Services
5722	TCP	RPC	Distributed File System Replication
6001	TCP	Information Store	Exchange Server 2003
6002	TCP	Directory Referral	Exchange Server 2003
6004	TCP	DSProxy/NSPI	Exchange Server 2003
42424	TCP	ASP.Net Session State	ASP.NET State Service
51515	TCP	MOM-Clear	Microsoft Operations Manager 2000

Port	Protocol	Application protocol	System service name
5985	TCP	HTTP	WinRM 2.0
5986	TCP	HTTPS	WinRM 2.0
1024-65535	TCP	RPC	Randomly allocated high TCP ports
135	TCP	WMI	Hyper-V service
random port number between 49152 - 65535	TCP	Randomly allocated high TCP ports	Hyper-V service
80	TCP	Kerberos Authentication (HTTP)	Hyper-V service
443	TCP	Certificate-based Authentication (HTTPS)	Hyper-V service
6600	TCP	Live Migration	Hyper-V Live Migration
445	TCP	SMB	Hyper-V Live Migration
3343	UDP	Cluster Service Traffic	Hyper-V Live Migration

Understanding the Registry

The *registry* is a central, secure database in which Windows stores all hardware configuration information, software configuration information, and system security policies. Components that use the registry include the Windows kernel, device drivers, setup programs, hardware profiles, and user profiles.

Most of the time, you will not need to access the registry because programs and applications typically make all the necessary changes automatically. For example, when you change your desktop background or change the default color for Windows, you access the Display settings within the Control Panel, and it will save the changes to the registry.

If you do need to access the registry and make changes to the registry, you should closely following the instructions from a reputable source since an incorrect change to your computer's registry could render your computer inoperable. However, there may be a time when you need to make a change in the registry because there is no interface or program to make the change. To view and manually change the registry, you will use the Registry Editor (Regedit.exe), which can be executed from the command prompt, Start Search box, or Run box. See Figure 2.29.

FIGURE 2.29 The Registry Editor

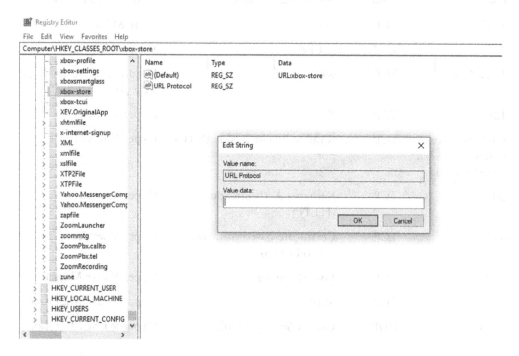

The Registry is split into a several logical sections, often referred to as hives, which are generally named by their Windows API definitions. The hives begin with HKEY and are often abbreviated to a three- or four-letter short name starting with "HK". For example, HKCU is HKEY_CURRENT_USER and HKLM is HKEY_LOCAL_MACHINE. There are 5 Root Keys/HKEYs:

- HKEY_CLASSES_ROOT—Stores information about registered application, such as file association that tells which default program opens a file with a certain extension.

- HKEY_CURRENT_USER—Stores settings that are specific to the currently logged-in user. When a user logs off, the HKEY_CURRENT_USER is saved to HKEY_USERS.

- HKEY_LOCAL_MACHINE—Stores settings that are specific to the local computer.

- HKEY_USERS—Contains subkeys corresponding to the HKEY_CURRENT_USER keys for each user profile actively loaded on the machine.

- HKEY_CURRENT_CONFIG—Contains information gathered at runtime. Information stored in this key is not permanently stored on disk, but rather regenerated at the boot time.

Registry keys are similar to folders, which can contain values or subkeys. The keys within the registry follow a syntax similar to Windows folder or file path using backslashes to separate each level. For example:

```
HKEY_LOCAL_MACHINE\Software\Microsoft\Windows
```

refers to the subkey "Windows" of the subkey "Microsoft" of the subkey "Software" of the HKEY_LOCAL_MACHINE key.

Registry Values include a name and a value. There are multiple types of values. Some of the common key types are shown in Table 2.3.

TABLE 2.3 Common Registry Key Types

Name	Data type	Description
Binary Value	REG_BINARY	Raw binary data. Most hardware component information is stored as binary data and is displayed in Registry Editor in hexadecimal format.
DWORD Value	REG_DWORD	Data represented by a number that is 4 bytes long (a 32-bit integer). Many parameters for device drivers and services are this type and are displayed in Registry Editor in binary, hexadecimal, or decimal format.
Expandable String Value	REG_EXPAND_SZ	A variable-length data string. This data type includes variables that are resolved when a program or service uses the data.
Multi-String Value	REG_MULTI_SZ	A multiple string. Values that contain lists or multiple values in a form that people can read are generally this type. Entries are separated by spaces, commas, or other marks.
String Value	REG_SZ	A fixed-length text string.
QWORD Value	REG_QWORD	Data represented by a number that is a 64-bit integer. This data is displayed in Registry Editor as a Binary Value and was introduced in Windows 2000.

Reg files (also known as Registration entries) are text files for storing portions of the registry. They have a .reg filename extension. If you double-click a reg file, it will add the registry entries into the registry. You can export any registry subkey by right-clicking the subkey and choosing Export. You can back up the entire registry to a reg file file by right-clicking Computer at the top of Regedit and selecting Export or you can back up the system state with Windows Backup.

Managing Server Core

After you install Server Core, you need to configure Server Core by connecting locally to execute traditional command-line tools using cmd.exe. From there, you can start PowerShell.exe and other programs to configure Windows. You can also configure Server Core remotely by using remote commands or MMC programs that can manage roles, features, or other programs remotely.

When you are connected to the system locally, you can use the following tools:

Cmd.exe   Allows you to run traditional command-line tools, such as ping.exe, ipconfig. exe, and netsh.exe.

PowerShell.exe   Opens a Windows PowerShell session so that you can execute Windows PowerShell commands. Windows Server 2016 comes with Windows PowerShell version 5.0 installed.

Sconfig.cmd   Functions as a command-line, menu-driven administrative tool that enables you to perform most common server administrative tasks, such as configuring networking, workgroups, and domains and configuring Windows Firewall.

Regedt32.exe   Opens the Registry Editor to change registry settings.

Msinfo32.exe: Allows you to view system information for the system.

Taskmgr.exe   Launches Task Manager.

Notepad.exe   A basic text editor.

To shut down or restart Windows Server 2016 Server Core, you need to use the shutdown.exe file. To shut down the computer, you would use the following command:

```
shutdown /s
```

To restart the computer, you can use the following command:

```
shutdown /r /t 0 or shutdown /r
```

The /r specifies reboot while the /t 0 (short for 0 seconds) indicates a reboot immediately.

To logoff, use:

```
shutdown /l
```

Because Server Core does not have a GUI interface, the GUI-based management tools and snap-ins cannot be installed on servers that are running the Server Core installation options of Windows Server 2016. Therefore, to install roles and features to Windows Server 2016 Server Core, you must use the Windows PowerShell Install-WindowsFeature cmdlet.

The Install-WindowsFeature cmdlet uses the following syntax:

```
Install-WindowsFeature -Name <feature_name>
-IncludeManagementTools -Restart
```

The Management tools and snap-ins are added by using the `IncludeManagementTools` parameter. The `Restart` command will restart the computer after the server role or feature is installed.

Install Roles and Features Using the *Install-WindowsFeature* Cmdlet

To install roles and features using the `Install-WindowsFeature` cmdlet on a computer running Windows Server 2016 Server Core, perform the following steps:

1. Log on with administrative privileges to a computer running Windows Server 2016 Server Core.

2. To open Windows PowerShell, from the command prompt, type **PowerShell.exe**.

3. To view the roles and features, execute the following command:

   ```
   Get-WindowsFeature
   ```

4. To install the Active Directory Domain Services role and the Group Policy Management feature on a remote server, execute the following command:

   ```
   Install-WindowsFeature -Name AD-Domain-Services, GPMC -IncludeManagementTools
   -Restart
   ```

Besides running these commands, there are a few simple but essential programs that are still available including:

- Notepad (notepad.exe)
- Task Manager (taskmgr.exe) command or pressing the Ctrl+Alt+Del keys
- Registry Editor (regedit.exe)
- System Information (msinfo32.exe)

After you have the server communicating on the network, you can connect to the server remotely using administrative tools based on the Microsoft Management Console including Computer Management and Server Manager consoles. To manage a Server Core server using an MMC snap-in:

1. Log on to a remote computer.

2. Start an MMC snap-in, such as Computer Management or Server Manager console.

3. In the left pane, right-click the top of the tree and click Connect to another computer. For example, in the Computer Management, you would right-click Computer Management (Local).

4. On another computer, type the computer name or IP address of the server running a Server Core installation and click OK.

To use the Disk Management MMC snap-in remotely on a Server Core computer, you must start the Virtual Disk Service on the Server Core computer by typing the **net start VDS** command at the command prompt.

Summary Skill Matrix

In this lesson you learned:

- Every computer must have a unique computer name assigned a network.

- A workgroup is usually associated with a peer-to-peer network where user accounts are decentralized and stored on each individual computer.

- A domain is a logical unit of computers that define a security boundary and is usually associated with Microsoft's Active Directory.

- The security of the domain is generally centralized and controlled by Windows servers acting as domain controllers.

- With Remote Assistance and Remote Desktop, you can access a computer running Windows with another computer that is connected to the same network or over the Internet just as you were sitting in front of the server.

- One of the simple tasks that need to be done is to make sure that the server has the correct date and time. It is essential for logging purposes and for security.

- Device drivers are programs that control a device. You can think of them as translator between the device and the operating system and programs that use the device.

- Plug and Play (PnP) allows you to install or connect a device, the device is automatically recognized, it is automatically configured, and the appropriate driver is installed.

- An interrupt is a signal sent by a device to get the attention of the processor when the device is ready to accept or send information. Each device must be assigned a unique IRQ number.

- A signed driver is a device driver that includes a digital signature, which is an electronic security mark that can indicate the publisher of the software and information that can show if a driver has been altered.

- A driver that lacks a valid digital signature, or was altered after it was signed, cannot be installed on 64-bit versions of Windows.

- Devices and Printers folder gives you a quick view of devices connected to your computer that you can connect or disconnect from your computer through a port or network connection.

- Device Manager provides you with a graphical view of the hardware (internal and external) that is installed your computer and gives you a way to manage and configure your devices.

- A down black arrow in Device Manager indicates a disabled device.

- A black exclamation point (!) in Device Manager on a yellow field indicates the device is in a problem state.

- Administrative Tools including Computer Management console and Server Manager console is a folder in the Control Panel that contains tools for system administrators and advanced users.

- To install Roles and Features in Windows Server 2016, you would use the Server Manager console.

- A service is a program, routine, or process that performs a specific system function to support other programs or to provide a network service. It runs in the system background without a user interface.

- The registry is a central, secure database in which Windows stores all hardware configuration information, software configuration information, and system security policies.

- After you install Server Core, you need to configure Server Core by connecting locally to execute traditional command-line tools using cmd.exe. From there, you can start PowerShell.exe and other programs to configure Windows. You can also configure Server Core remotely by using remote commands or MMC programs that can manage roles, features, or other programs remotely.

Knowledge Assessment

Fill in the Blank

1. The primary tool used to configure the Windows environment and hardware is Windows _____ and _____.

2. _____ is a feature that helps prevent a program making a change without you knowing about it.

3. Every computer should have a _____ computer name assigned to a network.

4. A _____ is a logical unit of computers that share the same security database and is usually associated with Microsoft's Active Directory.

5. _____ allows you to connect to a server remotely to run programs just as you were sitting in front of the computer.

6. For many security mechanisms to work, your computer needs to have the correct _____.

7. _____ are programs that control a device and act as a translator between the device and the operating system and programs that use the device.

8. _____ allows you to install or connect a device and the operating system will automatically recognize, configure and install the appropriate drivers for the device.

9. A _____ is a device driver that includes a digital signature proving who published the device driver and if the device driver has been altered.

10. _____ provides you with a graphical view of the hardware that is installed your computer and gives you a way to manage and configure your devices.

Multiple Choice

1. Which tool allows support personnel to interact with your session to help troubleshoot problems?
   A. Remote Desktop
   B. Remote Assistance
   C. Credential Manager
   D. Control Panel

2. If you connected to your internal network, what should you check if you cannot connect to web servers on the Internet?

   A. UAC

   B. Administrative rights

   C. Proxy settings

   D. NTFS permissions

3. What technology automatically configures IRQs, DMA channels, I/O port addresses, and memory address ranges for an expansion card?

   A. Credential Manager

   B. Signed drivers

   C. Services Manager

   D. Plug and Play

4. Which built-in account gives full access to the computer system?

   A. Local System

   B. Local Service

   C. Network Service

   D. Local user

5. What is a central secure database that stores all hardware configuration information, software configuration information, and system security configuration policies?

   A. Credential Manager

   B. The registry

   C. Server Manager

   D. Computer Management

6. When installing drivers on a 64-bit version of Windows Server 2016, you must
   _____.

   A. Install only signed drivers

   B. Install the driver with Device Manager

   C. First disable UAC

   D. Enable the Windows Installer service

7. To install a network role, you would use the _____.

   A. Computer Management console

   B. Server Manager console

   C. Device Manager

   D. Services console

8. What program would you use to assign IRQ for a device?

   A. Credential Manager

   B. Device Manager

   C. Registry Editor

   D. UAC

9. Which of the following is not a start-up type for a service?

   A. Automatic

   B. Manual

   C. Disable

   D. Self-configuring

10. Which registry key holds the specific settings of a local computer?

    A. HKEY_CLASSES_ROOT

    B. HKEY_CURRENT_USER

    C. HKEY_LOCAL_MACHINE

    D. HKEY_USERS

True/False

1. By default, UAC is disabled.

2. When you right-click Computer in Windows Server 2016, the Computer Management console will open.

3. You can install signed 32-bit drivers on Windows Server 2016.

4. A black exclamation point in the Device Manager means the device is disabled.

5. To connect to a remote computer running a Server Core, you can only use a command prompt escalated as an administrator.

Competency Assessment

Scenario 2-1: Managing Server Core

You just installed Windows Server 2016 Server Core to act as a web server. You now need to configure the server. What are all of the different tools you can use?

Scenario 2-2: Configuring Services

You are installing a new network program that will install a network service. You need to choose which account you want the service to run under. What are the guidelines in choosing the account?

Proficiency Assessment

Scenario 2-3: Using Device Manager

Open Device Manager. Verify that all devices are enabled and that all devices have the proper device driver. If necessary, find and install the correct drivers for any unknown devices.

Scenario 2-4: Configuring Network Adapter

1. Configure the following IP parameters (unless otherwise assigned by your instructor):

   IP address: 172.24.1.XX where XX is your student number. If you do not have a student number, use .31.

   Subnet Mask: 255.255.255.0

   Default Gateway: 172.24.1.20

   DNS Server: 172.24.24.1.30

2. Save your settings.

3. If necessary, change your settings back DHCP and save your settings.

 Real World Scenario

Workplace Ready: Configuring and Managing the Servers

Usually installing the server is a straightforward task. The real work comes when you have to patch Windows, install roles and features, install applications, and configure Windows and the applications. It also takes time to add users and grant permissions to the computers, folders, and applications. Backups will allow you to recovery any irreplaceable data and data that may take hours to re-create. It also allows you to restore a server that took many hours to install and configure if you have to replace or rebuild the server.

Lesson

3

Managing Storage

Objective Domain Matrix

Technology Skill	Objective Domain Description	Objective Domain Number
Identifying storage technologies.	Identify storage technologies.	4.1
Introducing Redundant Arrays of Independent Disks	Understand RAID.	4.2
Understanding Disk Structure.	Understand disk types.	4.3

Key Terms

FAT

FAT32

Fibre Channel

host bus adapter

hot spares

IDE drives

iSCSI

logical unit number (LUN)

network attached storage (NAS)

NTFS

partition

partition style

redundant array of independent disks (RAID)

Resilient File System (ReFS)

SATA

storage area network (SAN)

volume

 Real World Scenario

Lesson 3 Case

You just installed several new servers running Windows Server 2016 for the Acme Corporation, and they have been connected to your network. Now you need to expand several of these servers by adding drives to the servers and configuring a RAID array so that they can be fault tolerant. In addition, you need to connect to a SAN so that you can have several servers connect to a centralized storage device.

Identifying Storage Technologies

While you will need sufficient processing power and a sufficient amount of RAM, you will most likely need a large amount of storage. While simple servers have you install Windows Server on a local IDE (parallel and serial) or SCSI hard drive, more complex systems may use a form of RAID or an attached remote computer storage devices such as a storage array network (SAN) or network attached storage (NAS).

Certification Ready?

Which would you recommend on a server, IDE or SCSI? 4.1

Windows Server 2016 Storage Topologies

Software-defined storage for virtualized workloads

- Data Deduplication—Optimizes free space on a volume by examining the data on the volume for duplication. Once identified, duplicated portions of the volume's dataset are stored once and are (optionally) compressed for additional savings. Data deduplication optimizes redundancies without compromise data fidelity or integrity.
- Storage Quality of Service (QoS)—Centrally monitor and manage storage performance for virtual machines using Hyper-V and the Scale-Out File Server roles automatically improving storage resource fairness between multiple virtual machines using the same file server cluster.
- Storage Replica—Storage-agnostic, block-level, synchronous replication between clusters or servers for disaster preparedness and recovery, as well as stretching of a failover cluster across sites for high availability. Synchronous replication enables mirroring of data in physical sites with crash-consistent volumes, ensuring zero data loss at the file system level.
- Storage Spaces Direct—Directly attached local storage, including SATA and NVME devices, to optimize disk usage after adding new physical disks, and for faster virtual disk repair times.

General-purpose file servers

- DFS Namespaces—Group shared folders that are located on different servers into one or more logically structured namespaces. Each namespace appears to users as a single shared folder with a series of subfolders. The underlying structure of the namespace can consist of numerous file shares that are located on different servers and in multiple sites.
- DFS Replication—Replicates folders (including those referred to by a DFS namespace path) across multiple servers and sites. Uses a compression algorithm known as remote differential compression (RDC). RDC detects changes to the data in a file, and it enables DFS Replication to replicate only the changed file blocks instead of the entire file.
- File Server Resource Manager—Manages and classifies data stored on file servers.
- iSCSI Target Server—Provides block storage to other servers and applications on the network by using the Internet SCSI (iSCSI) standard. Can boot hundreds of computers from a single operating system image that is stored in a centralized location. This improves efficiency, manageability, availability, and security.

- Offline Files and Folder Redirection—Redirects the path of local folders to a network location, while caching the contents locally for increased speed and availability.

- Roaming User Profiles—Redirect a user profile to a network location.

- Storage Migration Service—Migrates servers to a newer version of Windows Server using a graphical tool that inventories data on servers, transfers the data and configuration to newer servers, and then optionally moves the identities of the old servers to the new servers so that apps and users don't have to change anything.

- Work Folders—Store and access work files on personal computers and devices, often referred to as bring-your-own device (BYOD), in addition to corporate computers. Users gain a convenient location to store work files, and they can access them from anywhere. Organizations maintain control over corporate data by storing the files on centrally managed file servers and can specify user device policies such as encryption and lock-screen passwords.

File systems and protocols

- BitLocker Drive Encryption—Stores data on volumes in an encrypted format, even if the computer is tampered with or when the operating system is not running. This can help protect against offline attacks, attacks made by disabling or circumventing the installed operating system, or made by physically removing the hard drive to attack the data separately.

- Network File System (NFS)—Provides a file sharing solution for enterprises that have heterogeneous environments that consist of both Windows and non-Windows computers.

- Resilient File System (ReFS)—A file system that maximizes data availability, scales efficiently to very large data sets across diverse workloads, and provides data integrity by means of resiliency to corruption (regardless of software or hardware failures).

- Server Message Block (SMB) protocol—A network file sharing protocol that allows applications on a computer to read and write to files and to request services from server programs in a computer network. The SMB protocol can be used on top of its TCP/IP protocol or other network protocols. Using the SMB protocol, an application (or the user of an application) can access files or other resources at a remote server. This allows applications to read, create, and update files on the remote server. It can also communicate with any server program that is set up to receive an SMB client request.

- Storage-class memory—Provides performance similar to computer memory, but with the data persistence of normal storage drives. Windows treats storage-class memory similar to normal drives, but there are some differences in the way device health is managed.

- Windows NT File System (NTFS)—The primary file system for recent versions of Windows and Windows Server—provides a full set of features including security descriptors, encryption, disk quotas, and rich metadata, and can be used with Cluster Shared Volumes (CSV) to provide continuously available volumes that can be accessed simultaneously from multiple nodes of a Failover Cluster.

Comparing IDE and SCSI Drives

Today's hard drives are either integrated drive electronics (IDE) or small computer system interface (SCSI), pronounced "skuzzy", drives. Even if you use RAID, a NAS, or a SAN, it is most likely still using IDE or SCSI drives.

IDE drives are designed as fast, low-cost drives. Traditional IDE drives were based on the parallel AT attachment (ATA) standard that used a parallel 40-pin/80-conductor connector. Today's IDE drives follow the *serial ATA standard (SATA)*, which uses a connector that is attached with only four wires and a smaller power connector. Although the serial ATA uses less wires/connectors, it provides faster throughput than parallel ATA IDE drives.

When configuring parallel IDE drives, you can connect two drives on the same ribbon cable. You then need to configure one drive as the master and the other drive as the slave using jumpers on the drive. You can also select a cable select that will automatically configure the drives. Today, if a system has parallel IDE drives, the motherboard will have two IDE connectors allowing you to connect 4 IDE drives. Since you can connect only one serial ATA drive to a cable, you do not need to configure the serial ATA drives.

Servers and high-performance workstations typically use SCSI drives. *SCSI drives* typically offer faster performance and throughput than IDE drives, and SCSI drives support a larger number of drives to be attached using the same interface. Legacy SCSI devices used a 50-pin connector. Newer drives are 68-pin if you are using copper cabling, and some SCSI drives support Fiber Channel for even faster throughput.

When connecting SCSI drives, each SCSI devices must have a unique SCSI ID number on the chain. In addition, both ends of the chain must be terminated with resistors. Today, most devices are auto-terminating, so you don't have to do much configuring.

Storage

Traditionally, hard drives are half-electronic/half-mechanical devices that store magnetic fields on rotating platters. Today, some hard drives, known as solid-state drives, are electronic devices with no mechanical components.

While most personal computers utilize local storage only, consisting of internal hard drives, servers may connect to external storage through a network-attached storage (NAS) or storage area network (SAN).

Optical disks traditionally were considered as read-only devices, but now many systems have burning capabilities that allow the user to write data to special disks. As an administrator, there are a number of questions to ask prior to setting up a server. These questions include:

- What type of disks should be used?
- What type of RAID sets should be made?
- What type of hardware platform should be purchased?

Introducing Redundant Arrays of Independent Disks

Since most drives are half-electronic and half-mechanical devices, you can connect multiple drives to special controllers to provide data production, system reliability, and better performance. *Redundant arrays of independent disks (RAID)* uses two or more drives in combination to create a fault tolerance system to protect against physical hard drive failure and to increase hard drive performance. A RAID can be accomplished with either hardware or software and is usually used with network servers.

Certification Ready?

Which level of RAID would you use on a server? 4.2

There are several levels of RAID available for use, based on your needs. RAID 0 stripes data across all drives. With stripping, all available hard drive are combined into a single large virtual file system, with the file system's blocks arrayed so they are spread evenly across all the drives. For example, if you have three 500 GB hard drives, RAID 0 provides for a 1.5 TB virtual hard drive. When you store files, they are written across all three drives. When a large file is written, a part of it may be written to the first drive, the next chunk to the second drive, more to the third drive, and perhaps more wrapping back to the first drive to start the sequence again. Unfortunately with RAID 0, there is no parity control or fault tolerance; therefore, it really is not a true form of RAID. If one drive fails, you lose all data on the array. However, RAID 0 does have several advantages because it has increased performance through load balancing.

A common RAID used in networked PCs and servers is RAID 1, known as disk mirroring. Disk mirroring copies a disk or partition onto a second hard drive. As information is written, it is written to both hard drives simultaneously. If one of the hard drives fails, the PC will still function because it can access the other hard drive. You can then replace the failed drive and data will be copied from the remaining good drive to the replaced drive.

Another common RAID is RAID 5, which is similar to stripping, except one of the hard drives is used for parity (error-correction) to provide fault tolerance. To increase performance, the error-correction is spread across all hard drives in the array to avoid the one drive of doing all of the work in calculating the parity bits. If one drive fails, you still keep working since the missing data can be filled in by doing parity calculations with the remaining drives. When the failed drive is replaced, the missing information will be rebuilt. However, if two drives fail, you will lose all data on the array. Generally speaking, RAID 5 has better performance than RAID 1. RAID 5 requires at least three drives, with more preferable. If you have 3×500 GB drives, you will have 2×500 GB=1,000 GB of disk space since one of the drives must be used for parity. If you have 6×500 GB drives, you will have 5×500 GB=2,500 GB of disk space.

There are two other forms of RAID worth mentioning, which are considered hybrid RAID or nested RAID.

- RAID 1+0 is a mirrored data set (RAID 1) which is then stripped (RAID 0). A RAID 1+0 array requires a minimum of four drives—two mirrored drives to hold half of the striped data, plus another two mirrored for the other half of the data. The array continues to operate with one or more drives failed in the same mirror set, but if drives fail on both sides of the mirror, the data on the RAID system is lost.

- RAID 0+1 is a stripped data set (RAID 0) which is then mirrored (RAID 1). Similar to RAID 1+0, RAID 0+1 requires a minimum of four drives: two to hold the striped data, plus another two to mirror the first pair. In a failed disk situation, RAID 1+0 performs better because all the remaining disks continue to be used. The array can sustain multiple drive losses so long as no mirror loses all its drives.

RAID can be implemented with hardware using a special controller that is built into the motherboard or an expansion card. The more expensive servers would typically use hardware RAID since software RAID requires some processing by the computer, whereas the hardware RAID is handled by the controller. One disadvantage of hardware RAID is that hardware usually requires a longer boot time.

RAID can also be implemented with software, specifically the operating system. Windows clients such as Windows XP, Windows Vista, and Windows 7 can support RAID 0 and RAID 1, whereas Windows Servers including Windows Server 2003 through Windows Server 2016 support RAID 0, RAID 1, and RAID 5.

A third form, which is sometimes difficult to distinguish, is firmware/driver-based RAID (sometimes referred to as FakeRAID). Adaptec calls them "HostRAID." With firmware/driver-based RAID, the RAID is initially implemented by the firmware and is taken over by the operating system when the appropriate driver is loaded. Therefore, firmware/driver can protect the boot process where some operating system–based RAID doesn't always protect the boot process. In addition, firmware/driver-based RAID is usually much less expensive than hardware RAID.

Introducing Hot Spares

Hot spares is much like it sounds. When having drives that need to be fault tolerant, you can have hot spare drives combined with your RAID. When a drive fails, the system will automatically grab the hot spare drive and replace the failed drive and rebuild or restore the missing data.

Remember that most hard drives are half-electronic/half-mechanical devices. Mechanical devices are considered high failure items because they fail more often than non-mechanical electronic devices. This is one of reasons servers use some form of RAID that provides fault tolerance.

To take it a step further, a hot spare drive is an extra drive installed within a RAID set that is inactive until an active drive fails. When a drive fails, the system automatically replaces the failed drive with the spare and rebuilds the array with the spare. Of course, any time you have to rebuild an array, it can take several hours especially on busy systems. A hot spare can be shared by multiple RAID sets.

Looking at Network Attached Storage and Storage Area Networks

For larger corporations, servers may connect to centralized devices that contain large amounts of storage. These devices offer better performance and better fault tolerance and offers quick recovery.

Network-attached storage (NAS) is a file-level data storage device that is connected to a computer network to provide shared drives or folders, usually using SMB/CIFS. NAS devices usually contain multiple drives in a form of RAID for fault tolerance and are managed usually using a web interface.

A *storage area network (SAN)* is an architecture used for disk arrays, tape libraries, and optical jukeboxes to appear as locally attached drives on a server. SANs always use some form of RAID and other technology to make the system redundant against drive failure and to offer high performance. They also usually contain spare drives. To provide a high-level of data throughput, SAN use the SCSI protocol and either iSCSI or Fibre Channel interface.

While SANs offer performance and redundancy, there are also other benefits to consider. Since you designate storage areas within the SAN and assign them to servers, if have problems with that server, you can quickly and easily move the storage areas to another server.

Some SANs also offer snapshotting and volume cloning. When you need to install or upgrade a component within a server, you can first take a snapshot, which is a temporary image at the time of the snapshot. You can then make changes or upgrades to the server. If you have a problem, you can roll back to the snapshot and continue on before you did the upgrade. The rolling back can take minutes.

Some SANs offer volume cloning. Volume cloning allows you to copy a storage area to another storage area within a SAN or to another SAN. This allows you to quickly create a test environment or to duplicate an environment. You can also establish storage replication between SAN units even if the SAN units are different locations.

A host adapter, sometimes referred to as host bus adapter (HBA), connects a host system such as a computer to a network or storage devices. It is primarily used to refer to connecting SCSI, Fibre Channel, and eSATA devices, but devices for connecting to IDE, Ethernet, FireWire, USB and other systems may also be called host adapters. Today, the term *host bus adapter* (HBA) is most often used to refer to a Fibre Channel interface card.

Logical Unit Numbers (usually referred to as *LUNs*) allow SANs to break its storage down into manageable pieces, which are then assigned to one or more servers in the SAN. It is a logical reference that can comprise a disk, a section of a disk, a whole disk array, or a section of a disk array. LUNs serve as logical identifiers through which you can assign access and control privileges. If a LUN is not mapped to a given server, that server cannot see or access the LUN. You only need to identify the server or cluster that will access the LUN and then select which HBA ports identified on the SAN by the World Wide Name on that server or cluster will be used for LUN traffic.

Introducing Fibre Channel

Optic fiber cabling is generally known for higher bandwidths and offers longer distances over copper cabling because signals travel along with less loss and is also immune to electromagnetic interference. Therefore, storage systems often use fiber cabling.

Fibre Channel or FC is a gigabit-speed technology primarily used for storage networking. It uses a Fibre Channel Protocol (FCP) as its transport protocol, which allows SCSI commands to be issued over Fibre Channel.

The network topology or layout used in Fibre Channel is known as a fabric, where devices are connected to each other through or more data paths. To provide redundancy and faster performance, Fibre Channel will use one or more Fibre Channel switches that allow servers and storage devices to connect to each other through virtual point-to-point connections. When a host or device communicates with another host or device, the fabric routes data from the source to the target.

A port much like in a network switch communicate over the network usually implemented in a device such as disk storage, an HBA on a server, or a Fibre Channel switch. The three major Fibre Channel topologies that describe how a number of ports are connected together are:

- Point-to-Point (FC-P2P)—The simplest topology where two devices are connected back to back.

- Arbitrated loop (FC-AL)—All devices are in a loop or ring, similar to token ring networking. Unfortunately, adding or removing a device from the loop causes communication on the loop to be interrupted as well as a failure of one of the devices, which causes a break in the ring. Some hubs can bypass failed devices.

- Switched fabric (FC-SW)—All devices or loops of devices are connected to Fibre Channel switches, similar to what you find on today's Ethernet network. The switches manage the state of the fabric to provide optimized connections. In an FC-SW, the media is not shared. Therefore, any device that communicates with another device communicates at full bus speed regardless of whether other devices and host are communicating. On advantage of FC-SW is that a failure of a port is isolated and should not affect operation of other ports.

The Fibre Channel and iSCSI fabrics include one or more Internet Storage Name Service (iSNS) servers to provide discoverability and partitioning of resources. When a host or device is powered on, it logs on to the fabric and is assigned a unique fabric address. When a host or device communicates with another device, it establishes a connection to that device before transmitting data. The switch then routes the packets in the fabric.

Each device including the Host Bus Adapter is called a node. Much like a MAC address used in network interface cards, each node has a fixed 64-bit worldwide name (WWN) assigned by the manufacturer and registered with the IEEE to ensure it is globally unique. Also similar to a server, each node can have multiple ports, each with a unique 64-bit port name and 24-bit port ID.

To make storage more manageable, Fibre Channel uses zoning and LUNs. Zoning is a method of restricting which ports or WWN can communicate with each other.

Introducing iSCSI

Internet Small Computing System Interface or iSCSI is an Internet Protocol (IP)–based storage networking standard for linking data storage facilities. iSCSI allows clients to send SCSI commands over a TCP/IP network using TCP port 3260. Similar to Fibre Channel, iSCSI can communicate using Gigabit Ethernet or Fibre and it can connect a SAN to multiple servers over a distance.

While iSCSI uses normal network technology to communicate, the network adaptor must be dedicated to iSCSI. This means that servers will typically need at least two set of networks cards, one for iSCSI and one for the network connection. However, similar to network connections, each iSCSI initiator can have one or more network adapters through which communication is established to provide increased bandwidth and redundancy. The iSCSI software could be built into the iSCSI host adapter or Host Bus Adapter allowing increased performance for the server.

After access is granted by the SAN, the iSCSI session emulates a SCSI hard disk so that to the server treats the LUN just like any other hard drive. Similar to Fibre Channel, you can define which servers can communicate with each LUN and the type of communication.

iSCSI initiators find storage devices by using the Internet Storage Name Service (iSNS) protocol to provide both naming and resource discovery services for storage devices on the IP network. The iSCSI uses the following to connect to the SAN:

- Hostname or IP Address
- Port Number (default port is 3260)
- iSCSI Name (For example, "iqn.2003-01.com.ibm:00.fcd0ab21.shark128")
- An optional CHAP Secret password.

    The iSCSI Name will follow one of the following formats:

- iSCSI Qualified Name (IQN)—IQN follows the iqn.yyyy-mm.{reversed domain name} format. For example, iqn.2001-04.com.acme:storage.tape.sys1.xyz). IQN addresses are the most common format.

- Extended Unique Identifier (EUI)—EUI follows the eui.{EUI 64-bit address} format. For example, eui.02004567A425678D. EUI is provided by the IEEE Registration authority in accordance with EUI-64 standard.

- T11 Network Address Authority (NAA)—NAA follows the naa.{NAA 64 or 128 bit identifier. For example, naa.52004567BA64678D). NAA is part OUI, which is provided by the IEEE Registration Authority. NAA name formats were added to iSCSI in RFC 3980, to provide compatibility with naming conventions used in Fibre Channel and SAS storage technologies.

iSCSI Initiator Software

Microsoft Windows Server 2016 includes two iSCSI Initiator software interfaces to connect an iSCSI storage array or volume of a storage array to a server and mount the array or volume as a local volume. They are:

- iSCSI Initiator located in the Administrative Tools and Control Panel
- iscsicli command interface

When you open the iSCSI Initiator program, you will see the following six tabs:

- Targets—Specifies which storage devices the server has access to and allows you to logon to those devices.

- Discovery—Specifies the location of the SAN and Internet Storage Name Service (iSNS) servers. Shown in Figure 3.1.

- Favorite Targets—Specifies which targets that reconnect each time you start your computer.

- Volumes and Devices—Shows volumes and devices that are connected to the server and allows you to bind or connect an iSCSI device to a volume.

- RADIUS—Specifies connect to RADIUS server for authentication

- Configuration—Allows you to configure settings globally that will affect any future connections made with the initiator.

FIGURE 3.1   iSCSI initiator included with Windows Server 2016

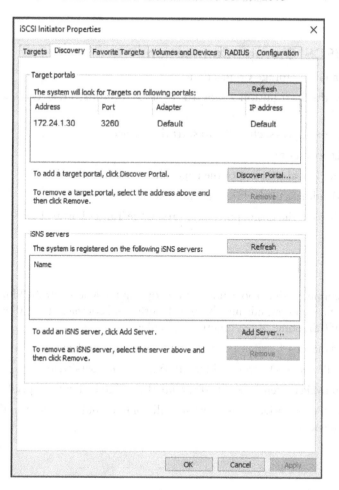

Connect to an iSCSI Array

To connect to an iSCSI target device by using Quick Connect:

1. Click Start, type iSCSI in Start Search, and then under Programs, click iSCSI Initiator.

2. If the UAC page appears, click Continue.

3. If this is the first time that you have launched Microsoft iSCSI Initiator, you receive a prompt that says the Microsoft iSCSI service is not running. You must start the service for Microsoft iSCSI Initiator to run correctly. Click Yes to start the service. The Microsoft iSCSI Initiator Properties dialog box opens, and the Targets tab is displayed.

4. On the Targets tab, type the name or the IP address of the target device in the Quick Connect text box, and then click Quick Connect. The Quick Connect dialog box is displayed.

5. If multiple targets are available at the target portal that is specified, a list is displayed. Click the desired target, and then click Connect.

6. Click Done.

Configure iSCSI Storage Connection

To configure an iSCSI Storage Connection:

1. Right-click the Start button ➤ Control Panel ➤ Administrative Tools ➤ iSCSI Initiator.

2. If a dialog box appears, click Yes to start the service.

3. Click the Discovery tab.

4. In the Target Portals portion of the page, click Discover Portal.

5. Enter the IP address of the target portal and click OK.

6. The IP address of the target portal appears in the Target Portals box.

7. Click OK.

iSCSICLI

iSCSICLI is a command-line tool suitable for scripting the Microsoft iSCSI initiator service. While some of these commands may become lengthy and complex, they allow you to access all features of iSCSI. Some of the functions include:

- iscsicli AddTarget—Creates a connection to a volume or device

- iscsicli AddPersistentDevices—Makes an iSCSI device persistent

- iscsicli RemovePersistentDevices—Prevents the reconnection to a specified volume

- iscsicli ClearPersistentDevices—Removes all volumes and devices from the list of persistent devices

Understanding Disk Structure

Before you use a disk, you must prepare the disk for usage including creating partitions or volumes and formatting the disk.

When you want to use a disk in Windows, you have several choices to make including the following:

- Disk partitioning style
- Disk type
- Type of volume
- File system

Traditionally, basic disks use partitions and logical drives. A partition is a defined storage space on a hard disk. To be usable, a hard disk needs to have at least one partition. A volume is a partition that has been formatted into a file system.

To keep track how the disk is divided, it uses a partition table. Formatting a disk prepares the volume's file system including creating a file allocation table so that can keep track of the files and folders on the volume.

Introducing Disk Partitioning Styles

Partition style refers to the method that Windows uses to organize partitions on the disk.

The MBR partition style has been around for quite a while, and all Windows operating systems support MBR partitions. The MBR is stored at a consistent location on a physical disk, enabling a computer's BIOS to reference it. After the computer examines the MBR to determine the active partition, it then loads the operating system startup files from the active partition.

But as with most legacy technologies, MBR partitions have their limitations, including the following:

- MBR partitions are limited to four basic partitions, and each partition is limited to 2 terabytes (TBs) in size.
- The four basic partitions can be either four primary partitions or three primary partitions with one extended partition, which can be further divided into multiple logical partitions.
- The MBR is a single point of failure. If it becomes corrupted or damaged, it could prevent the computer from starting.

A GPT partition style allows for more partitions and larger volume sizes. Features of GPT disks include:

- A disk initialized as a GPT partition style may contain up to 128 primary partitions.
- Each partition can be as large as 9.4 zetabytes (ZB). One zetabyte is equal to one billion terabytes.

You can implement GPT disks on Windows Server 2008 and newer versions, and Windows Vista and newer versions. You cannot use the GPT partition style on removable disks.

You can typically convert a basic disk to a dynamic disk without losing any data; however, you should back up all data before attempting the conversion just to be safe. If you have software or hardware that does not work with dynamic disks, you may need to convert a dynamic disk to basic.

When you initialize a disk, you specify if the disk will be MBR or GPT. To convert an MBR partition style to GPT, you can open Disk Management, right-click the disk, and choose Convert to GPT Disk. However, if the Convert to GPT Disk option is grayed out, you will need to back up the data, delete all partitions, and then convert MBR to GPT.

Comparing Types of Disks

Most versions of Windows servers including Windows Server 2016 support two types of hard disk storage: basic and dynamic. Basic disk is the traditional disk type while dynamic disks offer software-based RAID and the ability to resize volumes without rebooting.

Certification Ready?

What are the differences between basic and dynamic disks? 4.3

A basic disk under Windows Server 2016 is the same type of disk that you find under early versions of Windows. When using MBR, basic disks gave you the four primary partitions or 3 primary partitions and one extended partition. The partition table and master boot record is located on the first sector of each hard disk.

Dynamic disks were created to make a disk more flexible. Instead of the basic partition table found in the basic disk, the dynamic disk uses the Logical Disk Manager (LDR) database to store the information about the basic disk. Since it uses the LRD, it allows the disk to be divided up to 2,000 separate volumes. However it is recommended to keep the time for the system to boot, you should limit the number of volumes to 32.

Dynamic disks are meant to be dynamic, which means that you can extend a dynamic disk or shrink a dynamic disk without requiring a reboot. In addition, dynamic disks support five types of volumes:

- Simple volume—Consists of disk space on a single physical disk. It can consist of a single area on a disk or multiple areas on the same disk that are linked together.

- Spanned volumes—Consists of disk space from more than one physical disk. You can add more space to a spanned volume by extending it at any time. You can create spanned volumes on dynamic disks only and you need at least two dynamic disks to create a spanned volume. You can extend a spanned volume onto a maximum of 32 dynamic disk. Spanned volumes cannot be mirrored or striped. Spanned volumes are not fault tolerant.

- Striped volume—A striped volume (RAID 0) stores data in stripes on two or more physical disks. Data in a striped volume is allocated alternately and evenly (in stripes) to the disks contained within the striped volume. Striped volumes can substantially improve the speed of access to the data on disk. Striped volumes are not fault tolerant. You need at least two physical dynamic disks to create a striped volume and can be created a striped volume onto a maximum of 32 disks. If you need to make a striped volume larger by adding another disk, you first have to delete the volume and then re-create it.

- Mirrored volume—Uses volumes stored on two separate physical disks to "mirror" (write) the data onto both disks simultaneously and redundantly. This configuration is also referred to as RAID 1. If one of the disks in the mirrored configuration fails, Windows Server 2016 writes an event into the system log of the Event Viewer. The system will continue to function normally until the failed disk is replaced.

- RAID-5 volume—A form of RAID (striping with parity) that uses a minimum 3 disks (up to a maximum of 32 disks) to create a fault tolerant drive amount the drives. If one drive fails, you continue to work until you replace the drive.

You can create mirrored volumes and RAID-5 volumes only on dynamic disks running on Windows Server operating systems. Both mirrored volumes and RAID-5 volumes are considered fault tolerant because these configurations can handle a single disk failure and still function normally. Mirrored volumes and RAID-5 volumes both require that an equal amount of disk space be available on each disk that will be a part of these volumes. A mirrored volume must use two physical disks. A RAID-5 volume must use at least three physical hard disks up to a maximum of 32 physical disks.

Many network administrators and consultants agree that hardware-based fault-tolerant solutions are more robust and reliable than software-based fault-tolerant configurations. By installing one or more RAID controller adapter cards into a server, you can set up several different types of hardware fault tolerance, such as mirroring, RAID-5, RAID 10 (mirrored volumes that are part of a striped array set), and RAID 0+1 (striped volumes that are part of a mirrored set). When you use hardware RAID, you can retain basic disks or you can convert disks to dynamic; hardware RAID is hidden to Windows Server 2016. Of course, it's less expensive to implement a software solution, such as setting up mirrored volumes or RAID-5 volumes using the Disk Management console in Windows Server 2016, but often the performance, reliability, and flexibility of hardware-based RAID far outweighs its extra cost.

Solid State Drive (SSD) and Hard Disk Drive (HDD) Types and Comparisons

A solid-state drive (SSD) is a storage device that uses integrated circuit assemblies as memory to store data. It is also sometimes called a solid-state device or a solid-state disk. SSDs lack the physical spinning disks and movable read-write heads used by conventional electromechanical storage such as hard drives ("HDD") or floppy disks.

Compared with electromechanical drives, SSDs typically:

- Allow for quicker access time
- Offer lower latency
- Are more resistant to physical shock
- Run silently

A hard disk drive (HDD), hard disk, hard drive, or fixed disk, is an electro-mechanical data storage device that uses magnetic storage to store and retrieve information using one or more rigid rapidly rotating disks (platters) coated with magnetic material. The platters are paired with magnetic heads, usually arranged on a moving actuator arm, which read and write data to the platter surfaces. Data is accessed in a random-access manner, meaning that individual blocks of data can be stored or retrieved in any order and not only sequentially.

Introducing File Systems

A file system is a method of storing and organizing computer files and the data they contain to make it easy to find and access them. It also maintains the physical location of the files so that you can find and access the files in the future. Windows Server 2016 supports FAT16, FAT32, NTFS, and ReFS file systems on hard drives.

After you partition a disk, you then need to format the disk. You can format the disk as FAT16, FAT32, NTFS, or ReFS. Of these, NTFS is the preferred file system to be used in today's Windows operating systems.

FAT16, sometimes referred generically as *File Allocation Table (FAT)*, is a simple file that system that uses minimum memory and has been used with DOS. Originally it supported the 8.3 naming scheme, which allowed up to 8-character filename and 3-character filename extension. Later, it was revised to support long filenames. Unfortunately, FAT can only support up to 2 GB.

FAT32 was released with the second major release of Windows 95. While the file system can support larger drives, today's Windows support volumes up to 32 GB. It also supports long filenames.

As mentioned earlier, *NTFS* is the preferred file system that supports much larger hard disks up to 16 exabytes and large filenames. In addition, it is more fault tolerant than previous file systems used in Windows because it uses a journaling file system to make sure that a disk transaction is written to disk properly before recognized. Lastly, NTFS offers better security through permissions and encryption.

Resilient File System (ReFS) was introduced as an enhanced NTFS file system by offering larger volume sizes and files. ReFS also offers greater resiliency, meaning better data verification, error correction, and scalability. It is recommended that you should use ReFS for very large volumes and file shares. However, you cannot use ReFS for the boot volume. For maximum file name length, NTFS only supports 256 characters, whereas ReFS supports up to 32,000 characters.

Because ReFS uses a subset of NTFS features, it maintains backward compatibility with NTFS that can be accessed directly by Windows Server 2012 or higher, or Windows 8.1 or higher. Different from NTFS, ReFS has a fixed allocation unit size of 64 KB, and ReFS does not support Encrypting File System (EFS) for files.

When deciding which file system to use, you should always consider NTFS or ReFS. It is recommended to use ReFS for the following situations:

- Microsoft Hyper-V workloads. (ReFS has performance advantages when using both .vhd and .vhdx files.)

- Storage Spaces Direct when using shared direct attached storage. ReFS supports larger volumes and improved throughput.

- Archive data that you want to retain for long periods. Archived data can benefit from ReFS resiliency.

Table 3.1 compares the different file systems.

TABLE 3.1   Comparing File Systems

File System	Maximum Partition Size	Maximum File Size
FAT	2 GB	2 GB
FAT32	32 GB	4 GB
NTFS	256 TB*	Limited by the size of the volume on which it resides
ReFS	1 yobiByte (2^{80} bytes)	16 exbibytes (2^{64} bytes)
exFAT	128 pebiBtye (2^{50} bytes), However, Windows recommend a maximum size of 512 TB.	Limited by the size of the volume on which it resides

*with 64-KB clusters

Another file system to mention is the *Extended File Allocation Table (exFAT)*, which is a Microsoft file system optimized for flash drives. It is typically used where the NTFS file system is not ideal because of the data structure overhead. exFAT supports a larger volume than FAT or FAT32 supports. exFAT has been adopted by the SD Card Association as the default file system for SDXC cards larger than 32 GB.

Using Disk Management Tools

The main tool to manage disk in Windows Server 2016 is to use the MMC snap-in called Disk Management, which is also part of the Computer and Management consoles. In addition, you can use a diskpart.exe and the format command to partition and format a drive and Windows Explorer to format a drive.

Disk Management is a system utility for managing hard disks and the volumes or partitions that they contain. With Disk Management, you can initialize disks, create volumes, and format volumes with file systems. See Figure 3.2.

FIGURE 3.2   Disk Management snap-in

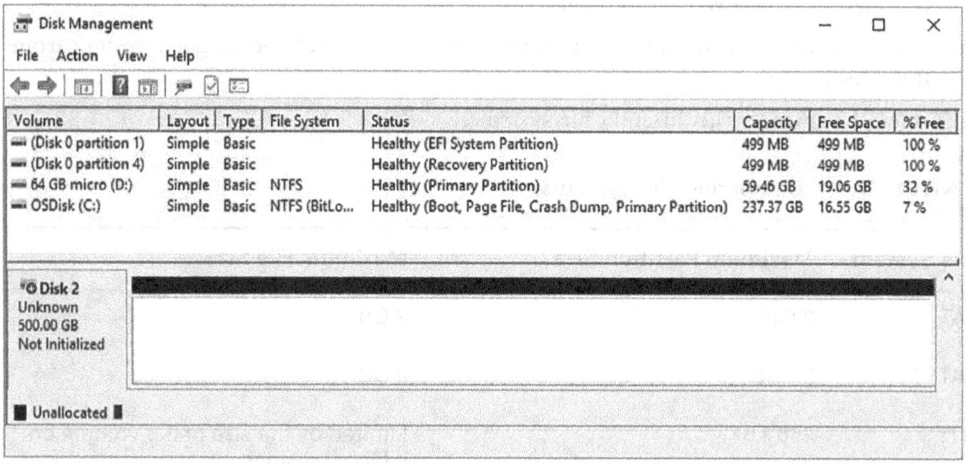

Any time you add a new disk (local hard drive or a virtual drive such as from a SAN) to a Windows Server 2016 system, you need open Disk Management and initialize the disk.

Initialize a New Disk

To initialize new disks:

1. Right-click the disk you want to initialize, and then click Initialize Disk.

2. In the Initialize Disk dialog box, select the disk(s) to initialize. You can select whether to use the master boot record (MBR) or GUID partition table (GPT) partition style. See Figure 3.3. Click the OK button.

If the disk that you want to initialize does not appear, you may need to right-click Disk Management and click refresh or Rescan Disks. If it still does not appear, you need to make sure the disk is connected properly and is running.

New disks will automatically start as basic disks. To convert a basic disk to dynamic disks, the disk must have at least 1 MB of unallocated space. Disk Management automatically reserves this space when creating partitions or volumes on a disk.

FIGURE 3.3   Initializing a disk

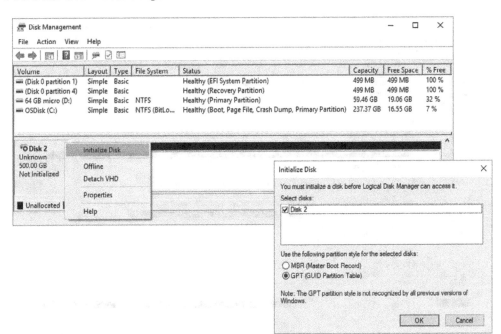

Convert a Basic Disk to a Dynamic Disk

To convert a basic disk to a dynamic disk from the Disk Management console, perform the following steps:

1. Open the Disk Management snap-in.

2. Right-click the basic disk you that want to convert to a dynamic disk and then click Convert to Dynamic Disk. See Figure 3.4.

When you convert a basic disk to a dynamic disk, any existing partitions or logical drives on the basic disk become simple volumes on the dynamic disk.

After you convert a basic disk to a dynamic disk, you cannot change the dynamic volumes back to a basic disk. Instead, you must delete all dynamic volumes on the disk and then use the Convert To Basic Disk command. If you want to keep your data, you must first back it up or move it to another volume.

FIGURE 3.4   Convert a basic disk to dynamic disk

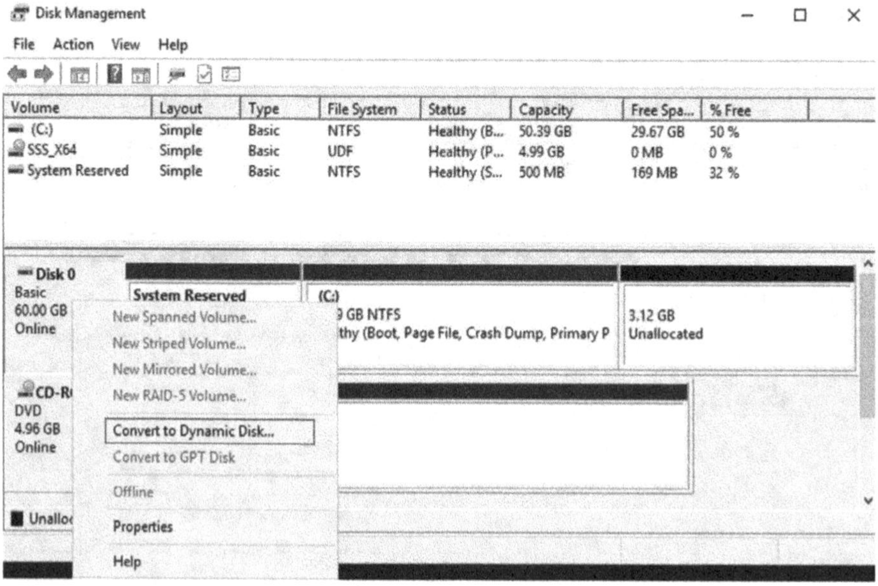

Create a Simple Volume

To create a simple volume, perform the following steps.

1. Open Disk Management in the Computer Management console. Right-click Start, choose Computer Management, and then click the Disk Management node.

2. Right-click an empty area (unallocated space) of a dynamic disk. The New Volume menu displays, similar to Figure 3.5. Choose New Simple Volume.

3. The New Simple Volume Wizard starts. Click Next on the welcome page.

4. Click Next to accept the default volume size.

5. On the Assign Drive Letter or Path page, assign a drive letter or path and then click Next.

6. On the Format Partition page (as shown in Figure 3.6), you can specify the file system, allocation unit size, and volume label. The file system choices (FAT, FAT32, NTFS, exFAT, or ReFS) are based on the size of the volume. There are two other options you can set: Perform a quick format (selected by default, which is a good idea) and Enable file and folder compression, which is not selected by default. Click Next.

7. On the Completing the New Simple Volume Wizard page, click Finish.

FIGURE 3.5   The New Volume menu

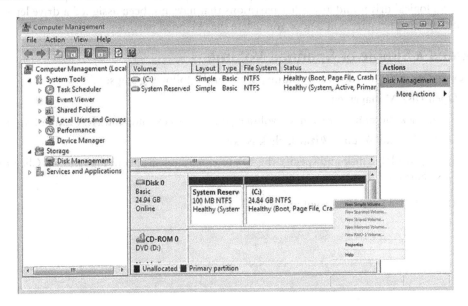

FIGURE 3.6   Formatting a partition

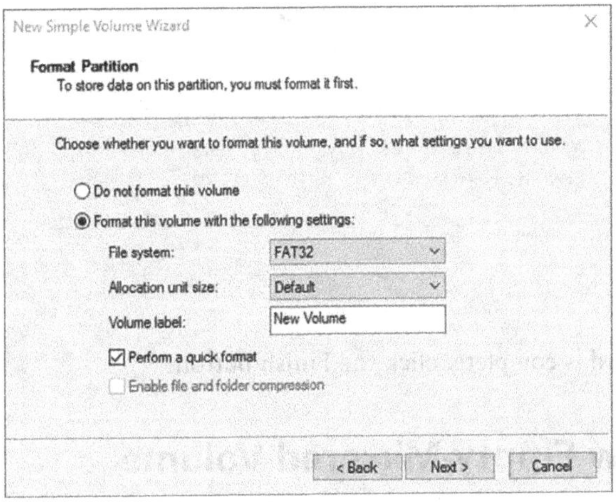

For basic disks, you must first create an extended partition before you can create a new logical drive, if no extended partition exists already.

If you choose to delete a partition, all data on the deleted partition or logical drive is lost unless you backed it up. In addition, you cannot delete the system partition, boot partition, or any partition that contains an active paging file. Windows Server 2016 requires that you delete all logical drives and any other partitions that have not been assigned a drive letter within an extended partition before you delete the extended partition itself.

Extend a Simple or Spanned Volume

To extend a simple or a spanned volume, perform the following steps:

1. Open Disk Management.
2. Right-click the simple or spanned volume you want to extend, and click Extend Volume.
3. On the Extend Volume Wizard, click Next.
4. Specify available disk and specify the size to extend (as shown in Figure 3.7). Click the Next button.

FIGURE 3.7   Extending a volume

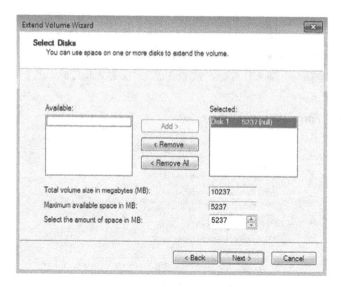

5. When the wizard is complete, click the Finish button.

Create a New Empty Mirrored Volume

To create a new empty mirrored volume from unallocated space, perform the following steps:

1. Open Disk Management.
2. Right-click an area of unallocated space on a disk and select New Mirrored Volume.
3. Click Next for the New Mirrored Wizard welcome window.
4. Select one of the available disks (as shown in Figure 3.8) and click Add.

FIGURE 3.8   Extending a volume

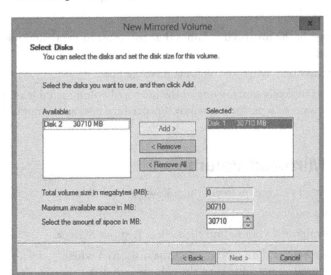

5. Enter the amount of storage space to be used (in MB) for this mirrored volume, up to the maximum available space on both disk that you selected, and then click Next.

6. Assign the new volume a drive letter, mount the volume in an empty NTFS folder, or choose not to assign the volume a drive letter or path and click Next.

7. Choose whether to format the new mirrored volume. If you choose to format the new volume, specify the following settings:

    ▪   File system (NTFS is the only option for dynamic volumes under the Disk Management console).

    ▪   Allocation unit size.

    ▪   Volume label.

    ▪   Mark the check box to Perform a Quick Format (if desired).

    ▪   Mark the check box to Enable File and Folder Compression (if desired).

8. Click Next to continue.

9. Click Finish to complete the New Volume Wizard.

10. If the volumes are not on dynamic disks, you will be asked if you want to convert the disks to dynamic disks and if you want to continue. Click Yes.

You can stop mirroring a volume by either breaking or removing the mirror. When you break a mirrored volume, each volume that makes up the mirror becomes an independent simple volume, and they are no longer fault tolerant. When you remove a mirrored volume, the removed mirrored volume becomes unallocated space on its disk, whereas the remaining mirrored volume becomes a simple volume that is no longer fault tolerant. All data that was stored on the removed mirrored volume is erased.

To break a mirrored volume, perform the following steps:

1. Open Disk Management.
2. Right-click one of the mirrored volumes that you want to break and select Break Mirrored Volume.
3. Click Yes in the Break Mirrored Volume message box.

If you want to completely destroy one of the mirrored volumes and leave just one of the volumes intact, you need to perform a removal procedure instead of simply breaking the mirrored volumes.

Remove a Mirrored Volume

To remove a mirrored volume, perform the following:

1. Open Disk Management.
2. Right-click a mirrored volume and then select Remove Mirror.
3. At the Remove Mirror dialog box, select the disk from which you want to completely erase the mirrored volume and turn the volume into unallocated space. The remaining volume will stay with all of its data intact as a simple volume.
4. Click the Remove Mirror button.
5. Click Yes to confirm the removal action at the Disk Management message box that appears.

Create a Striped Volume

To create a striped volume from unallocated space, perform the following steps:

1. Right-click unallocated space and select New Striped Volume.
2. When the Welcome screen appears, click the Next button.
3. Select the remaining disk and click the Add button. Click the Next button.
4. Assign the F drive and click the Next button.
5. When it asks to format the volume, click the Next button.
6. When the wizard is complete, click the Finish button.

Create a RAID-5 Volume

To create a RAID-5 volume using Disk Management, perform the following steps:

1. Open Disk Management. Be sure that the computer has three or more disks, each with unallocated space.
2. Right-click an area of unallocated space on one of the dynamic disks that you want to use for the RAID-5 volume and select New Volume.
3. Click Next for the Welcome to the New Volume Wizard window.

4. Select the RAID-5 option button and click Next.

5. Select each available disk that you want to use as part of the RAID-5 volume from within the Available list box and click Add for each one. You must select at least three disks and no more than 32 disks.

6. Select any disks that you do not want to use as part of the RAID-5 volume within the Selected list box and click Remove to remove any disks that you do not want to include as a part of the RAID-5 volume.

7. Enter the storage capacity that you want for the RAID-5 volume in the Select the Amount of Space in MB spin box and click Next to continue.

8. Choose to assign the volume a drive letter, mount the volume in an empty NTFS folder, or choose to not assign a drive letter or path to the new RAID-5 volume and click Next.

9. Choose whether to format the new RAID-5 volume. If you choose to format the new volume, specify the following settings:

   - File system (NTFS is the only option for dynamic volumes under the Disk Management console).
   - Allocation unit size.
   - Volume label.
   - Mark the check box to Perform a Quick Format (if desired).
   - Mark the check box to Enable File and Folder Compression (if desired).

10. Click Next to continue.

11. Click Finish to complete the New Volume Wizard.

12. If the volumes are not on dynamic disks, you will be asked if you want to convert the disks to dynamic disks and if you want to continue. Click Yes.

If one disk within a RAID-5 volume is intermittently failing, you can attempt to reactivate it by right-clicking the disk and selecting Reactivate Disk. If one disk within a RAID-5 volume appears to be permanently failed, you can replace that failed disk with another dynamic disk attached to the computer or you can install a new disk. To regenerate the RAID-5 volume, right-click the RAID-5 volume on the failed disk and select Repair Volume. The replacement disk must contain at least as much unallocated space as that used by the failed disk for the RAID-5 volume.

To format a disk, you can right-click the volume in Disk Management and select Format. You can also right-click the drive in Windows Explorer and select Format. You can then specify the volume label, the file system and the allocation unit size (the smallest space allocated to a file). You can also perform a quick format which only empties the FAT table and you can enable file and folder compression.

When you prepare a volume in Windows, you can assign a drive letter to the new volume or you can create a mount point the new volume as an empty NTFS folder. The drive letters are from drive C through drive Z (24 different drive letters). Drives A and B were reserved to floppy disk drives. To assign or change a drive letter to a volume, right-click the volume in the Disk Management console and select "Change drive letters and path." Then click either the Add or Change button.

By using volume mount points, you can graft, or mount, a target partition into a folder on another drive. The mounting is handled transparently to the user and applications. With the NTFS volume mount points feature, you can surpass the 26-drive-letter limitation.

Mount Points

With the ever-growing demand for storage, mount points are used to exceed the limitation of 26 drive letters and to join two volumes into a folder on a separate physical disk drive. A mount point allows an administrator to configure a volume to be accessed from a folder on another existing disk.

Using Disk Management, a mount point folder can be assigned to a drive instead of using a drive letter and can be used on basic or dynamic volumes that are formatted with NTFS. Mount point folders can only be created on empty folders within a volume.

Once created, mount point folder paths cannot be modified; they can be removed only once they have been created.

Assign a Mount-Point Folder Path

To assign a mount-point folder path to a drive by using the Windows interface:

1. In Disk Manager, right-click the partition or volume where you want to assign the mount-point folder path, and then click Change Drive Letter and Paths.

2. To assign a mount-point folder path, click Add. Click Mount in the following empty NTFS folder, type the path to an empty folder on an NTFS volume, or click Browse to locate it (as shown in Figure 3.9).

FIGURE 3.9   Assigning a mount-point folder path

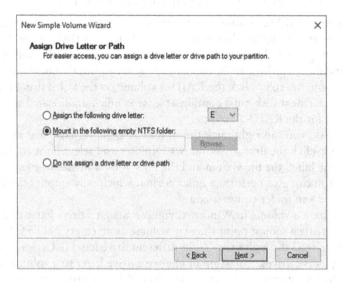

Understanding Distributed File System (DFS)

Distributed File System (DFS) in Windows Server 2016 offers an easy way for users to access files not at the same geographic location. DFS allows an administrator to set up a tree structure of virtual directories that allows users to connect to shared folders throughout the network.

Administrators have the ability to take shared folders that are located on separate servers and transparently connect them to one or more DFS namespaces. An advantage of using DFS is that if one of the folders becomes unavailable, there is a failover capability that will allow the users to connect to the data on a different server.

Administrators can use the DFS tools to choose which shared folders will show up in the namespace and also to decide how the names of these shared folders will appear in the virtual tree listing.

Advantages of DFS

An advantage of DFS is that when a user views this virtual tree or DFS namespace, the shared folders appear to be located on a single machine.

Here are some more advantages of DFS:

- Access-Based Enumeration (ABE)—This DFS feature (disabled by default) displays only the files and folders that a user has permissions to access. So, if a user does not have access to a folder, then Windows will hide the folder from the user's DFS view.

- Simplified Data Migration—DFS provides administrators with the ability to move data from one location to another without the user needing to know the physical location of the data.

- Security Integration Administrators do not need to configure additional security for the DFS shared folders. The shared folders use the NTFS and shared folder permissions that an administrator has already assigned when the share was set up.

Types of DFS

The following are types of DFS:

- DFS Namespace—This service is the virtual tree listing on the DFS server. An administrator can set up multiple namespaces on the DFS, allowing for multiple virtual trees within DFS. The DFS Namespace service was once called the Distributed File System.

- DFS Replication (DFSR)—Administrators have the ability to manage replication scheduling and bandwidth throttling using the DFS Management Console. Replication is the process of sharing data between multiple machines.

Mounting a Virtual Hard Disk (VHD)

Virtual hard disks (VHDs) are similar to the physical hard disk on a computer. Administrators have two types of VHD files:

- VHD (Virtual Hard Disk)—A VHD file represents a virtual hard disk drive. It can accommodate everything that is present on a physical HDD—disk partitions, file systems, data files, and folders. It is used as the hard disk of a virtual machine.

- VHDX (Hyper-V Virtual Hard Disk)—A VHDX format represents a Hyper-V Virtual Hard Disk Drive. It has a much larger storage capacity (64 TB as compared to VHD file, which has 2 TB storage limitation). It can protect data from corruption and extreme power failures.

There are several methods for mounting a virtual hard disk.

Method 1: Using Windows Explorer

This is the easiest way to mount/unmount a VHD/VHDX file.

- To mount a VHD/VHDX file: Right-click the VHD/VHDX file and select Mount. The VHD disk will be added to This PC as an additional drive. Can now copy, move, or access the required data from the drive. This will behave just like physical storage.

- To unmount a VHD/VHDX file: Go to the New Volume/drive, right-click, and select Eject to detach or unmount.

Method 2: Using Disk Management

Another way to mount/unmount a VHD/VHDX file is using Disk Management:

- To mount a VHD: Right-click This PC ➤ Manage ➤ Disk Management and click Attach VHD or click the Windows key and type **diskmgmt.msc** in the search box to open Disk Management. Expand Action menu and click Attach VHD.

- To mount VHD: Click Attach VHD and click Browse to load the VHD or VHDX file that is to be mounted. Click OK.

- To unmounts a VHD/VHDX file: Right-click the newly added volume and click Detach VHD.

Method 3: Using Command Prompt

This method can be used in Windows 10/8/7 to mount or unmount VHD/VHDX file.

1. Click Win+X, and click Command Prompt (Admin) mode.

2. In cmd, type **diskpart** and hit the Enter button. Type the following command to select the VHD/VHDX file by specifying its location:

   ```
   Select vdisk file = "location of VHD file"
   ```

3. Then, hit Enter.

4. To mount the VHD/VHDX file, type **attach vdisk** and hit Enter.

5. To unmount a VHD/VHDX file, type **detach vdisk** and hit Enter.

Method 4: Using PowerShell

An administrator can mount/unmount VHD/VHDX file in both Windows 10/8/7 and Windows Server 2016/2012/2008.

1. Launch PowerShell cmdlet as Administrator.

2. Type the following commands to mount/attach the VHD/VHDX files:

   ```
   Mount-DiskImage -ImagePath "location of VHD file"
   ```

3. Can unmount the virtual hard disk using:

   ```
   Dismount-DiskImage -ImagePath "location of VHD file:
   ```

Skill Summary

In this lesson you learned:

- Today's drives are either IDE (mostly found on consumer computers) or SCSI drives (mostly found in servers).

- Redundant arrays of inexpensive disks (RAID) uses two or more drives in combination to create a fault tolerance system to protect against physical hard drive failure and to increase hard drive performance.

- With stripping (RAID 0), all available hard drive are combined into a single large virtual file system, with the file system's blocks arrayed so they are spread evenly across all the drives. Unfortunately, striping offers no fault tolerance.

- Disk mirroring (RAID-1) copies a disk or partition onto a second hard drive. As information is written, it is written to both hard drives simultaneously.

- RAID 5, which is similar to stripping, except one of the hard drives is used for parity (error-correction) to provide fault tolerance.

- RAID 10 (1+0) is a mirrored data set (RAID 1) which is then stripped (RAID 0).

- When a drive fails, some systems use hot spares so that when a drive fails, the system will automatically grab the hot spare drive and replace the failed drive and rebuild or restore the missing data.

- Network-attached storage (NAS) is a file-level data storage device that is connected to a computer network to provide shared drives or folders, usually using SMB.

- A storage area network (SAN) is an architecture used for disk arrays, tape libraries and optical jukeboxes to appear as locally attached drives on a server.

- A host adapter, sometimes referred to as host bus adapter (HBA) connects a host system such as a computer to a network or storage devices.

- Logical Unit Numbers (usually referred to as LUNs) allow SANs to break its storage down into manageable pieces, which are then assigned to one or more servers in the SAN.

- Fibre Channel and iSCSI is a gigabit speed technology primarily used for storage networking.

- Microsoft Windows Server 2016 includes two iSCSI Initiator software interfaces (iSCSI Initiator and iscsicli command interface) to connect an iSCSI storage array or volume of a storage array to a server and mount the array or volume as a local volume.

- Partitioning is defining and dividing the physical or virtual disk into logical volumes called partitions. Each partition functions as if it were a separate disk drive that can be assigned drive letters.

- Formatting a disk prepares the disk's file system.

- Windows Server 2016 supports two types of disk partitioning styles: Master Boot Record (MBR) and GUID partition table (GPT).

- A basic disk under Windows Server 2016 is the same type of disk that you find under early versions of Windows.

- When using MBR, basic disks gave you the four primary partitions or 3 primary partitions and one extended partition.

- Dynamic disks were created to make a disk more flexible including up to 2,000 volumes and the ability to extend a dynamic disk or shrink a dynamic disk without requiring a reboot.

- Dynamic disks support five types of volumes: simple volumes, spanned volumes, striped volumes, mirrored volumes and RAID-5 volumes.

- A file system is a method of storing and organizing computer files and the data they contain to make it easy to find and access them. It also maintains the physical location of the files so that you can find and access the files in the future.

- NTFS is the preferred file system that supports much larger hard disk up to 16 exabytes and large filenames.

- NTFS is a journaling file system that makes sure that a disk transaction is written to disk properly before recognized.

- NTFS offers better security through permissions and encryption.

- Resilient File System (ReFS) was introduced as an enhanced NTFS file system by offering larger volume sizes and files. ReFS also offers greater resiliency, meaning better data verification, error correction, and scalability.

- The main tool to manage disk in Windows Server 2016 is to use the MMC snap-in called Disk Management, which is also part of the Computer Management console.

- When you prepare a volume in Windows, you can assign a drive letter to the new volume or you can create a mount point the new volume as an empty NTFS folder.

Knowledge Assessment

Fill in the Blank

1. _____ uses two or more drives used in combination to create a fault tolerance system.

2. _____ is a commonly used RAID technology does not provide fault tolerance.

3. _____ is an extra drive that can be automatically swapped when a drive fails.

4. A _____ is an architecture used for disk arrays, tape library, and optical jukeboxes based on networking technology.

5. The _____ sends SCSI commands to a SAN over a TCP/IP network.

6. _____ is an enhanced NTFS file system that offers larger volume sizes and files and supports file name lengths of 32,000 characters.

7. _____ is a method of storing and organizing computer files so that you can easily find them and access them.

8. NTFS can support up to _____ of storage space for each volume.

9. The _____ program is the command interface to partition drives.

10. A _____ uses volumes stored on two separate physical disk to write data onto both disks simultaneously and redundantly.

Multiple Choice

1. Which drives offer faster performance and is usually found on servers?
   A. SCSI
   B. IDE
   C. RLL
   D. MFM

2. Which common form of RAID uses 3 or more disk to provide fault tolerance?
   A. RAID 0
   B. RAID 1
   C. RAID 3
   D. RAID 5

3. How much disk space do you have when you use 4 2-TB drives in a RAID 5 configuration?
   A. 2 TB
   B. 4 TB
   C. 6 TB
   D. 8 TB

4. Which RAID uses a striped data set which is mirrored with RAID 1?
   A. RAID 4
   B. RAID 5
   C. RAID 10
   D. RAID 01

5. Which device is a file-level data storage drive that provides access to shared file and folders?
   A. SAN
   B. NAS
   C. RAID
   D. hot spare

6. What is the default port used by iSCSI?
   A. 3000
   B. 8080
   C. 3260
   D. 443

7. Windows Server 2016 uses a _____ to communicate to a SAN based on iSCSI?
   A. iSCSI connector
   B. iSCSI initiator
   C. iSCSI plug-in
   D. iSCSI snap-in

8. Which Fibre Channel topology provides optimized connection while isolate failed ports?
   A. FC-P2P
   B. FC-AL
   C. FC-SW
   D. FC-SNP

9. What units used in a SAN that can be assigned to a server?
   A. HBAs
   B. snapshots
   C. LUNs
   D. ANSIs

10. Which type of volume does dynamic disk not support?
    A. simple volume
    B. striped volume
    C. stripped mirror volume
    D. RAID-5 volume

True/False

1. When configuring IDE drives, you must configure a SCSI ID and you must terminate both ends of the chain.

2. Two volume types used by Windows Server 2016 is MBR and GPT.

3. NTFS is the preferred file used by Windows Server 2016.

4. Basic disks can be resized without rebooting.

5. GUID partition types can support up to 18 EB drives.

Competency Assessment

Scenario 3-1: Planning Your Disks

You are configuring a computer that is running Windows Server 2016 and will run Microsoft Exchange 2010. So far, you have a single 80 GB drive with Windows running on it. What drives and drive configuration should you add to the server to support Microsoft Exchange that requires 100 GB of mailboxes?

Scenario 3-2: Researching Disks

Disks are becoming faster and are having larger capacity every day. In addition, disks are starting to transition from mechanical magnetic disks to solid-state disks. Do a search on the Internet and pick the fastest disks and its features. List the drive and where you found the information and the highlights of the drive.

Proficiency Assessment

Scenario 3-3: Connecting a Second Hard Drive

Connect a second hard drive to your system. Then create a volume on the second drive that takes up half the space. Format the disk as an NTFS file system. Then expand the drive for the rest of the drive. When you can access the volume successfully, delete the volumes on the second hard drive.

Scenario 3-4: Create a Striped Volume

Using the free disk space on the first drive and the space on the second disk, create a striped volume.

 Real World Scenario

Workplace Ready: Disk Management Software

You can do a lot with the Disk Management snap-in and with the diskpart command. However, it is cannot do everything. For example, in some situations, you cannot extend certain disk because of something is in the way or it is a system disk in use. Tools such as Partition Magic can come in handy. Also while the Check Disk utility will help fix some basic errors, you may need to use a third-party tool to recover disks or rebuilt a disk.

Lesson 4

Monitoring and Troubleshooting Servers

Objective Domain Matrix

Technology Skill	Objective Domain Description	Objective Domain Number
Understanding Performance	Understand performance monitoring.	5.2
Using the Event Viewer	Understand logs and alerts.	5.3
Booting the System	Identify steps in the startup process.	6.1
Introducing Business Continuity	Understand business continuity.	6.2
Introducing Troubleshooting Methodology	Understand troubleshooting methodology.	6.4

Key Terms

active-passive cluster

Advanced Boot Options

backup

Boot Configuration Data (BCD)

Boot.ini file

cluster

differential backup

Event Viewer

failover cluster

full backup

Grandfather-father-son (GFS)

incremental backup

Information Technology Infrastructure
Library (ITIL)

Knowledge Base

last known good configuration

master boot record (MBR)

Microsoft TechNet

network load balancing (NLB)

paging file

Performance Monitor

Power-On Self Test (POST)

Resource Monitor

restore point

safe mode

shadow copies

System Information tool

Task Manager

teaming

uninterruptable power supply (UPS)

virtual memory

volume boot record (VBR)

WinPE

Windows Recovery Environment
(WinRE)

 Real World Scenario

Lesson 4 Case

You have been with the Acme Corporation for several months. Since then, you have upgraded several servers, installed several servers, and inventoried the servers and services you managed. Your boss comes up to you asks you if we had a disaster, how would you deal with the disaster. Unfortunately, you did not have a thorough answer for your boss. A couple of weeks later, one of your servers crashes and will no longer start.

Managing IT

For most companies, an Information Technology (IT) department can be very complex. With all of the network services and applications that are available, larger companies will usually need a team of people because of the workload and specialization needed. To help manage all of this, several standards have been created to give an organization some guidelines to follow.

When you are managing complicated systems that your company depends upon, you need to have processes in place to plan, design, implement, monitor and retire servers, services, and applications to ensure that your time and money are well managed and that the needs of your organization are met.

 Remember that the IT department is there to service the rest of the organization, not the other way around.

The *Information Technology Infrastructure Library (ITIL)* is a set of concepts and practices for managing Information Technology (IT) Services Management (ITSM), IT development, and IT operations. ITIL gives detailed descriptions of a number of important IT practices and provides comprehensive checklists, tasks, and procedures that any IT organization can tailor to its needs. ITIL is published in a series of books, each of which covers an IT management topic.

ITIL 4 was released in 2019 and focuses on automating processes, service management improvements, and how to better incorporate the IT department into a company. To adapt to the newest technology ITIL has updated their previous framework.

ITIL 4 contains nine basic fundamentals; these include:

- Be transparent
- Collaborate
- Design for experience
- Focus on value
- Keep it simple
- Observe directly
- Progress iteratively
- Start where you are
- Work holistically

The newest version of ITIL focuses on company culture and integrating IT into the overall business structure. It encourages collaboration between IT and other departments. ITIL 4 also highlights customer feedback.

The ITIL version v3 core books include and will remain essentially the same:

- Service Strategy - A view of ITIL that aligns business and IT together. It focuses on customer outcomes. Subsequent titles in the core set will link deliverables to meeting the business goals, requirements, and service management principles described in this publication.

- Service Design - Provides guidance on the production and maintenance of IT policies, architectures, and documents for the design of appropriate and innovative IT infrastructure service solutions and processes.

- Service Transition - Provides guidance and process activities for the transition of services in the operational business environment. It covers the broader, long-term change management role, release, and deployment practices, so that risks, benefits, delivery mechanisms, and the support of ongoing operational services are considered.

- Service Operation - Introduces, explains, and details delivery and control activities to achieve operational excellence on a day-to-day basis.

- Continual Service Improvement – Focusing on the process elements involved in identifying and introducing service management improvements, this publication also deals with issues surrounding service retirement.

These core books outline the entire ITIL Service Lifecycle, starting from identifying customer needs and IT requirements all the way through to the monitoring and improvement phase of the service.

The differences that distinguish ITIL V4 from the older versions are the addition of more best practices and new material on integration.

The new version supports fewer silos; greater collaboration, making it easier to communicate through the entire company; and the integration of Agile and DevOps into ITSM strategies.

ITIL V4 is designed to be even more flexible and customizable.

The updated framework focuses on facilitating value co-creation via a service value system (SVS). The SVS signifies how separate components can come together to smooth value creation through IT-enabled services.

More Information

For more information about the ITIL, visit the following two websites:

```
http://www.itil-officialsite.com

http://en.wikipedia.org/wiki/Information_Technology_Infrastructure_Library
```

In either case, the ITIL publications will give you a starting place in developing your organization's processes to help manage your IT department. You will also need to discuss the needs of the organization with various managers including managers of your core business and managers of other support departments such as human resources, accounting, and legal departments to gather what services your organization should provide and what other requirements you must follow.

For example, if you work with medical records, you have certain standards that you have to follow to keep the data secure such as the Health Insurance Portability and Accountability Act (HIPAA). As a trade public company, you have to follow certain financial requirements including archiving of data. Lastly, your own organization may have their own standards in place.

When you want to start using a server, service, or application, you should follow certain steps to implement the server, service, or application properly. They include:

- Collecting requirements
- Designing and planning
- Implementing
- Managing and monitoring

By collecting requirements, you define what the server, service, or application are supposed to do including its workload. Without properly collecting requirements, you may not select the correct hardware or software that will support your objectives. You must then plan and design the server, service, or application to make sure that the server, service, or application does what it is supposed to do without interfering with other server, service, or application. Next, you will implement the server, service, or application, which includes installing and configuring the server, service, or application. Lastly, you will need to manage and monitor the server, service, or application to make sure the server, service, or application does what it is intended to do and that the proper users and services can access the server, service, or application. If a problem occurs, you will need to fix and troubleshoot the problem. As you monitor the system, you should look at the performance of the system so that you know when the server, service, or application should be replaced. You should also need to identify potential problems to correct them before it affects the server, service, or application where it cannot be used or the server, service, or application is significantly degraded.

Most of the information available from Microsoft to design, plan, implement, manage, and monitor Microsoft products can be found at Microsoft's website, particular at *Microsoft TechNet* (http://technet.microsoft.com). It will include Microsoft Knowledge Base, service packs, security updates, resource kits, technical training, operations and deployment guides, white papers, and case studies.

Within these documents and websites, you should always pay attention to the Best Practices sections and documents. By following these guidelines, your system or application will run more efficiently, run more reliable, be more secure, and be more scalable. Some of the more complex software components including Microsoft Exchange and Microsoft SQL Server include Best Practices Analyzer software, which will automatically analyze the server and give recommendations.

When managing your servers, you can take one of two approaches: proactive and reactive. Being proactive means that you are planning ahead and anticipating problems before they disable or degrade your server, service, or application. Being reactive means that you are waiting for problems to occur before addressing them. In the long run, the best approach is to be proactive so that you can avoid system downtime. Of course, you must allocate some time and effort and possible additional hardware and software to help you to efficiently monitor your servers, services, and applications. Lastly, remember that while you make an effort to be proactive, you will still have to eventually deal with unforeseen or unexpected problems.

Introducing Troubleshooting Methodology

As a computer technician, a server administrator, or a network administrator, you will eventually have to deal with problems. Some problems will have obvious solutions and be easy to fix. Many problems will need to be figured out by following a troubleshooting methodology to efficiently resolve a problem.

Certification Ready?

What steps would you use to troubleshoot a problem? 6.4

The whole purpose for using an effective troubleshooting methodology is to reduce the amount of guesswork needed to troubleshoot and fix the problem in a timely manner. Microsoft Product Support Service engineers use the "detect method," which consists of the following six steps:

1. Discover the problem - Identify and document problem symptoms, and search technical information resources including searching Microsoft Knowledge Base (KB) articles to determine whether the problem is a known condition.

2. Evaluate system configuration - Ask the client or customer and check the system's documentation to determine if any hardware, software, or network changes have been made including any new additions. Also check any available logs including looking in the Event Viewer.

3. List or track possible solutions and try to isolate the problem by removing or disabling hardware or software components - You may also consider turning on additional logging or running diagnostic programs to gather more information and test certain components.

4. Execute a plan - Test potential solutions and have a contingency plan if these solutions do not work or have a negative impact on the computer. Of course, you don't want to make the problem worst, so if possible, back up any critical system or application files.

5. Check results - If the problem is not fixed, go back to track possible solutions.

6. Take a proactive approach - Document changes that you made along the way while troubleshooting the problem. Also notify the customer or client and document internal systems of the problem in case it happens in the future or if those changes that fixed the problem affect other areas.

So when troubleshooting problems, you do have several tools that can help isolate and fix the problems. The Device Manager was already discussed in an earlier chapter. Other tools include:

- System Information
- Event Viewer
- Task Manager
- Resource Monitor
- Performance Monitor
- System Configuration
- Memory Diagnostics tool
- Troubleshooting Wizard
- Boot Menu including Safe mode (if enabled)
- Windows Repair

When troubleshooting issues within Windows and related programs, you will eventually deal with problems that you do not know how to fix. Therefore, you may have to ask co-workers and research on the Internet. Using a good search engine such as Google and Bing are invaluable. You will also need to check the vendor websites including Microsoft's website (www.microsoft.com).

Microsoft also includes a *Knowledge Base* and several online forums (such as http:// social.microsoft.com/forums and http://social.technet.microsoft.com/Forums), where you can find help for a wide range of problems and allow you to leave messages for others to answer. The Microsoft Knowledge Base is a repository of thousands of articles made available to the public by Microsoft Corporation that contains information on problems encountered by users of Microsoft products. Each article bears an ID number, and articles are often referred to by their Knowledge Base (KB) ID. The Knowledge Base can be accessed by entering keywords or the ID at http://support.microsoft.com/search/.

System Information

When you first start troubleshooting a server, you need to know what is in the server such as the type and number of processors and the amount of RAM. You will also need to know what programs and services are running. The System properties will give you a quick glance of the processor found in the system and amount of RAM. You have also looked at Device Manager to see what hardware is recognized and what drivers are loaded. However, if you want a more detailed look at what your system consists of and what is running your system, you can use the System Information program.

System Information (also known as msinfo32.exe) shows details about your computer's hardware configuration, computer components, and software, including drivers. It was originally included with Windows to assist Microsoft support people in determining what is in a machine especially when talking to end-users.

System Information lists categories in the left pane and details about each category in the right pane. See Figure 4.1. The categories include:

- System Summary – Displays general information about your computer and the operating system, such as the computer name and manufacturer, the type of basic input/output system (BIOS) your computer uses, and the amount of memory that's installed.

- Hardware Resources – Displays advanced details about your computer's hardware and is intended for IT professionals.

- Components – Displays information about disk drives, sound devices, modems, and other components installed on your computer.

- Software Environment – Displays information about drivers, network connections, and other program-related details.

FIGURE 4.1   System Information

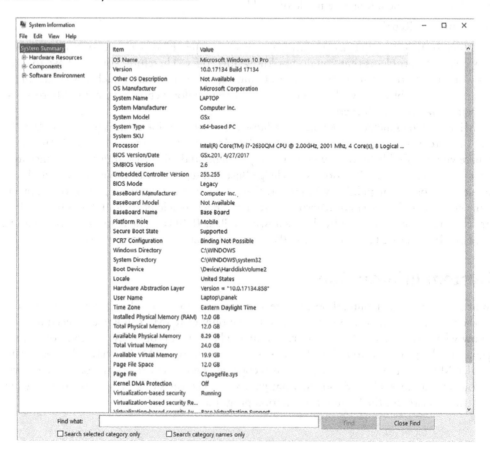

To find a specific detail in System Information, type the information you're looking for in the "Find what" box at the bottom of the window. For example, to find your computer's Internet protocol (IP) address, type **ip address** in the "Find what" box, and then click Find.

Using the Event Viewer

One of the most useful troubleshooting tools is the Event Viewer MMC snap-in, which essentially is a log viewer. Any time you have problems, you should look in the Event Viewer to see any errors or warning, which may reveal what a problem is.

Certification Ready?

How you would see the errors and warnings in the Windows logs? 5.3

The *Event Viewer* is a Microsoft Management Console (MMC) snap-in that enables you to browse and manage event logs. It is included in the Computer Management and Server Manager MMC and is included in Administrative Tools as a stand-alone console. You can also execute the eventvwr.msc command.

Event Viewer enables you to perform the following tasks:

- View events from multiple event logs, as shown in Figure 4.2
- Save useful event filters as custom views that can be reused
- Schedule a task to run in response to an event
- Create and manage event subscriptions

FIGURE 4.2   Windows Event Viewer

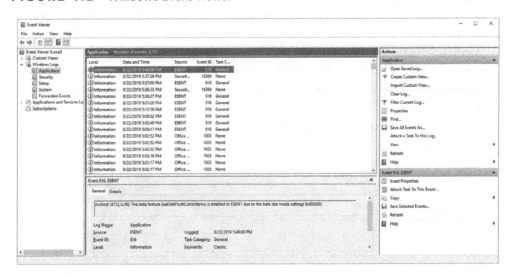

The Event Viewer is broken down into three categories:

- Custom View
- Windows Logs
- Applications and Services Logs

The Custom Views include logs for server roles such as Hyper-V, Remote Desktop Services, Web Server (IIS), and Windows Server Update Services. It also includes Administrative Events, which shows all critical, error, and warning events from all the Windows logs including Application, Security, System, Hardware Events, Internet Explorer, Key Management Services, Microsoft, and Windows PowerShell.

The Windows Logs category includes the logs that were available on previous versions of Windows. They include:

- Application log - Contains events logged by applications or programs.

- Security log - Contains events such as valid and invalid logon attempts and access to designated objects such as file and folders, printers, and Active Directory objects. By default, the Security log is empty until you enable auditing.

- Setup log - Contains events related to application setup.

- System log - Contains events logged by Windows system components including errors displayed by Windows during boot and errors with services.

- Forwarded Events log - Used to store events collected from remote computers. To collect events from remote computers, you must create an event subscription.

Applications and Services logs were first introduced with Windows Vista. These logs store events from a single application or component rather than events that might have system-wide impact.

- Admin – These events are primarily targeted at end users, administrators, and support personnel. The events that are found in the Admin channels indicate a problem and a well-defined solution that an administrator can act on.

- Operational – Operational events are used for analyzing and diagnosing a problem or occurrence. They can be used to trigger tools or tasks based on the problem or occurrence.

- Analytic – Analytic events are published in high volume. They describe program operation and indicate problems that cannot be handled by user intervention.

- Debug – Debug events are used by developers troubleshooting issues with their programs.

Table 4.1 shows the common fields displayed in the Event Viewer logs.

TABLE 4.1   Common fields displayed in the Event Viewer logs

Property Name	Description
Source	The software that logged the event, which can be either a program name, such as "SQL Server", or a component of the system or of a large program, such as a driver name.
Event ID	A number identifying the particular event type.
Level	A classification of the event severity. • Information – Indicates that a change in an application or component has occurred, such as an operation has successfully completed, a resource has been created, or a service started. • Warning – Indicates that an issue has occurred that can impact service or result in a more serious problem if action is not taken. • Error – Indicates that a problem has occurred, which might impact functionality that is external to the application or component that triggered the event. • Critical – Indicates that a failure has occurred from which the application or component that triggered the event cannot automatically recover. • Success Audit –Shown in security logs to indicate that the exercise of a user right. • Failure Audit – Shown in security logs to indicate that the exercise of a user right has failed.

When you open any of these logs, particularly the Application, Security, and System, they may have thousands of entries. Unfortunately, this may take some time to find what you are looking for if you look entry by entry. To cut down on the time to find what you want, you can use a filter to cut the entries down. To filter a log, open the Action menu and click Filter Current Log.

There are always going to be errors and warnings in the event log, and you will not be able to solve all of them. Instead, you should use the Event Viewer to troubleshoot problems when encountered. You should also view the Event Viewer from time to time so that you can get a better understanding of what warnings and errors are benign so that you can ignore those when dealing with a real problem.

Event Viewer enables you to view events on a single remote computer. However, troubleshooting an issue might require you to examine a set of events stored in multiple logs on multiple computers.

Today's Event Viewer can be used to collect copies of events from multiple remote computers and store them locally. To specify which events to collect, you create an event subscription. Among other details, the subscription specifies exactly which events will be collected and in which log they will be stored locally. Once a subscription is active and events are being collected, you can view and manipulate these forwarded events as you would any other locally stored events.

Booting the System

One of the most frustrating problems to troubleshoot is when Windows does not boot and you cannot log into Windows to troubleshoot the computer. To overcome these problems, you need to understand how the computer boots and be familiar with the tools available during boot up.

Certification Ready?

If you server fails to start properly, do you know how to isolate where it fails at? 6.1

What Is Basic Input Output System (BIOS)?

Basic Input Output System (BIOS) is software stored on a small memory chip on the motherboard. An administrator may need to access BIOS to change how the device works or to assist in troubleshooting a problem.

The BIOS is responsible for the POST and is the first software to be run when a computer is started. The BIOS firmware is considered non-volatile (the settings are saved and recoverable even after power has been removed from the device).

BIOS is used to instruct a computer on how to perform a number of basic functions such as booting and keyboard control. It is also used to identify and configure the hardware in a computer such as the hard drives, optical drive, CPU, memory, etc.

The BIOS is accessed and configured through the BIOS Setup Utility. The BIOS is pre-installed when the computer is purchased. It can be accessed in various ways depending on the computer or motherboard make and model.

The BIOS contains many hardware configuration options that can be changed using the setup utility. Saving these changes and restarting the computer applies the changes to the BIOS and alters the way BIOS instructs the hardware to function.

What Is Unified Extensible Firmware Interface (UEFI)?

By 2020, Intel has announced that it has plans to replace the BIOS with UEFI. Both UEFI and BIOS are software that starts when a computer is booted. UEFI is a current solution that supports larger hard drives, quicker boot times, provides additional security features, and cursors for graphics and mouse.

UEFI replaces the traditional BIOS on computers. There's no way to switch from BIOS to UEFI on an existing computers. An administrator would need to buy new hardware that supports and includes UEFI. Most UEFI machines now provide a BIOS emulation so that an administrator can choose to install and boot old operating systems that look for a BIOS instead of UEFI, so they are backwards compatible.

The UEFI firmware can boot from drives of 2.2 TB or larger. UEFI uses the GPT partitioning scheme instead of MBR.

UEFI can run in 32-bit or 64-bit mode and has more addressable address space than BIOS. UEFI setup screens include graphics and mouse cursor support.

UEFI supports Secure Boot, which means the operating system can be checked for validity to ensure that there is no malware that has tampered with the boot process. It can aid in remote troubleshooting and configuration.

An administrator may need to access the UEFI settings screen through the Windows boot options menu rather than pressing a key when the computer boots.

What Is Trusted Platform Module (TPM)?

TPM is a special-purpose microprocessor that provides cryptographic services. It is designed to provide hardware-based, security-related functions. A TPM chip is a secure crypto-processor that is designed to carry out cryptographic operations. The chip includes multiple physical security mechanisms to make it tamper resistant, and malware is unable to tamper with it.

Some key advantages of using TPM technology:

- Can generate, store, and limit the use of cryptographic keys.
- Can help ensure platform integrity by taking and storing security measurements.
- Can use TPM technology for platform device authentication by using the TPM's unique RSA key, which is burned into itself.

During the boot process, the boot code (including the firmware and the operating system components) can be measured and recorded in the TPM. The integrity measurements can then be used as evidence for how a system started and to make sure that a TPM-based key was used only when the correct software was used to boot the system.

TPM-based keys can be configured in a number of ways:

- Make a TPM-based key unavailable outside the TPM. This is useful in alleviating phishing attacks because it prevents the key from being copied and used without the TPM.
- TPM-based keys can also be configured to require an authorization value to use them. If too many wrong authorization guesses occur, then the TPM will activate its dictionary attack logic and prevent further authorization value guesses.

Startup Process

Booting is a process in which a computer gets initialized. This process includes initializing all of the hardware components on a computer and gets them to work together to load the operating system.

All computers running Windows utilizes the same startup phases:

▪ Power On Self Test (POST)

▪ Boot loader

▪ Detect and configure hardware

▪ Kernel loading

▪ Logon

Every time you turn on a computer, the computer goes through the *Power-On Self Test (POST)*, which initializes hardware and finds an operating system to load. The POST includes the following steps:

1. Computer does a quick power check to make sure it has enough to power to supply the system.

2. When the processor receives a power good signal, the processor initializes and tests essential PC components as specified in the System ROM BIOS.

3. If a problem is found, it will identify the problem with a series of beeps based on the system ROM BIOS.

4. The processor then initializes the video card and starts sending information to the monitor. The system will then initialize additional components. If a problem is discovered, it will display a message to indicate the problem.

5. The system will search for a boot device (such as a hard drive, optical disk or USB flash drive) to boot from.

6. The system will read the master boot record on a boot device to determine operating system boot files.

If the system is running Windows 7, Windows 8/8.1, Windows 10, Windows Server 2012, Windows Server 2012 R2, or Windows Server 2016, the system will go through the following steps:

1. BOOTMGR is loaded and accesses the Boot Configuration Data Store to display the boot menu or to boot from a partition or volume.

2. WINLoad is the operating system boot loader that loads the rest of the operating system.

3. NTOSKERNL.EXE is the main part of Windows and is responsible for various system services and process and memory management.

4. Boot-class Device Drivers implements a number of functions that are implemented in different ways by different hardware platforms based on processor and chipset.

A *master boot record (MBR)* is the first 512-byte boot sector of a partitioned data storage device such as a hard disk. It is used to hold the disk's primary partition table, contains the code to bootstrap an operating system that usually passes control to the volume boot record, and uniquely identifies the disk media. By default, the master boot record contains the primary partition entries in its partition table.

A volume boot record (VBR), also known as a volume boot sector or a partition boot sector, is a type of boot sector, stored in a disk volume on a hard disk, floppy disk, or similar data storage device, that contains code for booting an operating system such as NTLDR and BOOTMGR.

The active partition is the partition or volume that is marked as the partition to boot from. The active partition or volume that contains the boot file (NTLDR or BOOTMGR) is known as the system partition/volume. The partition or volume that contains the Windows operating system files (usually the Windows or WINNT folder) is called the boot partition. It is common for the systems to have one drive and one partition/volume, which makes the partition the system partition and the boot partition.

The %SystemRoot% variable is a special system-wide environment variable found on Microsoft Windows systems. Its value is the location of the system folder, including the drive and path. By default, on a clean installation of Windows, the %SystemRoot% is C:\Windows.

Understanding BCDEdit

Boot Configuration Data (BCD) is a firmware-independent database for boot-time configuration data used by Microsoft's Windows Boot Manager found with Windows 7, Windows 8/8.1, Windows 10, Windows Server 2012, Windows Server 2012 R2, and Windows Server 2016. To edit the Boot Configuration, you would typically use Bcdedit.exe.

Different from older versions of Windows, which used the Boot.ini file to designate the boot configuration, newer versions of Windows store the configuration in a \Boot\bcd on the system volume on machines that use IBM PC compatible firmware. To edit the Windows Boot Menu Options, the Boot Configuration Data Editor (Bcdedit) is used.

The Bcdedit.exe command-line tool can be used to add, delete, and edit entries in the BCD store, which contains objects. Each object is identified by a GUID (Globally Unique Identifier). Every drive or partition on the system will have its own GUID and could be {legacy} (to describe a drive or partition on which a pre-Windows Vista operating system), {default} (to describe the drive or partition containing the current default operating system), or {current} (to describe the current drive or partition one is booted to), or for example {c34b751a-ff09-11d9-9e6e-0030482375e7} (to describe another drive or partition on which an operating system has been installed).

Some of the options available for the BCDEdit command are:

- /createstore—Creates a new empty BCD store.
- /export—Exports the contents of the system BCD store to a specified file.

- `/import`—Restores the state of the system BCD store from a specified file.
- `/copy`—Makes copies of boot entries.
- `/create`—Creates new boot entries.
- `/delete`—Deletes boot entries.
- `/deletevalue`—Deletes elements from a boot entry.
- `/set`—Creates or modifies a boot entry's elements.
- `/enum`—Lists the boot entries in a store.
- `/bootsequence`—Specifies a one-time boot sequence.
- `/default`—Specifies the default boot entry.
- `/displayorder`—Specifies the order in which Boot Manager displays its menu.
- `/timeout`—Specifies the Boot Manager Timeout value.
- `/toolsdisplayorder`—Specifies the order in which Boot Manager displays the tools menu.
- `/bootems`—Enables or disables Emergency Management Services (EMS) for a specified boot application.
- `/ems`—Enables or disables EMS for an operating system boot entry.
- `/emssettings`—Specifies global EMS parameters.
- `/store`—Specifies the BCD store upon which a command acts.

Of course, you can use bcdedit /? to see the available options.

To change the title of the boot menu entry such as to the type, you would use the following command to change the title to Windows Server 2012 R2 from "Earlier Windows Version"

```
bcdedit /set {ntldr} description "Windows Server 2012 R2"
```

To change the timeout on showing boot menu:

```
bcdedit /timeout 5
```

To change the default OS to boot first:

```
bcdedit /default {ntldr}
```

More Information

For more information about Bcdedit, visit the following websites: https://docs
.microsoft.com/en-us/windows-hardware/manufacture/desktop/bcdedit-
command-line-options and https://docs.microsoft.com/en-us/windows-server/
administration/windows-commands/bcdedit.

When using Windows 7 or higher and Windows Server 2008 or higher, you can modify the default operating system and the time the list of operating system appears by right-clicking Computer, selecting Properties, clicking Advanced system settings, selecting the Advanced tab, and clicking the Settings button in the Startup and Recovery section. You can also specify what type of dump occurs during a system failure.

Understanding Advanced Startup Options

If you have issues that occur during boot up, you may need to take some extra steps to get the computer in a usable state so that you can fix the problem.

To get into Advanced Startup Options, you used to be able to press F8 as the system was booting up. However, you cannot use the F8 option in Windows Server 2016 unless you enable it; it is disabled by default. I will discuss how to enable F8 in Windows Server 2016 a little later in this section.

To utilize the Advanced Startup Options to recover the Windows Server 2016 operating system (see Figure 4.3):

1. Click the Start button and select Settings.

2. In Windows Settings select Update & Security.

3. Select Recovery.

4. Click Restart and then select a reason for the shutdown. Click Continue.

FIGURE 4.3   Advanced Startup

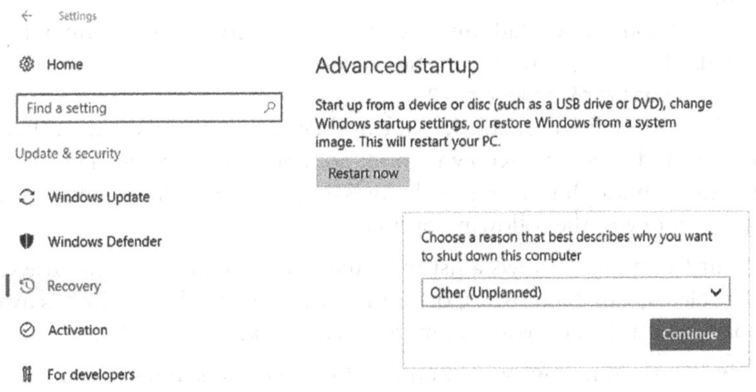

Once you press the Continue button the Advanced Options Menu will appear—you can choose options such as Continue, Troubleshoot, and Turn off your PC. If you select the Troubleshoot option, you will see the Advanced options (see Figure 4.4).

FIGURE 4.4 Advanced Startup Options

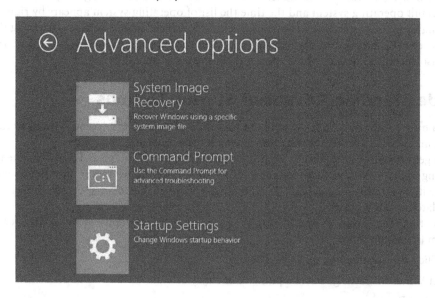

To enable the F8 functionality on Windows Server 2016, an administrator needs to go to an elevated command prompt.

If, however, the server will not boot (thus the need for F8), then boot off of a Windows Server install DVD and select the Repair Your Computer option, Troubleshooting, then Command Prompt.

Once at a Command Prompt (administrator), enter the following commands:

```
bcdedit /set {bootmgr} displaybootmenu yes
bcdedit /set {bootmgr} timeout 10
```

Once the F8 functionality is enabled, you can then reboot the machine utilizing the older functions of Safe Mode and Last Known Good. So, once F8 has been enabled, you can then access the Advanced Boot Options screen by pressing F8 before the Windows logo appears. You can then select one of the following options:

- Repair Your Computer - Shows a list of system recovery tools you can use to repair startup problems, run diagnostics, or restore your system. This option is available only if the tools are installed on your computer's hard disk.

- Safe Mode - Starts Windows with a minimal set of drivers and services. If you make a change to the system and Windows no longer boots, you can try safe mode.

- Safe Mode with Networking - Starts Windows in safe mode and includes the network drivers and services needed to access the Internet or other computers on your network.

- Safe Mode with Command Prompt - Starts Windows in safe mode with a command prompt window instead of the usual Windows interface.

- Enable Boot Logging - Creates a file, ntbtlog.txt, that lists all the drivers that are installed during startup and that might be useful for advanced troubleshooting.

- Enable low-resolution video (640×480) - Starts Windows using your current video driver and using low resolution (640×480) and refresh rate settings. You can use this mode to reset your display settings.
- Last Known Good Configuration (advanced) - Starts Windows with the last registry and driver configuration that worked successfully, usually marked at the last successful login.
- Directory Services Restore Mode - Starts Windows domain controller running Active Directory so that the directory service can be restored. This option will only show on domain controllers.
- Debugging Mode - Starts Windows in an advanced troubleshooting mode intended for IT professionals and system administrators.
- Disable automatic restart on system failure - Prevents Windows from automatically restarting if an error causes Windows to fail. Choose this option only if Windows is stuck in a loop where Windows fails, attempts to restart, and fails again repeatedly.
- Disable Driver Signature Enforcement - Allows drivers containing improper signatures to be loaded.
- Disable Early Launch Anti-Malware Driver – Allows drivers to initialize without being measured by the anti-malware driver.
- Start Windows Normally - Starts Windows in its normal mode.

Safe mode is useful for troubleshooting problems with programs and drivers that might not start correctly or that might prevent Windows from starting correctly. If a problem doesn't reappear when you start in safe mode, you can eliminate the default settings and basic device drivers as possible causes. If a recently installed program, device, or driver prevents Windows from running correctly, you can start your computer in safe mode and then remove the program that's causing the problem.

While in safe mode, you access the Control Panel to access the Device Manager, Event Viewer, System Information, command prompt, Registry Editor.

Devices and drivers that start in safe mode:

- Floppy disk drives (internal and USB)
- Internal CD-ROM drives (ATA, SCSI)
- External CD-ROM drives (USB)
- Internal DVD-ROM drives (ATA, SCSI)
- External DVD-ROM drives (USB)
- Internal hard disk drives (ATA, SATA, SCSI)
- External hard disk drives (USB)
- Keyboards (USB, PS/2, serial)
- Mice (USB, PS/2, serial)
- VGA video cards (PCI, AGP)

Windows services that start in safe mode:

- Windows event log
- Plug and Play
- Remote procedure call (RPC)
- Cryptographic Services
- Windows Management Instrumentation (WMI)

Devices and services that start in safe mode with networking:

- Network adapters (wired Ethernet and wireless 802.11x)
- Dynamic Host Configuration Protocol (DHCP)
- DNS
- Network connections
- TCP/IP-NetBIOS Helper
- Windows Firewall

Using the System Configuration Tool

While safe mode can allow you to boot Windows when it would not boot before due to a bad driver, service, or application that loads when Windows boots, the System Configuration tool allows you to select or deselect which service or application automatically start when you start Windows.

System Configuration (msconfig.exe) is a tool that can help identify problems that might prevent Windows from starting correctly. See Figure 4.5. When a problem occurs and assuming you can successfully start and log into Windows, you can open System Configuration and disable certain startup programs or services. If the problem goes away when you restart Windows, you know that the problem is caused by the program or service that you disabled.

FIGURE 4.5   System Configuration tool showing the General tab

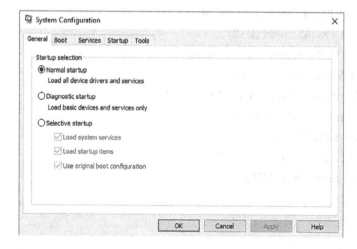

The following tabs and options are available in System Configuration:

- General tab – Shows the startup selection:
    - Normal startup – Starts Windows in the usual manner.
    - Diagnostic startup – Starts Windows with basic services and drivers only.
    - Selective startup – Starts Windows with basic services and drivers and the other services and startup programs that you select.
- Boot tab – Shows configuration options for the operating system and advanced debugging settings (as shown in Figure 4.6), including:
    - Safe boot: Minimal – On startup, opens the Windows graphical user interface (Windows Explorer) in safe mode running only critical system services. Networking is disabled.
    - Safe boot: Alternate shell – On startup, opens the Windows command prompt in safe mode running only critical system services. Networking and the graphical user interface are disabled.
    - Safe boot: Active Directory repair – On startup, opens the Windows graphical user interface in safe mode running critical system services and Active Directory.
    - Safe boot: Network – On startup, opens the Windows graphical user interface in safe mode running only critical system services. Networking is enabled.
    - No GUI boot – Does not display the Windows Welcome screen when starting.
    - Boot log – Stores all information from the startup process in the file %SystemRoot%Ntbtlog.txt.
    - Base video – On startup, opens the Windows graphical user interface in minimal VGA mode. This loads standard VGA drivers instead of display drivers specific to the video hardware on the computer.
    - OS boot information – Shows driver names as drivers are being loaded during the startup process.
    - Make all boot settings permanent – Doesn't track changes made in System Configuration. Options can be changed later using System Configuration, but must be changed manually. When this option is selected, you can't roll back your changes by selecting Normal startup on the General tab.
- Advanced boot options – Allows you to configure Windows to load quicker or slower based on your needs.
    - Number of processors – Limits the number of processors used on a multiprocessor system. If the check box is selected, the system boots using only the number of processors in the drop-down list. One processor is selected by default.
    - Maximum memory – Specifies the maximum amount of physical memory used by the operating system to simulate a low memory configuration. The value in the text box is megabytes (MB).
    - PCI Lock – Prevents Windows from reallocating I/O and IRQ resources on the PCI bus. The I/O and memory resources set by the BIOS are preserved.
    - Debug – Enables kernel-mode debugging for device driver development.

- Services tab – Lists all of the services that start when the computer starts, along with their current status (Running or Stopped). Use the Services tab to enable or disable individual services at startup to troubleshoot which services might be contributing to startup problems. You can also select the "Hide all Microsoft services" option to show only third-party applications in the services list.

FIGURE 4.6   System Configuration tool showing the Boot tab

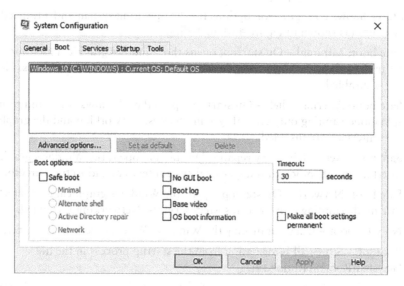

Understanding Performance

Performance is the overall effectiveness of how data moves through the system. Of course, it is important to select the proper hardware (processor, memory, disk system, and network) to satisfy the expected performance goals. Without the proper hardware, hardware bottle-necks limit the effectiveness of software.

Certification Ready?

When your system is slow, what would you use to see why it is slow? 5.2.

When a component limits performance, the component is known as a bottleneck. When you relieve one bottleneck, you may cause other bottlenecks. For example, one of the most common bottlenecks is the amount of memory the system has. By increasing the memory, you can often increase the overall performance of a system (up to a point). However, when you add more RAM, then RAM needs to be fed more data from the disk, and now the disk becomes the bottleneck or the processor now cannot keep up with the additional data. Overall, the system will become faster, but if your performance is still not where you want it to be, you will need to then look for the possibility of another bottleneck.

Many performance problems cannot be identified by just looking at performance at a quick glance. Instead, you need a baseline, which is done by analyzing the performance when the system is running normal and within design specifications. Then when a problem occurs, you compare the current performance to your baseline to see what is different. Since performance can also change gradually over time, it is highly recommended that you baseline your server regularly so that you can chart your performance measures and identify trends. Therefore, you will have an idea when the server needs to be upgraded or replaced or the workload of the server reduced.

There are several tools available with Windows for you to analyze performance. They include:

- Task Manager
- Performance Monitor
- Resource Monitor

Performance Logs and Alerts

An important part of monitoring performance is that it should be done over a given period of time. This is referred to as a baseline.

When viewing information in Performance Monitor, an administrator has two main options in respect to the data being displayed:

- View Current Activity - When Performance Monitor is first opened, the default option is to view data obtained from current system information. This method of viewing measures and displays various real-time statistics on the system's performance.

- View Log File Data - This option allows an administrator to view information that was previously saved to a log file. Although the performance objects, counters, and instances may appear to be the same as those viewed using the View Current Activity option, the information itself was actually captured from a previous point in time and stored onto a log file. These log files are created in the Performance Logs And Alerts section of the Windows Server 2016 Performance tool.

There are three items that allow an administrator to customize how the data is collected for the log files:

- Counter Logs - record performance statistics based on the various performance objects, counters, and instances available in Performance Monitor. The values are updated based on a time interval setting and are saved to a file for later analysis.

- Circular Logging - the data that is stored within a file is overwritten as new data is entered into the log. This is a useful method of logging to record information only for a certain time frame. Circular logging also conserves disk space by ensuring that the performance log file will not continue to grow over certain limits.

- Linear Logging - data is never deleted from the log files, and new information is added to the end of the log file. The result is a log file that continually grows. The benefit is that all historical information is retained.

Understanding Virtual Memory and Paging File

If your computer lacks RAM needed to run a program or perform an operation, Windows uses *virtual memory* to compensate. Virtual memory combines your computer's RAM with temporary space on your hard disk. When RAM runs low, virtual memory moves data from RAM to space called a *paging file*. By default, the paging file is stored as C:\pagefile.sys.

Moving data to and from the paging file frees up RAM so your computer can complete its work. Unfortunately, when something needs to be accessed from the virtual memory on disk, it is much slower than accessing it directly from RAM. With an ample amount of RAM you have, you will not need as much virtual memory.

Manage Your Paging File

To manage your paging file in Windows, you will do the following:

1. Right-click the Start button, and click System. Alternatively, you can right-click Computer and select Properties.

2. In the left pane, click Advanced system settings. If you are prompted for an administrator password or confirmation, type the password or provide confirmation.

3. On the Advanced tab, under Performance, click Settings.

4. In the Performance Options dialog box, click the Advanced tab, and then, under virtual memory, click Change.

5. Under Virtual memory, click Change.

6. Clear the "Automatically manage paging file size for all drives" check box, as shown in Figure 4.7.

7. Under Drive {Volume Label], click the drive that contains the paging file you want to change.

8. Click Custom size, type a new size in megabytes in the Initial size (MB) or Maximum size (MB) box, click Set, and then click OK.

FIGURE 4.7   Managing Paging Files

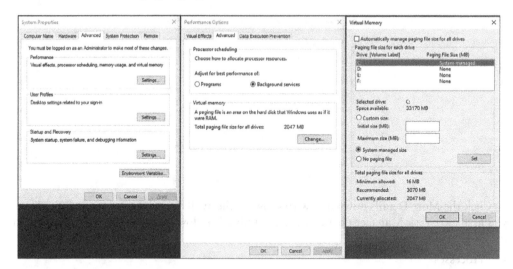

By default, Windows automatically manages the size of this file. It starts small and grows larger as needed. In addition, if you have multiple physical drives, you can move the paging file from the boot volume to another volume. Increases in size usually don't require a restart for the changes to take effect, but if you decrease the size, you will need to restart your computer. It is recommended that you don't disable or delete the paging file. In addition, if you have multiple physical drives, you can move the paging file from the boot volume to another volume.

Windows also uses the paging file as a placeholder for *memory dumps*. A memory dump is the process in which the contents of memory are stored in the event of an application or system crash and that can be used to diagnose, identify, and resolve the problem that led to the application or system failure. Since Windows writes the crash dump to the memory dump first, you will need to ensure that the paging file can store the necessary memory dump. For a complete memory dump, the paging file needs to be the RAM size + 257 MB.

Using Task Manager

Task Manager gives you a quick glance at performance and provides information about programs and processes running on your computer. A *process* is an instance of a program that is being executed.

Task Manager is one of the handiest programs you can use to take a quick glance at performance to see which programs are using the most system resources on your computer. You can see the status of running programs and of programs that have stopped responding, so you can stop a program running in memory.

To start Task Manager, right-click the empty space on the taskbar and choose Task Manager (or you can open the Security menu by pressing Ctrl+Alt+Del and choosing Task Manager). When Task Manager starts, it displays only the running applications (see Figure 4.8).

FIGURE 4.8 Using Task Manager

Click the More Details down arrow to show all the available tabs (see Figure 4.9). When you first start Task Manager on a computer running Windows Server 2016, tabs are opened for Task Manager:

- Processes
- Performance
- App history
- Startup
- Users
- Details
- Services

FIGURE 4.9 Viewing the Task Manager tabs

Task Manager				
File Options View				
Processes Performance App history Startup Users Details Services				
Name	3% CPU	23% Memory	1% Disk	0% Network
Apps (4)				
> ☑ Microsoft Word (32 bit) (2)	0%	40.1 MB	0 MB/s	0 Mbps
> 🗗 Task Manager	0.1%	11.7 MB	0 MB/s	0 Mbps
> 🗔 Windows Explorer	1.0%	51.4 MB	0 MB/s	0 Mbps
> 🖼 Windows Photo Viewer	0.1%	23.7 MB	0.1 MB/s	0 Mbps
Background processes (71)				
> ☐ Adobe Acrobat Update Service (...	0%	0.8 MB	0 MB/s	0 Mbps
🖼 Application Frame Host	0%	8.2 MB	0 MB/s	0 Mbps
> 🖼 Bonjour Service	0%	1.9 MB	0 MB/s	0 Mbps
🌐 Cisco AnyConnect User Interfac...	0%	16.8 MB	0 MB/s	0 Mbps
🖼 COM Surrogate	0%	0.8 MB	0 MB/s	0 Mbps
◎ Cortana	0%	68.5 MB	0 MB/s	0 Mbps
⌃ Fewer details				End task

The Processes tab shows all processes running in memory and how much processing and memory each process uses. The processes display applications (as designated by Apps), background processes, and Windows Processes. On the Processes tab, you can perform the following tasks:

- To see the processes that use the highest percentage of CPU utilization, click the CPU column header.

- To stop a process, right-click the process and choose End task.

- To jump to the Details tab for a particular process, right-click the process and choose Go to details.

- If you want to see the executable that is running the processes, right-click the process and choose Open file location.

To add or remove additional columns, right-click a column header and select or deselect the desired column (such as Process Identification (PID) or process name).

The Performance tab (as shown in Figure 4.10) displays the amount of CPU usage, physical Memory usage, and Ethernet throughput. For CPU usage, a high percentage indicates the programs or processes are requiring a lot of CPU resources, which can slow your computer. If the percentage seems frozen at or near 100%, a program might not be responding.

FIGURE 4.10   Viewing CPU usage

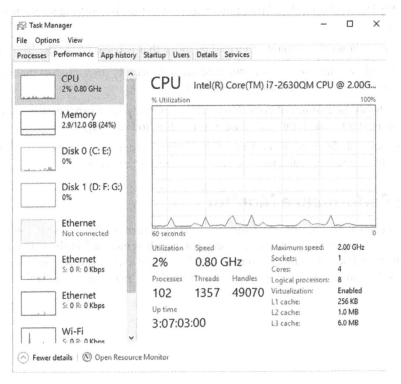

Click Memory to display how much of the paging file is being used (*In use* and *Available*), the amount of Committed and Cached memory, Paged pool, and Non-paged pool. It also shows you the total amount of RAM, the speed of the RAM, and the number of slots used for memory on the motherboard.

The Users tab displays the users who are currently logged on, the amount of CPU and memory usage that each user is using, and the processes the users are running. It also gives you the ability to disconnect them.

The Details tab displays a more detailed look at the processes running on the computer, including the Process Identification (PID). The PID is composed of unique numbers that identify a process while it is running. Similarly, you can stop the process, and you can increase or decrease the process priority.

If you are an advanced user, you might want to view other advanced memory values on the Details tab. To do so, right-click the column heading and choose Select Columns and then select or deselect values to be displayed or not displayed. While there are nearly 40 columns to display, some of the more useful values include the following:

Working Set (Memory)   Shows the amount of memory in the private working set plus the amount of memory the process is using that can be shared by other processes.

Peak Working Set (Memory)   Shows the maximum amount of working set memory used by the process.

Working Set Delta (Memory)   Shows the amount of change in working set memory used by the process.

Commit Size   Shows the amount of virtual memory that is reserved for use by a process.

Paged Pool   Shows the amount of committed virtual memory for a process that can be written to another storage medium, such as the hard disk.

NP Pool   Shows the amount of committed virtual memory for a process that can't be written to another storage medium. (NP is an abbreviation for non-paged.)

The Services tab displays all services on the computer that are running and not running. Similar to the Services console, you can start, stop, or restart services.

Using Performance Monitor

Windows *Performance Monitor* is a Microsoft Management Console (MMC) snap-in that provides tools for analyzing system performance. It is included in the Computer Management and Server Manager consoles, and it can be executed using perfmon. From a single console, you can monitor application and hardware performance in real time, specify which data you want to collect in logs, define thresholds for alerts and automatic actions, generate reports, and view past performance data in a variety of ways.

Performance Monitor provides a visual display of built-in Windows performance counters, either in real time or as a way to review historical data. See Figure 4.11.

FIGURE 4.11 Performance Monitor

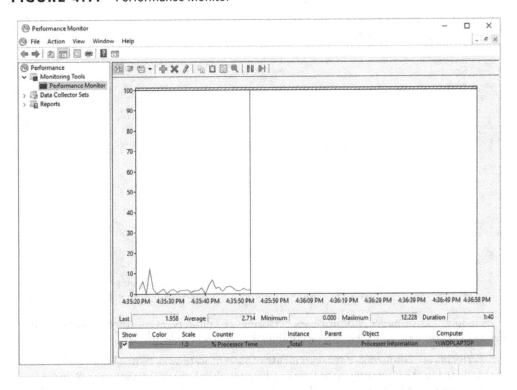

You can add performance counters to Performance Monitor by right-clicking the main pane and choosing Add Counters. Another way to add performance counters is to create and use custom Data Collector Sets. (Data Collector Sets are explained later in this lesson.) Figure 4.12 shows the Add Counters dialog box. You can create custom views that can be exported as Data Collector Sets for use with performance and logging features.

FIGURE 4.12 Performance Monitor counters

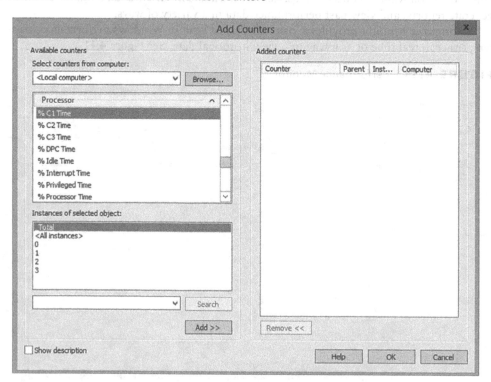

Windows Performance Monitor uses performance counters, event trace data, and configuration information, which can be combined into Data Collector Sets.

- Performance counters are measurements of system state or activity. They can be included in the operating system or can be part of individual applications. Windows Performance Monitor requests the current value of performance counters at specified time intervals.

- Event trace data is collected from trace providers, which are components of the operating system or of individual applications that report actions or events. Output from multiple trace providers can be combined into a trace session.

- Configuration Information is collected from key values in the Windows registry. Windows Performance Monitor can record the value of a registry key at a specified time or interval as part of a file.

There are hundreds of counters that can be added. Often you can look at the Task Manager. Others can only be found in the Performance Monitor. They include:

- Processor:%Processor Time measures how busy the processor is. Although the processor may jump to 100% processor usage, the processor should not be above 80% most of the time. If not, you should upgrade the processor (using a faster processor or add additional processors) or move some of the services to other systems.
- A page fault occurs when a process attempts to access a virtual memory page that is not available in its working set in RAM. If the pages/sec is 20 or higher, you should increase the memory.
- If the paging file is 1 times RAM (or higher for specialized applications), you should increase the memory.
- Physical Disk:%Avg. Disk Queue Length is the average number of read requests or write requests queued for the disk in question. A sustained average higher than 2 indicates that the disk is being over utilized.

Using Performance Monitor

1. Right-click the Start and choose Run. Type in Perfmon.exe and hit the Enter key.
2. On the left-hand side under Monitoring Tools, click Performance Monitor.
3. In the center window, click the green plus sign. This will allow you to add a counter.
4. Under Available Counters, make sure Local Computer is chosen. Then expand Processor and choose % Processor Time. Click the Add button. Click OK.
5. Choose any other counters to watch. An administrator can change the view by using the pull-down arrow next to the green plus sign.
6. Once completed, close Performance Monitor.

Creating an Alert

Alerts are used for monitoring when a predefined threshold has been reached. An administrator can create an alert by following these steps:

1. Open the Performance Management Console and locate Performance Logs and Alerts.
2. Right-click the Alerts icon and select New Alert Settings. Name the alert and click Add below the counters field.
3. Select the counter to use and click Add below the counters field, then click Close.
4. Choose Over from the drop-down box next to Alert when the value is. Set the limit and the Interval.
5. When done, click OK. Will see a new icon in the Contents pane of the MMC.

Now that an alert has been created, the administrator will be alerted whenever the counter exceeds the specified threshold. Now, the administrator will need to determine the actions to be taken when the alert occurs:

1. Open the Performance MMC. Click the Performance Logs and Alerts icon and expand down to the Alerts icon.

2. Right-click the alert that was made previously and select it. Then click the Action tab.

3. By default the alert is logged to the Application Event log. The administrator can leave this but must check the log regularly to see if the threshold has been exceeded.

4. The administrator can send an alert to the Administrator (or another user) by selecting "Send a network message to" and typing in the username.

5. The administrator can also select the start performance data log. When the drop-down menu is pulled down, the administrator will find the log that was created. Click it.

Data Collector Sets

Data Collector Sets are a tool that work with Performance Monitor performance logs that tell Performance Monitor where the logs are stored and when the log needs to run. The Data Collector Sets also define the credentials used to run the set. These were discussed earlier in the chapter.

Using Resource Monitor

Windows Resource Monitor is a system tool that allows you to view information about the use of hardware (CPU, memory, disk, and network) and software (file handles and modules) resources in real time. You can filter the results according to specific processes or services that you want to monitor. In addition, you can use Resource Monitor to start, stop, suspend, and resume processes and services, and to troubleshoot when an application does not respond as expected.

Windows *Resource Monitor* is a powerful tool for understanding how your system resources are used by processes and services. In addition to monitoring resource usage in real time, Resource Monitor can help you analyze unresponsive processes, identify which applications are using files, and control processes and services. To start Resource Monitor, perform one of the following:

▪ Execute the resmon.exe command.

▪ From Task Manager Performance tab, click Open Resource Monitor

▪ Open from Windows Administrative Tools

Figure 4.13 shows the Resource Monitor.

FIGURE 4.13   Resource Monitor

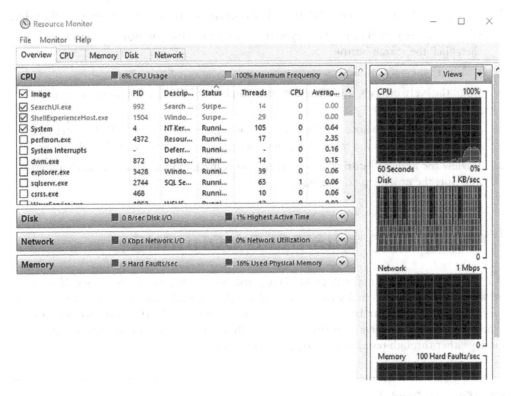

Resource Monitor includes five tabs: Overview, CPU, Memory, Disk, and Network. The Overview tab displays basic system resource usage information; the other tabs display information about each specific resource. Each tab in Resource Monitor includes multiple tables that provide detailed information about the resource featured on that tab.

To identify the process with the highest current CPU usage, follow these steps:

1. Click the CPU tab.

2. In Processes, click CPU to sort processes by current CPU resource consumption.

To view service CPU usage by process, follow these steps:

1. Click the CPU tab.

2. In Processes, in the Image column, select the check box next to the name of the service for which you want to see usage details. You can select multiple services. Selected services are moved to the top of the column.

3. Click the title bar of Services to expand the table. Review the data in Services to see the list of processes hosted by the selected services, and to view their CPU usage.

To identify the process that is using a file, follow these steps:

1. Click the CPU tab, and then click the title bar of Associated Handles to expand the table.
2. Click in the Search Handles box, type the name of the file you want to search for, and then click the search button.

To identify the network address that a process is connected to

1. Click the Network tab, and then click the title bar of TCP Connections to expand the table.
2. Locate the process whose network connection you want to identify. If there are a large number of entries in the table, you can click Image to sort by executable file name.
3. Review the Remote Address and Remote Port columns to see which network address and port the process is connected to.

Introducing Business Continuity

When a server goes down, it will most likely cause your company to lose money. If your network contains an external website or database that controls your sales, ordering, inventory, or production, it can be detrimental to these business needs. If it is an internal server, it may not allow your users to perform their job. In either case, your company is losing money either through revenue or through productivity.

Certification Ready?

If a server failed, do you know how you could have prevented the server from failing? 6.2

As a server administrator, you need to minimize downtime by identifying potential failures and taking steps to avoid those failures and to reduce the effect of those failures.

High availability is a system design protocol and associated implementation that ensures a certain degree of operational continuity during a given measurement period. Generally, the term downtime is used to refer to periods when a system is unavailable. Availability is usually expressed as a percentage of uptime in a given year as shown in Table 4.2.

TABLE 4.2 Availability guidelines

Availability %	Downtime per year	Downtime per month
99%	3.65 days	7.20 hours
99.9% ("three nines")	8.76 hours	43.2 minutes

Availability %	Downtime per year	Downtime per month
99.99% ("four nines")	52.6 minutes	4.32 minutes
99.999% ("five nines")	5.26 minutes	25.9 seconds
99.9999% ("six nines")	31.5 seconds	2.59 seconds

Often when designing servers and the services they provide, they are assigned service level agreements (SLA) that state how much a server or services must be available. Of course, having a server design that can support five or six nines is going to much more expensive than supporting an availability of 99%.

Introducing Fault Tolerance Components

To make a server more fault tolerant, you should first look at what components are the most likely to fail and implement technology to make a system more fault tolerant.

Some of the components that are made redundant within a system are usually:

- Disks – Use some form or RAID and hot spares.
- Power supplies – Use redundant power supplies.
- Network cards – Use redundant network cards.

RAID and hot spare disks have already been discussed in Lesson 3.

It has already been mentioned in this book that mechanical devices fail more often than mechanical devices. A power supply is another mechanical device that converts AC power into clean DC power and includes fans for cooling. For systems that cannot afford to be down, these systems should have redundant power supplies.

While you cannot install fault tolerant processors and redundant memory, high-end servers have additional features to make the server more resistant to hardware failure and have additional monitoring of key components including processors, RAM, motherboards, and storage. For example, high-end servers use a more expensive Error Correcting Code (ECC) memory that includes special circuitry for testing the accuracy of data as it passes in and out of memory. In addition, ECC memory corrects a single failed bit in a 64-bit block. Some of these servers when combined with Windows Server 2016 Enterprise and Datacenter versions allow you to hot-add or hot-replace processors and memory without taking the server down.

Teaming of Network Cards

NIC *teaming* is the process of grouping together two or more physical NICs into one single logical NIC, which can be used for network fault tolerance and increased bandwidth through load balancing. To make a system truly fault tolerant, you should also have redundant switches where one network card of a team is connected to one switch and the other network card of the team is connected to another switch. This way, if the switch fails, you can still communicate over the network.

To support NIC teaming, the network card, network card driver, and switch must support the same teaming technology such as 802.3ad link aggregation. You will then most likely have to install and configure specialized software to activate the team.

Understanding Clustering

A computer *cluster* is a group of linked computers that work together as one computer. Based on the technology used, clusters can provide fault tolerance (often referred to as availability), load balancing, or both. If the system fails including the processor, memory, or motherboard, a cluster that provides fault tolerance can still service requests.

The two most popular forms of clusters are failover clusters and load balancing clusters. A common use of clusters would include:

- A failover cluster for the backend servers such as a database (such as SQL server) or mail server (such as Exchange server).

- A load balancing cluster for the front-end that provides the web interface to the back end servers.

Introducing Failover Clusters

A *failover cluster* is a set of independent computers that work together to increase the availability of services and applications. The clustered servers (called nodes) are connected by physical cables and by software. If one of the nodes fails, another node begins to provide services (a process known as failover). Failover clusters can be used for wide range of network services including database applications such as Exchange Server or SQL server, file servers, print services, or network services such as DHCP services.

The most common fail-over cluster is the *active-passive cluster*. In an active-passive cluster, both servers are configured to work as one, but only one at a time. The active node provides the network services, while the passive node waits for something to happen to the active node where it cannot provide network services. If the active node goes down, the passive node becomes the active node and resumes providing the network services.

Another type of failover cluster is the Active-Active node that is designed to provide fault tolerance and load-balancing. The network services are split into two groups. One cluster node will run one set of network services, while the other cluster node will run the other set of network services. Both nodes are active. If one of the nodes fails, the remaining node will take over providing all of the network services.

To create a failover using Windows Server 2016, you will need two servers that is compatible with Windows Server 2016 and that have identical hardware components. In addition, the server must run the same Windows Server 2016 Enterprise or Windows Server 2016 Datacenter including the same hardware version, such as 32-bit or 64-bit, and the servers should have the same software updates and service packs. In addition, the servers must be part of the same domain.

Cluster nodes are kept aware of the status of the other nodes and services through the user of heartbeats that are sent through a dedicated network card. Therefore, you need to have at least two network adapters, one for the heartbeat and one to link normal network traffic. Since the servers provide access to the same files or databases, they will often use the same central storage such as a SAN.

To create a cluster in Windows Server 2016, you would first install the Failover Cluster feature. You then validate your hardware configuration and then create a cluster using the Failover Cluster Manager.

Introducing Load Balancing Clusters

Load balancing/*network load balancing (NLB)* is when multiple computers are configured as one virtual server to share the workload among multiple computers. As far as the users are concerned, they are accessing the virtual machine, and the requests are distributed among the nodes within the cluster. NLB enhances the availability and scalability of Internet server applications such as those used on Web, FTP, firewall, proxy, virtual private network (VPN), and other mission-critical servers.

Each node in the NLB cluster is assigned a unique set of cluster IP addresses so that users can access the cluster and the requests are distributed among the various nodes. In addition, each node will have its own dedicated IP addresses for each host. For load-balanced applications, when a host fails or goes offline, the load is automatically redistributed among the computers that are still operating.

For each node to keep track of the status of each other, the NLB cluster exchanges heartbeat messages. By default, when a host fails to send heartbeat messages within five seconds, it has failed. When a host has failed, the remaining hosts in the cluster converge will determine which hosts are still active members, elect the host with the highest priority as the new default host, and ensure that all new client requests are handled by the surviving hosts. Convergence generally takes only a few seconds, so interruption in client service by the cluster is minimal. During convergence, hosts that are still active continue handling client requests without affecting existing connections. Convergence ends when all hosts report a consistent view of the cluster membership and distribution map for several heartbeat periods.

Understanding Power

Without electricity, the server will not run. Even if you have redundant power supplies, redundant power supplies will not protect against a power outage or other forms of power fluctuations. In these situations, your company should look at uninterruptable power supplies and power generators to provide power when there is no power available from the power company.

An *uninterruptible power supply* or UPS is an electrical device consisting of one or more batteries to provide backup power when a power outage occurs. UPS units range in size from units designed to protect a single computer without a video monitor (around 200 VA rating) to large units powering entire data centers or buildings. For server rooms that contain many servers, you will most likely install one or more racks full of batteries or UPS devices. For smaller deployments, you may have a single UPS connected to an individual server or essential computer. You also need the UPS to protect other key systems and devices such as primary routers, switches, and telecommunication devices.

What most people new to IT do not realize is that UPS are not usually designed to provide power for lengthy periods of time. Instead, they are usually designed to provide power for momentary power outages and to perform a proper shutdown a server or to allow adequate time to switch over to a power generator.

A power generator or a standby power generator is a backup electrical system that operates automatically within seconds of a power outage. Automatic standby generator systems may also be required by building codes for critical safety systems such as elevators in high-rise buildings, fire protection systems, standby lighting, or medical and life support equipment.

Of course, since power is such a critical component for your server and network, you will need to do periodical tests to make sure that the UPS can supply sufficient power for the necessary time and that the power generator can turn on as needed.

Understanding Backups

Data stored on a computer or stored on the network is vital to the users and the organization. It represents hours of work, and its data is sometimes irreplaceable. One of the most essential components of any server design is backups. No matter how much effort, hardware, and software you put into a system, you will eventually have a failure. Sometimes when the downtime occurs, you may have data loss.

A *backup* or the process of backing up refers to making copies of data so that these additional copies may be used to restore the original after a data loss event. They can be used to restore entire systems following a disaster or to restore a small set of files that were accidentally deleted or corrupted.

 The best method for data recovery is backup, backup, backup.

When planning your backups, you also need to plan of where backup files are going to be stored. If you have files stored throughout your corporation including users keeping their files on their local computers, it is very difficult to back up all of these files. Therefore, you most likely will need to use some form of technology that will keep your files within a limited number of locations. For example, you can use file redirection for Desktop and My Documents to be stored on a file server by configuring the user profiles.

There are multiple technologies available to help centralize your data. Microsoft offers Distributed File System (DFS), which can be used to replicate shared folders to other servers. In addition, both Microsoft SQL server and Microsoft Exchange Server have technology to replicate the databases to other servers including servers in other locations.

Introducing Backup Media

With early networks and servers, a backup was done with floppy disks. Unfortunately, floppy disks were very limited in size, speed, and life span. Eventually, magnetic tapes were developed and become the standard mechanism use for corporations to perform backup and storage. More recently, competing technology has been hard disk storage, and optical disks have become more common for backups.

Traditionally, magnetic tapes have been the most commonly used medium for bulk data storage, backup, and archiving. Tape is a sequential access medium, so even though access times may be poor, the rate of continuously writing or reading data can actually be very fast. For larger organizations, you may use multiple tape drives connected together with a tape library that can automatically swap and manage tapes.

Recently because of increased capacity at lower cost, hard drives have become a viable option for backups. Hard disks can be included in the SAN, NAS, internal hard drives, and external hard drives. Some disk-based backup systems, such as virtual tape libraries, support data de-duplication, which can dramatically reduce the amount of disk storage capacity consumed by daily and weekly backup data.

Usually when using hard disks for backups, hard disks are used to provide a backup of recent data, and the data will be copied to tape and taken offsite for longer-term storage and archiving. If a failure occurs, you can quickly restore from the disks. If you need to recovery or read data from the past, you will then have to retrieve the tapes from offsite and read the tapes.

Another media that is becoming more popular for backups is to use recordable optical disks such as CDs, DVDs, and even Blu-ray. Unfortunately, the newer formats tend to cost more, which may prohibit its use for backups. There is also some concern on the lifetime of a selected optical disk since some optical disks to degrade and lose data within a couple of years.

Introducing Backup Items

When a novice thinks of backups, he or she will most likely think of backing up data files such as Microsoft Word or Excel documents. However, there are more than just data files. You have the program files that make computer do what it needs to do. You also have mailboxes, email databases, SQL databases, and other data types that may need special software to read and back up. In addition when determining what and often to back up, you should also look at the time it would take to reinstall, reconfigure, or recover the item. For example, Microsoft Exchange may take days to install and configure but only a relatively short time to reinstall from backup.

When planning backups, you should isolate your program files and your data files. Program files usually do not change, and so they do not have to be backed up often. Data files change often so they should be backed up more often. If you isolate them in different areas, you can create different backup policies for each area.

Databases usually consist of one or more database files and one or more log files. The primary data file is the starting point of the database and points to the other files in the database. Every database has one or more primary data file. The recommended file name extension for primary data files is .mdf.

Log files hold all the log information that is used to recover the database. For example, you can restore from backup the entire database as is or back up to a point in time if you have the complete log files. The recommended file name extension for log files is .ldf.

Another item that must be covered is the system state. The Windows system state is a collection of system components that are not contained in a simple file but can be backed up easily. It includes:

- Boot files (Boot.ini, NDTLDR, NTDetect.com)
- DLLScache folder
- Registry - Including COM settings
- SYSVOL - Group Policy and Logon Scripts
- Active Directory NTDS.DIT (Domain Controllers)
- Certificate Store (If the service is installed)
- User profiles
- COM+ and WMI information
- IIS metabase

Windows backup and most commercial backup software packages will back up the Windows system state. If you want to perform a complete restore of a system running Windows, you will need to back up all files on the drive and the system state.

Understanding Backup Methods

When planning and implementing backups, you will need to determine when and how often you are going to back up, what hardware and software you are going to use, where you are going to store the backups and how long you are going to store the backups.

Media Management Methods

When you plan a backup, you plan needs to balance between accessibility, security, and cost. Larger organizations will often combine one of the following management methods:

- On-line - The most accessible type of data storage usually using hard disks or disk arrays. Restore can begin in milliseconds time, but can be relatively expensive. In addition, on-line storage can be easily deleted or overwritten by accident or intentional.

- Near-line - Typically less accessible and less expensive than on-line storage, usually consisting of a tape library with the restore time beginning with seconds or minutes.

- Off-line - Requires some direct human action to physical load tapes in a tape library or drive. Access time can vary from minutes to hours or even days if you have to order tapes from an offsite storage area.

- Backup site or DR site- In the event of a disaster, you can switch to the backup site/ DR site while you fix or repair the primary site. Unfortunately, this method is the most expensive solution and the most difficult to implement properly.

Looking at Backup Types

When planning and performing a backup, backup software will include different types of backups, each varying on the time it takes to do a backup and restore. The traditional backups include:

- Full backup
- Full backup with incremental backups
- Full backup with differential backup

Full backups back up all files and data that have been designated. For files, it will shut off an archive attribute bit to indicate that the file has been backed up. For example, you will do a full backup once a day, once a week, or once a month depending on the importance of the data and how often it changes. To perform a restore from a full backup, you just need to grab the last full backup. A full backup offers the fastest restore.

Full backups with *incremental backups* start with a full backup followed by several incremental backups. For example, once a week, you will perform a full backup on Friday night, which will shut off the archive attribute indicating that the files were backed up. Then any new files or changed files will have the archive attribute turned on. You will then perform an incremental backup Monday, Tuesday, Wednesday, and Thursday nights, which will only back up new and changed files and shut off the archive attribute. When you do a restore, you restore the last full backup and then restore each incremental backup from oldest to newest. Full backups with incremental backups offers fastest backup.

Full backup with *differential backup* starts with a full backup followed by several differential backups. For example, once a week, you will perform a full backup on Friday night, which will shut off the archive attribute indicating that the files were backed up. Then any new files or changed files will have the archive attribute turned on. You will then perform a differential backup Monday, Tuesday, Wednesday, and Thursday nights, which will only back up new and change files since the last full backup but will not turn off the archive attribute. When you do a restore, you restore the last full backup and the last differential backup.

Another backup type that is available from backup software packages including Microsoft's backup software is the copy backup. A copy backup backs up the designated files but does not shut off the archive attribute. This is used for impromptu backups such as before you make a system or application change. Since it does not modify the archive attribute, it will not interfere with your normal backup schedules.

Looking at Backup Rotation Schemes

One of the questions you should ask yourself is how often should you do a backup? The answer will vary based on your needs. You must first look at how important your data is and how much effort it would require to re-create the data. You should also consider what it will do to your company if the data is lost. Important or critical data will backed up nightly. Data that does not change much can be backed up weekly and data that does not change at all can be backed up monthly.

The next question should be how often should you keep you backups? That question is not easy to answer because it is really based on the needs of your organization including legal requirements that your organization must follow.

Another consideration you should keep in mind is that backups do fail from time to time. Therefore, you should periodically test your backups by doing a restore to make sure that a backup is working and that you are backing up the necessary files. Second, you should have some type of rotation.

One common backup rotation scheme is the *Grandfather-father-son (GFS)*. The son backup is done once a day, and those backups are rotated on a daily backup. At the end of the week, the daily backup is promoted to a weekly backup. The weekly or father backups are rotated on a weekly basis with one graduating to grandfather status each month. The monthly backups would traditionally be placed offsite; of course, this is based on your needs of what needs to be sent offsite.

Introducing Microsoft Windows Backup

Windows includes Microsoft Windows Backup, which will allow you to back up a system. However, third-party backup software packages usually offer more features and options.

To access the backup and recovery tools for Windows Server 2016, you must install the Windows Server Backup Command-line Tools and Windows PowerShell items that are available in the Add Features Wizard in Server Manager. To run the Windows Server Backup, you must be a member of the Backup Operators or Administrators group.

You can create a backup using the Backup Schedule Wizard or by using the Backup Once option. You can back up to any local drive or to a shared folder on another server.

Create a Backup Schedule

To create a backup schedule using the Windows Server Backup user interface:

1. Click Start, and click Server Manager.
2. Open the Tools menu, and click Windows Server Backup.
3. In the Actions pane of the snap-in default page, under Windows Server Backup, click Backup Schedule. This opens the Backup Schedule Wizard.
4. On the Getting started page, click Next.
5. On the Select Backup configuration page, click Full Server or Custom Backup and click Next. See Figure 4.14. Select Full Server to back up all volumes on the server. Click Custom to back up just certain volumes, and then click Next.

FIGURE 4.14 Selecting Backup Configuration

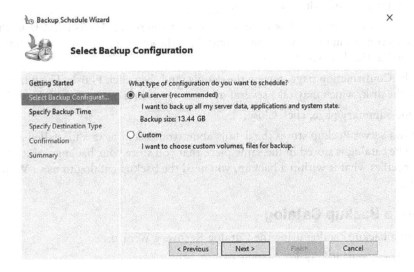

6. On the Specify Backup Time page, click Once a day (as shown in Figure 4.15) or click More than once a day. Then enter the time or times to start the backups. When completed, click Next.

FIGURE 4.15 Specify Backup Time

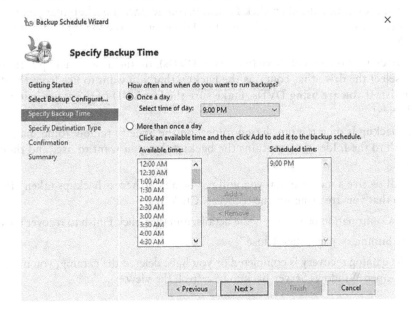

7. On the Select destination disk page, select the check box for the disk that you attached for this purpose, and then click Next.

8. On the Label destination disk page, the disk that you selected is listed. A label that includes your computer name, the current date, the current time, and a disk name is assigned to the disk. Click Next.

9. On the Confirmation page, review the details, and then click Finish. The wizard formats the disk, which may take several minutes depending on the size of the disk.

10. On the Summary page, click Close.

Windows Server Backup stores the details about your backups in a file called a backup catalog. The catalog is stored in the same place that you store your backups. Since the catalog specifies what is within a backup, you need the backup catalog to use a Windows backup file.

Recover a Backup Catalog

To recover a backup catalog using the Catalog Recovery Wizard:

1. Click Start, and click Server Manager.

2. Open the Tools menu, and click Windows Server Backup.

3. In the Actions pane of the snap-in default page, under Windows Server Backup, click Recover Catalog. This opens the Catalog Recovery Wizard.

4. On the Specify storage type page, if you do not have a backup that you can use to recover the catalog, and just want to delete the catalog, click I don't have any usable backups, click Next, and then click Finish. If you do have a backup that you can use, specify whether the backup is on a local drive or remote shared folder, and then click Next.

5. If the backup is on a local drive (including DVDs), on the Select backup location page, select the drive that contains the backup that you want to use from the drop-down list. If you are using DVDs, make sure the last DVD of the series is in the drive. Click Next.

6. If the backup is on a remote shared folder, on the Specify remote folder page, type the path to the folder that contains the backup that you want to use, and then click Next.

7. You will receive a message that you will not be able to access backups taken after the backup that you are using for the recovery. Click Yes.

8. On the Confirmation page, review the details, and then click Finish to recover the catalog.

9. On the Summary page, click Close.

Once the catalog recovery is completed or you have deleted the catalog, you must close and then re-open Windows Server Backup to refresh the view.

Shadow Copy (Volume Snapshot Service or Volume Shadow copy Service or VSS) is a technology included in Microsoft Windows that allows you take a snapshot of data, even if it has a lock on a specific volume at a specific point in time so that the file can be backed up. Today, most backup software uses VSS to make backups of files within Windows.

Understanding Shadow Copies of Shared Folders and Restore Points

Windows Server 2003 introduces a new feature called shadow copies of shared folders, which is also used in Windows Server 2016. Shadow copies, when configured, automatically create backup copies of the data stored in shared folders on specific NTFS drive volumes at scheduled times.

Shadow copies allow users to retrieve previous versions of files and folders on their own, without requiring IT personnel to restore files or folders from backup media. Of course, you need to have sufficient disk space to store the shadow copies, at least 100 MB of free space.

Shadow copies are copies of files and folders that Windows saves as part of a restore point. Typically, restore points are created once a day if System Protection is enabled. If enabled, Windows will automatically create shadow copies of files that have been changed since the last restore point.

One benefit of using restore points and shadow copies is the capability to restore file and folders using the Previous Versions tab. When you click a folder and then choose Properties, you will see the Previous Versions tab. This is where you can restore a folder. This will be explained a little later in this section.

Restore points contain registry and system information as it was at a certain point in time. Restore points are created after a specified period of time. Restore points can be created either:

- Weekly
- Prior to installing applications or drivers
- Prior to significant system events
- Prior to performing a System Restore to restore files (so, if necessary, can undo the changes)
- Manually (upon request)

Create a Restore Point

If you'd like to create a restore point, follow these steps:

1. Click Start ➤ Windows System ➤ Control Panel ➤ System ➤ System Protection.
2. Click the Create button on the bottom of the screen. (See Figure 4.16.)

3. At the System Protection dialog box, enter a description for the restore point. Click Create.

4. A dialog box states that the restore point was created. Click Close.

FIGURE 4.16 Using System Restore

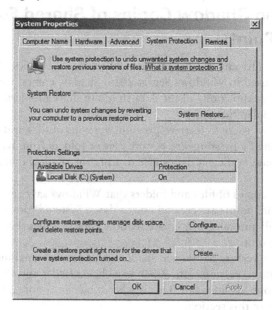

You can restore an earlier created restore point by using System Restore. This will restore system files and settings but will not affect the personal files. System Restore will remove any programs that have been installed since the restore point was created.

To return your computer's configuration to a previously captured restore point, follow these steps:

1. Click Start ➢ Windows System ➢ Control Panel ➢ System ➢ System Protection.

2. Click the System Restore button, then click Next at the Restore System Files And Settings screen to continue.

3. Choose the restore point created and click Next to continue.

4. Review the restore point selection and click Finish.

5. Click Yes to confirm.

6. The System Restore will restore the system and reboot the computer to apply the changes. You will get a message showing that the System Restore has restored the computer. Click OK to close.

One issue of creating multiple restore points is that they will eventually take up a huge amount of hard disk space. Occasionally, you will want to clean up the older restore points.

This can be done by utilizing the Disk Cleanup utility. This utility helps remove temporary files, cleans out the Recycle Bin, and removes older system files that are no longer needed.

To use the Disk Cleanup utility, click Start ➤ Windows System ➤ Control Panel ➤ Administrative Tools ➤ Disk Cleanup.

Restore a Previous Version of a File or Folder

To restore a previous version of a file or folder:

1. Locate the file or folder that you want to restore, right-click the file or older, and click Properties. The Properties dialog box will appear.

2. Click the Previous Versions tab, click the version of the file that you want to restore, and then click Restore. A warning message about restoring a previous version will appear. Click Restore to complete the procedure. See Figure 4.17.

FIGURE 4.17   Restoring a Previous Version

Restoring a previous version will delete the current version. If you choose to restore a previous version of a folder, the folder will be restored to its state at the date and time of the version you selected. You will lose any changes that you have made to files in the folder since that time. Instead, if you do not want to delete the current version of a file or folder, click Copy to copy the previous version to a different location.

Recovering Servers with WinRE

If you experience problems that prevent Windows Server 2012 from booting, you can use the *Windows Recovery Environment (WinRE)* to troubleshoot and repair the system.

There are several ways to access the Windows Recovery Environment (WinRE) in Windows Server 2016:

- The server enters WinRE in situations after two consecutive failed attempts to start Windows, after two consecutive shutdowns that were unexpected, or due to secure boot errors. Secure boot is a security feature built into Windows Server that captures a signature of the operating system. Windows checks against the signature the last time it booted up. If the signatures don't match, the system enters WinRE.

- Press the Shift key and keep it pressed. Then click the Start ➤ Power ➤ Restart. If it asks for the reason for the reboot, click Continue.

- Boot the server from Windows installation media and select Repair Computer.

- Enter the command shutdown /r /o from a command prompt.

Upon entering the WinRE environment, you have the following options as shown in Figure 4.18.

FIGURE 4.18 Exploring the Windows Recovery Environment (WinRE)

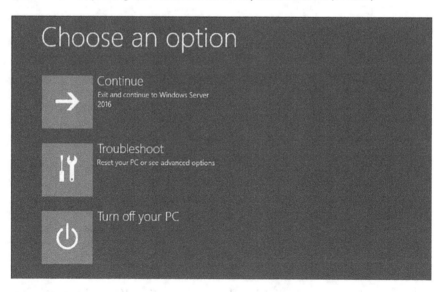

Continue   Exits the WinRE environment and continues to the Windows Server 2016 operating system.

Troubleshoot   Provides access to the following tools as shown in Figure 4.19.

FIGURE 4.19 Troubleshooting using the Windows Recovery Environment (WinRE) tools

If you select Advanced options from the troubleshooting menu you will see the Advanced options that are available for use with the Widows Recovery Environment (WinRE). See Figure 4.20.

FIGURE 4.20 Advanced Options using the Windows Recovery Environment (WinRE) tools

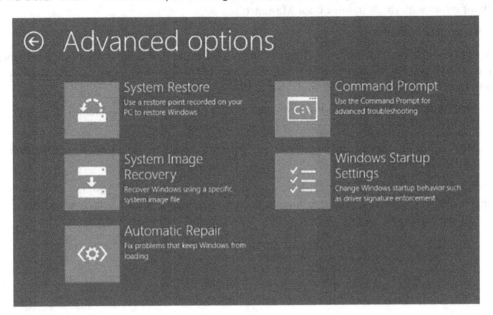

Turn off PC   Shuts down the server.

System Restore   This feature can repair certain types of computer crashes and other computer related issues. Can use system restore to revert a computer's state to a previous point in time, called a restore point. Restore points contain Windows system files, applications, Windows Registry, and system settings.

System Image Recovery   Restores the entire system to a previous state by using an image created by Windows Backup. This option should be a used only after you try other options and assumes you have a current backup of your server to restore from.

Automatic Repair   The Automatic Repair tool automates diagnostic and repair tasks for non-bootable operating system installations. It will start if a computer fails over into Windows RE due to a detected boot failure. If automatic failover to an on-disk instance of WinRE is not available, then users can start Automatic Repair as a manual recovery tool from a Windows RE CD or DVD.

Command Prompt   Provides command-line access with administrator privileges to the Windows Server file system. You can use it for tools such as Diskpart, System File Checker, bootrec, bcdedit, and format.

Windows Startup Settings   Provides access to the Advanced Boot options menu.

If you select the Command Prompt option, you have access to several different tools that can assist you in recovering a server that will not boot into the operating system:

Bootrec   Troubleshoots and repairs the master boot record, boot sector, and Boot Configuration Data (BCD) store.

Bcdedit   Displays how Windows is configured to boot and can also be used to troubleshoot issues with the Windows Boot Manager.

Format   Formats partitions.

System File Checker   Checks the integrity of your hard drive. If a file is missing or corrupt, it can be restored with this tool. SFC validates the digital signatures of all the Windows system files and restores any that it finds that are incorrect.

Sfc /scannow   Scans all of your protected system files and repair problems it finds by replacing incorrect versions with the correct Microsoft versions.

Sfc /verifyonly   Scans for integrity of all protected system files but does not perform a repair operation.

Diskpart   Loads the Windows Disk management program. Using this program, you can shrink, expand, create, and delete existing partitions as well as gather information about your hard drives.

In Windows Server 2016, you can boot into safe mode by using one of the options discussed previously. Starting in *safe mode* allows you to troubleshoot situations where you cannot access the system due to faulty hardware, software, device drivers, and virus infections.

Safe mode loads a minimal set of drivers and services; therefore, if you can boot into safe mode but can't boot normally, the system most likely has a conflict with hardware settings, services, drivers, or some type of registry corruption.

Once you can access your system via safe mode, you should check the Event Viewer (System and Application logs) for errors. You can also run the Windows System Information tool (msinfo32.exe) to gather details about the computer, operating system, and software including drivers. You can also search for problem devices.

You can review the ntbtlog (see Figure 4.21) located in the %systemroot% folder. You can open this file using a text editor (Notepad) to review the devices and services that loaded and did not load. The file shows the path of each item and identifies them as BOOTLOG_LOADED or BOOTLOG_NOT_LOADED.

FIGURE 4.21   Reviewing the sample ntbtlog.txt file

```
ntbtlog - Notepad                                              —    □    ×
File  Edit  Format  View  Help
BOOTLOG_LOADED  \SystemRoot\system32\ntoskrnl.exe
BOOTLOG_LOADED  \SystemRoot\system32\hal.dll
BOOTLOG_LOADED  \SystemRoot\system32\kd.dll
BOOTLOG_LOADED  \SystemRoot\system32\mcupdate_GenuineIntel.dll
BOOTLOG_LOADED  \SystemRoot\System32\drivers\werkernel.sys
BOOTLOG_LOADED  \SystemRoot\System32\drivers\CLFS.SYS
BOOTLOG_LOADED  \SystemRoot\System32\drivers\tm.sys
BOOTLOG_LOADED  \SystemRoot\system32\PSHED.dll
BOOTLOG_LOADED  \SystemRoot\System32\BOOTVID.dll
BOOTLOG_LOADED  \SystemRoot\System32\drivers\cmimcext.sys
BOOTLOG_LOADED  \SystemRoot\System32\drivers\ntosext.sys
BOOTLOG_LOADED  \SystemRoot\System32\CI.dll
BOOTLOG_LOADED  \SystemRoot\System32\drivers\msrpc.sys
BOOTLOG_LOADED  \SystemRoot\system32\drivers\FLTMGR.SYS
BOOTLOG_LOADED  \SystemRoot\System32\drivers\ksecdd.sys
BOOTLOG_LOADED  \SystemRoot\System32\drivers\clipsp.sys
BOOTLOG_LOADED  \SystemRoot\system32\drivers\Wdf01000.sys
BOOTLOG_LOADED  \SystemRoot\system32\drivers\WDFLDR.SYS
BOOTLOG_LOADED  \SystemRoot\System32\Drivers\acpiex.sys
BOOTLOG_LOADED  \SystemRoot\System32\Drivers\WppRecorder.sys
BOOTLOG_LOADED  \SystemRoot\System32\Drivers\cng.sys
BOOTLOG_LOADED  \SystemRoot\System32\drivers\ACPI.sys
```

Another option is to run MSConfig and use the process of elimination to identify the source of the problem that is keeping Windows from booting correctly. *MSConfig* (also called *System Configuration*) is a tool used to troubleshoot the system startup process (see Figure 4.22). It can be used to disable, enable, software, device drivers, and services that run at startup. MSconfig can also be used to change boot parameters if necessary.

FIGURE 4.22 Using MSCONFIG to troubleshoot

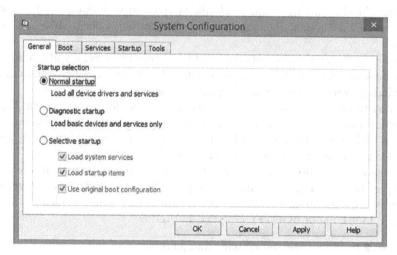

The general process for troubleshooting using MSConfig is as follows:

1. Start Windows in Diagnostic startup mode in the General tab. If the problem occurs during a diagnostic startup, files and drivers are suspect. If the problem does not occur, proceed to Step 2.

2. Start Windows in Select startup mode in the General tab.

3. Select the services tab and disable each service one at a time and restart the server. If the problem does not go away, you can eliminate the services as the source.

4. Select the *Startup* tab and turn off all startup items except the first one. Reboot the server. This process can be used to isolate a startup item.

Boot into Safe Mode

To boot into safe mode on Server01, perform the following steps:

1. Log in to LON-SVR1 and enter the following at a command prompt:

shutdown /r /o

 The /r switch tells the server to restart; the /o option tells the server to end the current Windows session and open the Advanced Boot options menu.

2. Select Close when prompted; the system will shut down in less than a minute.

3. Select the Troubleshoot tile.

4. Select the Startup Settings tile.

5. Select Restart.

6. Select Safe Mode and press Enter.

7. Enter the password for the Administrator account and press Enter.

8. Confirm your system is now in safe mode. The words "safe mode" should appear on each corner of your desktop.

9. Select the Windows logo key + R to open the Run dialog box.

10. Enter **MSConfig** and select OK.

11. Review each tab of the System Configuration tool for options you can configure and then close the dialog box.

12. Select the Windows logo key + R to open the Run dialog box.

13. Enter compmgmt.msc to open the Computer Management console.

14. Expand Event Viewer ➢ Windows logs and review the System and Application logs. Close the Computer Management console.

15. Use File Explorer to navigate to %systemroot% and locate the ntbtlog.txt file.

16. Open the ntbtlog.txt file to view its contents.

17. Restart the computer by running the following from a command prompt (do not use the /o switch):

    shutdown /r

Skill Summary

In this lesson you learned:

- You need to have processes in place to plan, design, implement, monitor, and retire servers, services, and applications.

- The Information Technology Infrastructure Library (ITIL) is a set of concepts and practices for managing Information Technology (IT) services (ITSM), IT development, and IT operations.

- An effective troubleshooting methodology is to reduce the amount of guesswork and random solutions so that you can troubleshoot and fix the problem in a timely manner.

- System Information (also known as msinfo32.exe) shows details about your computer's hardware configuration, computer components, and software, including drivers.

- The Event Viewer is a Microsoft Management Console (MMC) snap-in that enables you to browse and manage event logs.

- Every time you turn on a computer, the computer goes through the Power-On Self Test (POST), which initializes hardware and finds an operating system to load.

- When you load Windows 7, Windows 8/8.1, Windows 10, Windows Server 2012, Windows Server 2012 R2, and Windows Server 2016, you will be loading BOOTMGR, WINLoad, NTOSKERNL.EXE, and Boot-class Device Drivers.

- A master boot record (MBR) is the first 512-byte boot sector of a partitioned data storage device such as a hard disk. It is used to hold the disk's primary partition table, contains the code to bootstrap an operating system that usually passes control to the volume boot record, and uniquely identifies the disk media.

- A volume boot record (VBR), also known as a volume boot sector or a partition boot sector, is a type of boot sector, stored in a disk volume on a hard disk, floppy disk, or similar data storage device, that contains code for booting an operating system such as NTLDR and BOOTMGR.

- Boot Configuration Data (BCD) is a firmware-independent database for boot-time configuration data used by Microsoft's Windows Boot Manager found with Windows Vista, Windows 7, Windows Server 2008, and Windows Server 2016.

- When you have some problems that occur during bootup, you may need to take some extra steps to get the computer in a usable state so that you can fix the problem. Since Windows XP, you can access the Advanced Boot Options to access advanced troubleshooting modes including safe mode and Last Known Good Configuration.

- To access the Advanced Boot Options screen, you turn your computer on and press the F8 before the Windows logo appears.

- Safe Mode starts Windows with a minimal set of drivers and services. If you make a change to the system and Windows no longer boots, you can try safe mode.

- Last Known Good Configuration starts Windows with the last registry and driver configuration that worked successfully, usually marked at the last successful login.

- System Configuration (msconfig.exe) is a tool that can help identify problems that might prevent Windows from starting correctly by disabling programs and services that start automatically when Windows starts.

- Performance is the overall effectiveness of how data moves through the system.

- If your computer lacks RAM needed to run a program or perform an operation, Windows uses virtual memory to compensate.

- When RAM runs low, virtual memory moves data from RAM to space called a paging file. Moving data to and from the paging frees up RAM so your computer can complete its work.

- Task Manager gives you a quick glance on performance and provides information about programs and processes running on your computer.

- Windows Performance Monitor is a Microsoft Management Console (MMC) snap-in that provides tools for analyzing system performance.

- Windows Resource Monitor is a system tool that allows you to view information about the use of hardware (CPU, memory, disk, and network) and software (file handles and modules) resources in real time.

- As a server administrator, you need to minimize downtime by identifying potential failures and taking steps to avoid those failures and to reduce the effect of those failures.

- NIC teaming is the process of grouping together two or more physical NICs into one single logical NIC, which can be used for network fault tolerance and increased bandwidth through load balancing.

- Computer cluster is a group of linked computers that work together as one computer. Based on the technology used, clusters can provide fault tolerance (often referred to as availability), load balancing, or both.

- A failover cluster is a set of independent computers that work together to increase and availability of services and applications. The clustered servers (called nodes) are connected by physical cables and by software.

- In an active-passive cluster, both servers are configured to work as one, but only one at a time.

- Network load balancing (NLB) is when multiple computers are configured as one virtual server to share the workload among multiple computers.

- A common use of clusters would include a failover cluster for the backend servers such as a database (such as SQL server) or mail server (such as Exchange server) and a load balancing cluster for the front-end that provide the web interface to the back-end servers.

- An uninterruptible power supply or UPS is an electrical device consisting of one or more batteries to provide backup power when a power outage occurs.

- A backup or the process of backing up refers to making copies of data so that these additional copies may be used to restore the original after a data loss event.

- The best method for data recovery is backup, backup, backup.

- The Windows system state is a collection of system components that are not contained in a simple file that can be backed up easily. It includes boot files and the registry.

- Full backups back up all files and data that has been designated.

- Full backups with incremental backups start with a full backup followed by several incremental backups. When you do a restore, you restore the last full backup and then restore each incremental backup from oldest to newest. Full backups with incremental backups offer the fastest backup.

- Full backups with differential backup start with a full backup followed by several differential backups. When you do a restore, you restore the last full backup and the last differential backup.

- Shadow copies, when configured, automatically create backup copies of the data stored in shared folders on specific NTFS drive volumes at scheduled times.

Knowledge Assessment

Fill in the Blank

1. The _____ is the first 512-byte boot sector of a partitioned data storage device such as a hard disk.

2. _____ starts Windows with a minimal set of drivers and servers.

3. The _____ tool can be used to easily disable individual startup programs.

4. In Windows, virtual memory uses a _____ file.

5. _____ is the combining of network cards to provide fault tolerance.

6. A _____ is a group of computers that work together as one virtual computer to provide fault tolerance or increased performance.

7. The most common failover cluster is the _____ cluster where only one server is active at a time.

8. In a cluster, an individual computer is known as a _____.

9. A _____ is a electrical device to provide temporary power during power outages.

Multiple Choice

1. What publications includes a set of concepts and practices for managing IT services, development, and operations?
   A. Red book
   B. IT Development Guide
   C. ITIL core books
   D. IT Transition Guidebook

2. What tool is used to view the hardware and software loaded on a Windows server?
   A. System Information
   B. System Configuration
   C. KB tool
   D. POST

3. Where would you find NTLDR or BOOTMGR on a hard drive?
   A. MBR
   B. VBR
   C. boot.ini
   D. WINNT folder

4. What determines which operating system to load when running Windows 10 or Windows Server 2016?

   A. RAID

   B. GUID

   C. boot.ini

   D. BCD

5. You loaded a program and rebooted Windows. Unfortunately, Windows no longer boots. What should you try first?

   A. Enable boot logging.

   B. Load Last Known Good Configuration

   C. Disable the boot.ini file.

   D. Reinstall Windows.

6. What program gives you a quick look at system performances and the processes that are running?

   A. Task Manager

   B. Performance Monitor

   C. Resource Monitor

   D. System Information

7. _____ is multiple computers configured as one virtual server to share the workload.

   A. Network load balancing

   B. Active passive cluster

   C. SAN cluster

   D. Terminal server

8. _____ is making copies of data so that these additional copies may be used to restore the original after a data loss event.

   A. DFS

   B. RAID

   C. Backup

   D. EMS

9. Which type of backup backs up all designated files and turns off the archive attribute?

   A. full

   B. differential

   C. incremental

   D. copy

10. Which type of backup is the longest to restore

   A. full

   B. differential

   C. incremental

   D. copy

True/False

1. The best method for data recovery is backup, backup, backup.

2. Shadow copies are only available under older file systems.

3. To view Windows log, use the Log Viewer application.

4. 99.9999 availability means that a system can be down for 4.32 minutes a year.

5. Clusters nodes will protect against faulty power supplies, faulty processors, and faulty RAM.

Competency Assessment

Scenario 4-1: Using a Troubleshooting Methodology

Your computer does not boot. The computer has no lights, and you hear no beeps. What would the steps be in troubleshooting this problem?

Scenario 4-2: Planning a backup strategy

You have several servers that all include important data that change often. Unfortunately, when you try to back up these servers, it takes about 30 hours to back up. What would you recommend as a backup strategy?

Proficiency Assessment

Scenario 4-3: Looking at Backups

You have setup backups, and you perform full backups once a week and incremental Monday through Thursday. So what should you do next?

Scenario 4-4: Looking at Event Viewer

You experiencing some problems on a server running Windows Server 2016. You log in and open the Server Management console and decide to look at the System logs in the Event Viewer. Unfortunately, you see many errors and warnings. What should you have done before you had problems to get the most of the Event Viewer?

 Real World Scenario

Workplace Ready: Monitoring and Managing Servers

After a server is built and configured, it takes a lot of work to keep the server working as efficiently as it should be so that it can perform its job properly. Keeping the system updated can be time-consuming, especially if you have many servers to keep patched.

Therefore, you should invest in some kind of monitoring software such as the Microsoft System Center Operations Manager (SCOM). SCOM makes sure the server is up by constantly contacting the agent running on the server. It will also constantly check the event viewer for errors. Lastly, depending on the roles that the server has and the management packs loaded on the SCOM server, it can constantly test key components to make sure they are up and running.

Lesson

5

Essential Services

Objective Domain Matrix

Skills/Concepts	Objective Domain Description	Objective Domain Number
Looking at Objects Introducing Groups	Understand accounts and groups.	3.1
Introducing Domains, Trees, and Forests Introducing Organizational Units	Understand organizational units (OUs) and containers.	3.2
Introducing Directory Services with Active Directory	Understand Active Directory infrastructure.	3.3
Introducing Group Policies	Understand group policy.	3.4

Key Terms

Active Directory

built-in group

computer account

directory service

distribution group

domain controller

domain local group

Domain Name System (DNS)

Dynamic Host Configuration Protocol (DHCP)

Flexible Single Master Operations (FSMO) roles

forest

fully qualified domain name (FQDN)

functional level

global catalog

global group

group

group policy

hosts file

Lightweight Directory Access Protocol (LDAP)

member server

object

organizational unit

Passport

permission

right

security group

site

tree

trusts relationship

universal group

user account

Windows Internet Name Service (WINS)

 Real World Scenario

Lesson 5 Case

You are building a new network, and you need to get things started. You figure the best place to begin is to create servers that will host essential services, including DHCP and DNS. Then, when those servers are in place, you can create a domain controller so that you can begin establishing user and computer accounts and assigning rights and permissions to those users and computers.

Naming Resolution

In today's networks, you assign logical addresses, such as with IP addressing. Unfortunately, these addresses tend to be hard to remember, especially in the case of newer, more complicated IPv6 addresses. Therefore, you need to use some form of naming service that will allow you to translate logical names, which are easier to remember, into logical addresses. The most common naming service is *Domain Name System*, or DNS.

There are two types of names to translate. The first type consists of hostnames, which reside in the Domain Name System and are the same names used on the Internet. When you type the name of a Web site or a server that is on the Internet, such as `www.microsoft.com` or `www.cnn.com`, you are specifying a domain/hostname. The second type of name is your computer name, also known as the NetBIOS name. If you are on a corporate network or your home network, the hostname is usually the computer name. In fact, for most computers, the hostname and the NetBIOS/computer name are the same.

Understanding HOSTS and LMHOSTS Files

Early TCP/IP networks used hosts (used with domain/hostnames associated with DNS) and lmhost (used with NetBIOS/computer names associated with WINS) files, which were text files that would list a name and its associated IP address. However, with this system, every time you needed to add or modify a name and address, you would have to go to every computer and modify the text file each required to know the address. For larger organizations, this was incredibly inefficient, because it might involve hundreds if not thousands of computers and extremely large text files.

In Windows, both of these files are located in the C:\WINDOWS\system32\drivers\ etc folder. The *hosts file* (see Figure 5.1) can be edited and is ready to use. The lmhosts .sam file is a sample file, and it will have to be copied as lmhosts without the .sam filename extension.

Although the hosts and lmhosts files are considered legacy methods for naming resolution, they still come in handy when troubleshooting or testing because name resolution will check these two files before contacting naming servers. For example, say you just installed a new server but do not want to make it available to everyone else. In this situation, you can add an entry in your local hosts file so that when your computer resolves a certain name, it will resolve to the IP address of the new server. This avoids changing the DNS entry, which would affect all users on your organization's network, until you are ready.

FIGURE 5.1   A sample hosts file

```
hosts - Notepad                                                           —   □   ×
File  Edit  Format  View  Help
# Copyright (c) 1993-2009 Microsoft Corp.
#
# This is a sample HOSTS file used by Microsoft TCP/IP for Windows.
#
# This file contains the mappings of IP addresses to host names. Each
# entry should be kept on an individual line. The IP address should
# be placed in the first column followed by the corresponding host name.
# The IP address and the host name should be separated by at least one
# space.
#
# Additionally, comments (such as these) may be inserted on individual
# lines or following the machine name denoted by a '#' symbol.
#
# For example:
#
#      102.54.94.97     rhino.acme.com        # source server
#      38.25.63.10      x.acme.com            # x client host

# localhost name resolution is handled within DNS itself.
#      127.0.0.1        localhost
#      ::1              localhost

127.0.0.1        google.com
```

Exploring DNS

DNS is short for Domain Name System. DNS is a hierarchical client/server-based distributed database management system that translates domain/hosts names to IP addresses. In other words, your organization most likely has one or more DNS servers that provide name resolution for your company. At home, your ISP provides a DNS server so that when you type in a URL or try to connect to a server over the Internet, your computer can find the hosting server's IP address. What makes DNS so powerful and scalable is that all of the DNS servers on the Internet are linked together to provide worldwide naming resolution while allowing you to manage the DNS for your organization. Because DNS servers provide name resolution, they are sometimes referred to as name servers.

The top of the tree is known as the root domain. Below the root domain, you will find top-level domains, such as .com, .edu, .org, and .net, as well as two-letter country codes, such as .uk, .ca, and .us. Below the top-level domains, you will find the registered variable name that corresponds to an organization or other registered name. The second-level domain name must be registered by an authorized party, such as www.networksolutions.com or www.godaddy.com.

For example, www.microsoft.com is registered to the Microsoft Corporation. When you search for this URL, your computer will first contact the .com DNS servers to determine the name server for microsoft.com. It will then contact the microsoft.com DNS servers to determine the address that is assigned to microsoft.com. Larger organizations may subdivide their DNS name space into subdomains, such as technet.microsoft.com, msdn.microsoft.com, or social.microsoft.com.

A hostname is a name assigned to a specific computer within a domain or subdomain to identify the TCP/IP host. Multiple hostnames can be assigned to the same IP address, although only one name can be assigned to a physical computer or virtual computer.

A *fully qualified domain name* (FQDN) describes the exact position of a host with the DNS hierarchy. Examples of FQDNs include the following:

- `www.microsoft.com`
- `technet.microsoft.com`
- `server1.sales.microsoft.com`

Then, within a DNS zone, there are resource records (RR) that provide name resolution. See Figure 5.2 to show resource records in a forward lookup zone. These RRs are as follows:

SOA (Start of Authority)   Identifies the name server that is the authoritative source of information for a DNS domain or zone. It also includes parameters for how long DNS entries should be cached in a system.

NS (Name Server)   Provides a list of names servers that are assigned to a domain.

A (Host Address)   Provides a hostname to an IPv4 address.

AAA (Host Address)   Provides a hostname to an IPv6 address.

PTR   Resolves an IP address to a hostname (reverse mapping).

CNAME (Canonical Name)   Creates an alias or alternate DNS domain name for a specified hostname. Examples include `www.acme.com` or `ftp.acme.com`, which point to a server on the `acme.com` network, such as `server01.acme.com`. This type of RR is often used with virtual servers that point to multiple servers, such as servers that provide network load balancing so that work can be distributed.

SRV (Service)   Locates servers that are hosting a particular service, including LDAP servers or domain controllers.

MX (Mail Exchanger)   Identifies which mail exchanger should contact a specified domain and in what order to use each mail host.

FIGURE 5.2   Resource records shown in a forward lookup zone

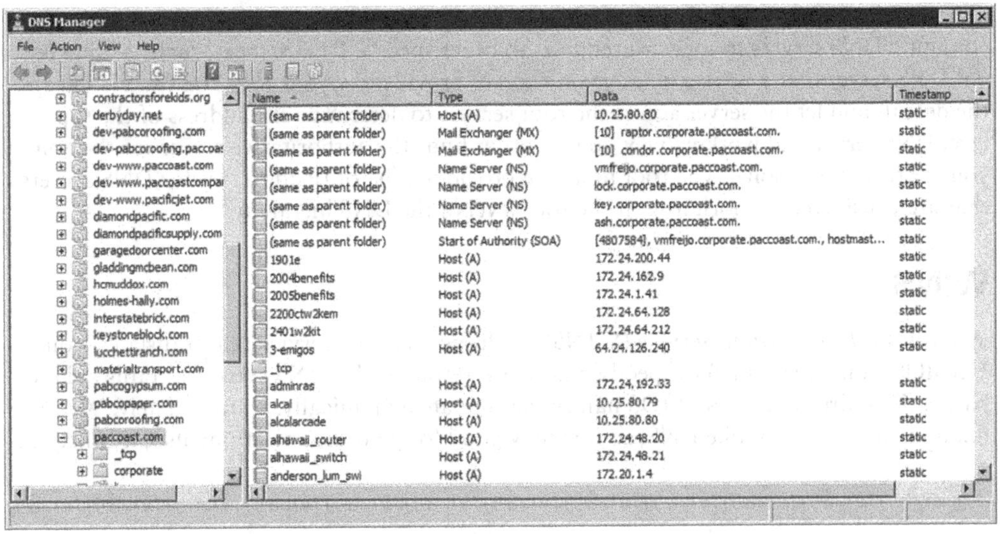

When you define DNS zones, you create the zone as either a forward lookup zone or a reverse lookup zone. The forward lookup zone (such as technet.microsoft.com or microsoft.com) has the majority of the resource records, including A and CNAME records, whereas the reverse lookup zone has PTR records. The reverse lookup zone is defined by reverse lookup format. For example, if you have a 172.24.1.x subnet, it will be shown as 1.24.172.

DNS servers use a mechanism called round-robin to share and distribute loads for a network resource. Round-robin rotates the order of resource records with the same name that point to different IP addresses.

UNIX and Linux systems used BIND implementations of DNS, which support two types of zones: a standard primary zone and a standard secondary zone. The standard primary zone is the master copy of a new zone that is replicated to standard secondary zones. Thus, if you need to make a change, that change should be made on the primary zone so that it can be replicated to the secondary zones.

Since the release of Windows Server 2000, there has also been an Active Directory integrated zone that is stored in Active Directory instead of a file. With Active Directory integrated zones, each server acts as a peer primary server, meaning you can update any server running the Active Directory integrated zones and the changes will be replicated as part of Active Directory replication to the other DNS servers. By using Active Directory integrated zones, the zones have increased fault tolerance (assuming you have two or more DNS servers with integrated Active Directory zones), have minimal traffic for zone replication, and are more secure.

DNS queries and DNS transfers between primary and secondary zones occur over TCP/UDP port 53. So, if you have any firewall between servers (including firewalls running on the servers), you will need to open port 53.

Since DNS has become the primary naming resolution tool, Dynamic DNS has been created. Dynamic DNS uses and will automatically register and update a DNS server's resource records when a host gets an IP address. For servers that have static addresses, you should add static entries.

When you configure a DNS server to handle name resolution for your organization, the DNS server is usually the authority for your organization. If you need to resolve a name for another organization, it will have to forward the request to another DNS server. You can configure DNS servers to forward requests to other specific DNS servers, such as an external DNS server that you also manage or a server provided by your ISP. You can also keep the default and let the server access the root servers to determine the address of the top-level DNS server and work its way down until it finds the authoritative server for the zone you are trying to resolve. The root hints file provides a list of IP addresses for DNS servers that are considered authoritative at the root level of the DNS hierarchy.

WINS

Windows Internet Name Service (WINS) is a legacy naming service that translates from NetBIOS (computer name) to specify a network resource. A WINS server contains a database of IP addresses and NetBIOS names that update dynamically. Unfortunately, WINS is not a hierarchy system like DNS, so it is only good for your organization; also, it functions only for Windows operating systems. Typically, other network devices and services cannot register with a WINS server. Therefore, you have to add static entries for these devices if you want name resolution using WINS.

When a WINS client starts up, it registers its name, IP address, and type of services within the WINS server database. See Figure 5.3. The type of service is designated by a hexadecimal value:

00h: workstation

03h: messenger

20h: file server

The NetBIOS name can be only up to 15 characters long, not counting the hexadecimal value.

FIGURE 5.3   WINS server

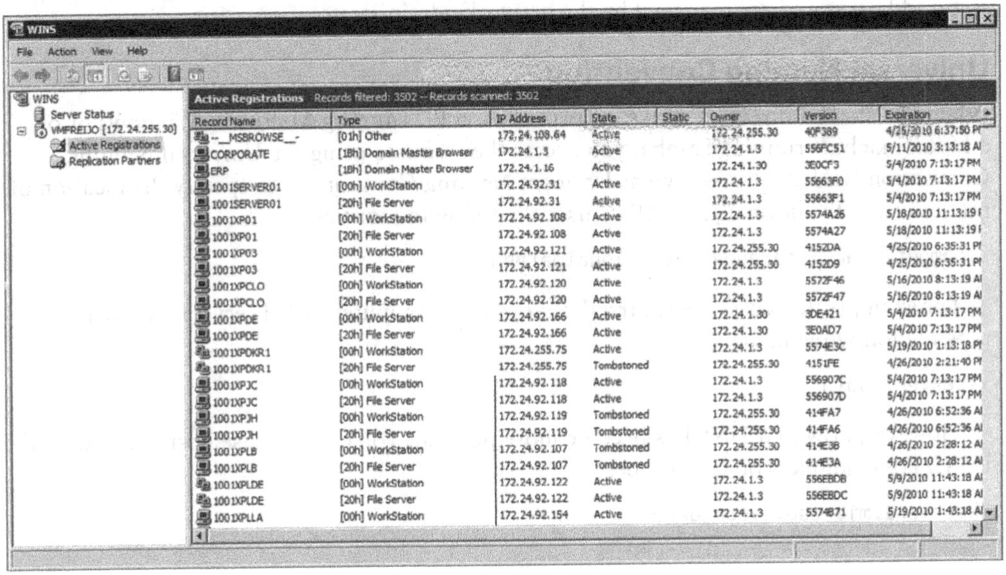

To provide fault tolerance, you should have more than one WINS server with the same WINS database. A WINS replication partner can be added and configured as either a pull partner, a push partner, or a push/pull partner. A pull partner is a WINS server that requests new database entries from its partner on a normal time interval. A push partner is a WINS server that sends update notification messages based on the number of changes to the WINS database. A push/pull partner does a push update based on the number of changes and a pull partner updates on a normal time interval.

If you configure WINS and the clients to use broadcast (known as b-node) to find a WINS server, you need to configure a WINS proxy agent to listen on remote subnets where a WINS server does not exist and forward those requests directly to a WINS server. WINS proxies are typically not needed for most networks because most clients are configured as peer node (known as p-node), which will send a packet directly to the WINS server instead of a broadcast.

DNS GlobalName Zones

Most of the time, when specifying an FQDN, you need only specify the hostname, and each client will have a DNS suffix search list that it appends to the hostname. Therefore, when you want to connect to server01, the client will append a DNS suffix search domain such as acme.com to make it server01.acme.com.

One advantage of WINS is its use of a single-label name instead of FQDNs that require the full name, including the domain. Unfortunately, NetBIOS names/single-label names are not supported with IPv6.

To help an organization retire WINS, Windows Server 2016 supports a specially named zone called GlobalNames, which allows you to define static global records with single-label names without relying on WINS. These entries will typically be used for servers that have static addresses and are managed by the network administrator.

Universal Naming Convention

When you share a directory, drive, or printer on a PC running Microsoft Windows or on a Linux machine running Samba, you access the resource using the Universal Naming Convention (UNC), also known as Uniform Naming Convention, to specify the location of the resource. Traditionally, the UNC uses the following format:

```
\\computername\sharednamed\optionalpathname
```

For example, to access the shared directory on a computer called server1, you would type the following name:

```
\\server1\data
```

However, now that DNS has become more popular, you can also use hostnames with the UNC. For example, you could type:

```
\\server1.microsoft.com\data
```

DHCP Services

As explained in an earlier lesson, it would take hours to configure every host IP configuration, including IP address, addresses of DNS and WINS servers, and any other parameters. Thus, most organizations use *Dynamic Host Configuration Protocol (DHCP)* services to automatically assign IP addresses and related parameters (including subnet mask and default gateway and length of the lease) so that a host can immediately communicate on an IP network when it starts.

A DHCP server maintains a list of IP addresses called a pool. When a DHCP client starts and needs an IP address assigned to it, it broadcasts to a DHCP server asking for a leased address. The client sends messages to UDP port 67, and the server sends messages to UDP port 68.

Here is a high-level overview of what happens with DHCP-enabled clients (sometimes referred to as DORA):

1. **Discovery:** The DHCP-enabled client starts and broadcasts a request for an IP address over the network.

2. **Offer:** Any DHCP servers that receive the request review their pool of IP addresses (DHCP scope) and select one to offer to the client.

3. **Request:** The client reviews the offers and broadcasts a message to the servers, letting them know which IP address it has accepted.

4. **Acknowledge:** All DHCP servers see the message. Those whose offers are not accepted place the IP address back into their pool for a future client request. The server the client accepted acknowledges and provides additional information to complete the client configuration (default gateway, DNS information, and so on).

After a client receives an IP address and additional configuration information, it has it for a specific period of time called the *lease period*. When the lease is 50% expired, the client tries to renew it with the DHCP server. If the client cannot renew the lease, it tries again before the lease expires. At this point, if it cannot renew the lease, it tries to contact an alternate DHCP server. If all attempts fail and the client cannot obtain a new IP address, it autoconfigures with a Microsoft Class B subnet (169.254.0.0/255.255.0.0).

Before it chooses an IP address in this network, the client checks to make sure no other client is using the address it wants to assign by sending an Address Resolution Protocol (ARP) request to the address that it has been assigned. If a reply is received, the address is already being used, and the lease process starts over.

Install DHCP Service Role

To install the DHCP Server service on a Windows Server 2016 computer with Server Manager, perform the following steps.

1. Log on to a server running Windows Server 2016 as **adatum\administrator** with the password of **Pa$$w0rd**.

2. Click Start and click Server Manager.

3. Click Manage ➤ Add Roles and Features. The Add Roles and Features Wizard starts, displaying the Before You Begin page.

4. Click Next. The Select Installation Type page appears.

5. Leave the "Role-based or feature-based installation" radio button selected and click Next. The Select Destination Server page appears.

6. Select the server on which you want to install the roles and/or features and click Next. The Select Server Roles page appears.

7. Select the DHCP Server check box. An Add features that are required for DHCP Server dialog box opens.

8. Click Add Features. Then, click Next. The Select Features page appears.

If your computer does not have a static IP address, a message box appears, recommending that you reconfigure the TCP/IP client with a static address before you install the DHCP Server role.

9. Click Next. The DHCP Server page appears.

10. Click Next. The Confirm Installation Selections page appears.

11. Click Install. The Installation Progress page appears as the wizard installs the role.

12. Click Close. The wizard closes.

Before your DHCP server can provide IP address leases, you have to define a scope that includes a range of IP addresses that can be distributed. See Figure 5.4. A scope will define a single physical subnet on your network to which DHCP services are offered. For the DHCP server to hand out addresses to a subnet, it has to be physically connected to the subnet, or you have to install a DHCP relay agent on the subnet that will relay the DHCP requests to the DHCP server. The DHCP relay agent could be a Windows server or workstation or built into a router or switch.

FIGURE 5.4   DHCP console in Windows Server 2016

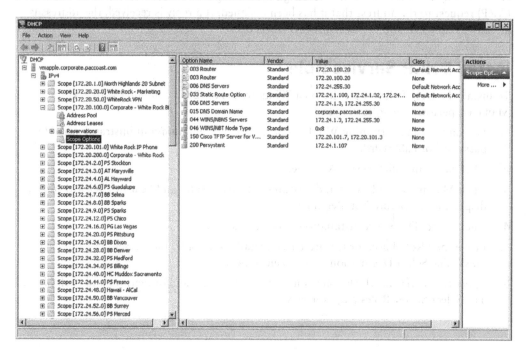

A DHCP server can have only one scope per subnet for each DHCP server. However, you can assign a range of addresses and excluded addresses within the scope for those addresses that are manually assigned to servers or other network devices. After you create a scope, you must activate the scope so that it will be available for lease assignments. To activate a scope in the DHCP console, right-click the console and select Activate.

When a host receives an IP address and related IP configuration from a DHCP server, it assigns them a lease time, which specifies how long the address is assigned to the host. When a DHCP lease has reached 50% of the lease time, the client will automatically attempt to renew the lease in the background. The default lease time is eight days. If, for some reason, the host cannot contact the DHCP server, it will try again and again on the remaining lease time until either it contacts the DHCP server or the lease time runs out.

If you have a client that must always use the same address, you can reserve that address using a client reservation. With a client reservation, the address is reserved for a specific host and will not be assigned to other hosts. If there are multiple DHCP servers handing out addresses, you will have to reserve the same addresses on each DHCP server.

Introducing Directory Services with Active Directory

A *directory service* stores, organizes, and provides access to information in a directory. Directory services are used for locating, managing, administering, and organizing common items and network resources, such as volumes, folders, files, printers, users, groups, devices, telephone numbers, and other objects. One popular directory service used by many organizations is Microsoft's Active Directory.

Certification Ready?

How is a domain used to manage network resources? 3.3

Active Directory is a technology created by Microsoft that provides a variety of network services, including the following:

- LDAP
- Kerberos-based and single sign-on authentication
- DNS-based naming and other network information
- A central location for network administration and delegation of authority

The *Lightweight Directory Access Protocol*, or *LDAP*, is an application protocol for querying and modifying data using directory services running over TCP/IP. Within the directory, the sets of objects are organized in a logical hierarchical manner so that you can easily find and manage them. The structure can reflect geographical or organizational boundaries, although it tends to use DNS names for structuring the topmost levels of the hierarchy. Deeper inside the directory, there might be entries representing people, organizational units, printers, documents, groups of people, or anything else that represents a given tree entry (or multiple entries). LDAP uses TCP port 389.

Kerberos is a computer network authentication protocol, which allows hosts to prove their identity over a nonsecure network in a secure manner. It can also provide mutual authentication so that both the user and server verify each other's identity. For security reasons, Kerberos protocol messages are protected against eavesdropping and replay attacks.

Single sign-on (SSO) allows you to log on once and access multiple related but independent software systems without having to log in again. As you log on with Windows using Active Directory, you are assigned a token, which can then be used to sign on to other systems automatically.

Finally, Active Directory allows you to organize all of your network resources, including users, groups, printers, computers, and other objects, so that you can assign passwords, permissions, and rights to the users on your network. You can also assign who can manage a group of objects.

Introducing Domains, Trees, and Forests

Active Directory domains, trees, and forests are logical representations of your network organization, which allow you to organize them in the best way to manage them. To identify domains, trees, and forests, Active Directory is closely tied to DNS.

Certification Ready?

For what reasons would you use OUs in your domain? 3.2

 Without DNS and SRV records, Active Directory will not be able to function properly.

As mentioned earlier, a Windows domain is a logical unit of computers and network resources that define a security boundary. A domain uses a single Active Directory database to share its common security and user account information for all computers within the domain, allowing centralized administration of all users, groups, and resources on the network.

Because some organizations contain thousands of users and thousands of computers, it might make sense to break an organization into more than one domain. An Active Directory forest contains one or more transitive, trust-linked trees, with each tree linked in a transitive trust hierarchy, so that users and computers from one domain can access resources in another domain. Active Directory is very closely tied to DNS and, in fact, requires it.

A *tree* is made of one or more domains (although most people think of a tree as two or more domains) with contiguous name space. For example, you could have one domain assigned to an organization's developers and another domain assigned to its salespeople:

```
Developers.microsoft.com
```

```
Sales.microsoft.com
```

The Developers and Sales domains would both be child domains of the `microsoft.com` domain.

One of the advantages to using domains is the ability to have a child domains, which are a subdomain of another domain. An administrator can build child domains based on physical locations, departments, etc. Child domains provide greater scalability.

Active Directory has the ability to store millions of objects within a single domain, but child domains allow an administrator the flexibility to design a structure that meets an organization's needs. An example, you may have a site located in a different state. Creating a child domain for that office allows that office to be an independent domain, and thus they can have their own security and domain settings. One or more domains that follow the same contiguous namespace are called a tree.

When an administrator sets up child domains, the parent and child domains automatically establish a trust relationship. Trusts allow users to be granted access to resources in a domain even when their accounts reside in a different domain (we will discuss trusts a little later on in this chapter). To make administration of trust relationships easier, Microsoft has made transitive two-way trusts the default relationship between domains within a forest. A forest is all the trees that are part of the Active Directory structure, and they share a schema and global catalog. This means that by default all domains within the same forest automatically trust one another.

A *forest* is made of one or more trees (although most people think of a forest as two or more trees). A forest differs from a tree because it uses disjointed namespaces between the trees. For example, in a forest, you could have microsoft.com as the root for one tree. Say that Microsoft then purchases another company called Acme (acme.com), and acme.com then becomes the root of another tree. Both trees could be combined into a forest, yet each tree's identity could be kept separate.

To allow users in one domain to access resources in another domain, Active Directory uses *trust relationships*. As mentioned earlier, domains with a tree and forest are automatically created as two-way transitive trusts. A transitive trust is based on the following concept:

> If domain A trusts domain B, and domain B trusts domain C, then domain A trusts domain C.

However, if you have a partnership with another company and you need users from one domain within one organization to access resources in another domain, you can configure an explicit non-transitive trust to be either one way or two way.

Introducing Sites and Domain Controllers

Although domains, trees, and forests are logical representations of your organization, sites and domain controllers represent the physical structure of your network.

A *site* is one or more IP subnets that are connected by a high-speed link, typically defined by a geographical location. For example, say you have a four-story office building. Although the building includes several subnets, all of the computers within the building use layer-2 and layer-3 switches to communicate with each other. If you have multiple sites, each site is connected to other sites over a much slower WAN link (at least slower than the LAN speeds you would find within an individual site). You can then define various network traffic patterns based on how the sites are defined.

When a user logs on, Active Directory clients locate an Active Directory server (using the DNS SRV resource records) known as a domain controller in the same site as the computer. Each domain has its own set of domain controllers to provide access to the domain resources, such as users and computers.

For fault tolerance, a site should have two or more domain controllers. That way, if one domain controller fails, the other domain controller can still service the clients. Note that whenever an object (such as a username or password) is modified, it is automatically replicated to the other domain controllers within a domain.

A *domain controller* is a Windows server that stores a replica of the account and security information for the domain and defines the domain boundaries. To make a computer running Windows Server 2016 a domain controller, you must install the Active Directory Domain Services and execute the dcpromo (short for dc promotion) command.

After you have promoted a computer to a domain controller, you can use several MMC snap-in consoles to manage Active Directory. These consoles are as follows:

Active Directory Users and Computers   Used to manage users, groups, computers, and organizational units.

Active Directory Domains and Trusts   Used to administer domain trusts, domain and forest functional levels, and user principal name (UPN) suffixes.

Active Directory Sites and Services   Used to administer replication of directory data among all sites in an Active Directory Domain Services (AD DS) forest (Figure 5.5).

Active Directory Administrative Center   Used to administer and publish information in the directory, including managing users, groups, computers, domains, domain controllers, and organizational units.

Group Policy Management Console (GPMC)   Provides a single administrative tool for managing Group Policy across the enterprise. GPMC is automatically installed in Windows Server 2016 and subsequent domain controllers but must be downloaded and installed on Windows Server 2003 domain controllers.

FIGURE 5.5   Active Directory Sites and Services console

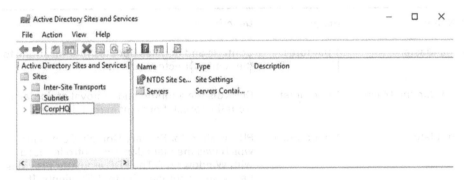

Although these tools are installed on domain controllers, they can also be installed on client PCs so that you can manage Active Directory without logging on to a domain controller.

A server that is not running as a domain controller is known as a *member server*. To demote a domain controller to a member server, you would rerun the dcpromo program.

The replication path, or site topology, within a site is automatically managed by a service called the Knowledge Consistency Checker (KCC). Typically, replication within sites happens more quickly than replication between sites. The Active Directory Sites and Services MMC snap-in allows you to control intersite replication. You can use it to create site-link bridge objects and to configure replication patterns.

Within Active Directory, you need to define each subnet. Once you have done this, Active Directory can figure out the best way to replicate information locally and between sites.

To minimize traffic across a WAN link, bridgehead servers perform directory replication between two sites, whereas only two designated domain controllers talk to each other. If you have domain controllers from multiple domains, you will have a bridgehead server for each domain.

Flexible Single Master Operations

Active Directory uses multimaster replication, which means that there is no master domain controller, commonly referred to as a primary domain controller within Windows NT domains. However, because there are certain functions that can be handled by only one domain controller at a time, Active Directory uses *Flexible Single Master Operations (FSMO) roles*, also known as operations master roles. See Table 5.1 and Figure 5.6.

TABLE 5.1   FSMO roles

Role Name	Scope	Description
Schema Master	1 per forest	Controls and handles updates/modifications to the Active Directory schema.
Domain Naming Master	1 per forest	Controls the addition and removal of domains from the forest if present in root domain.
PDC Emulator	1 per domain	PDC is short for Primary Domain Controller, which was the main domain controller used with Windows NT. The PDC emulator provides backwards compatibility for NT4 clients. It also acts as the primary server for password changes and as the master time server within the domain.
RID Master	1 per domain	Allocates pools of unique identifiers to domain controllers for use when creating objects.
Infrastructure Master	1 per domain	Synchronizes cross-domain group membership changes. The infrastructure master cannot run on a global catalog server unless all DCs are also GCs.

FIGURE 5.6   Domain-level FMSO roles

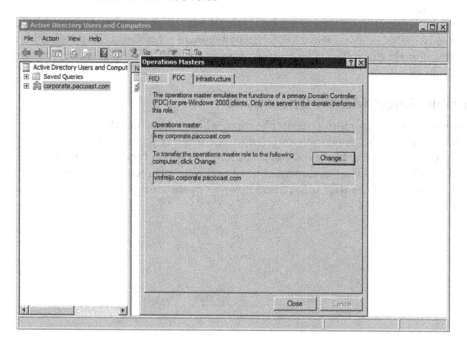

Looking at Global Catalogs

Because the domain controller only has information for the domain and does not store a copy of the objects for other domains, you still need a way to find and access objects in other domains within your tree and forest. A *global catalog* replicates the information of every object in a tree and forest. However, instead of storing the entire object, it stores just those attributes that are most frequently used in search operations, such as a user's first and last name, computer name, and so forth. By default, a global catalog is created automatically on the first domain controller in the forest, but any domain controller can be made into a global catalog. See Figure 5.7.

FIGURE 5.7   Configuring a domain controller as a global catalog

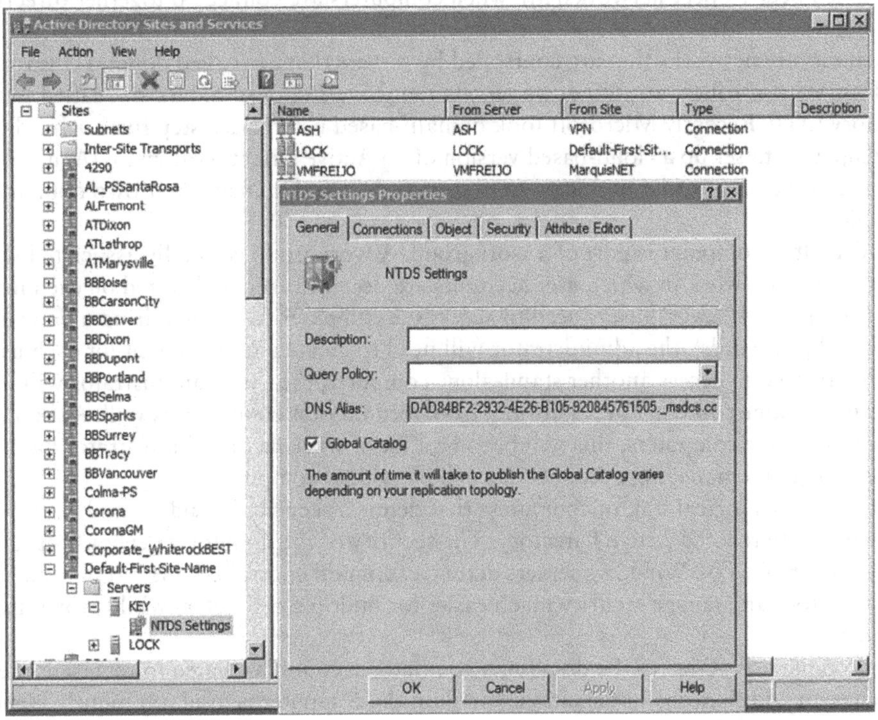

Beyond being used to find objects in a forest, global catalogs are also used during user authentication as follows:

- In Windows 2000 native mode and above domain functional levels, domain controllers must request universal group membership enumeration from a global catalog server.

- When a user principal name (UPN) is used at logon and the forest has more than one domain, a global catalog server is required to resolve the name. A UPN follows the same format as an email address (i.e., username@domainname.ext).

Lastly, a global catalog is needed for universal group membership caching. In a forest that has more than one domain, and in sites that have domain users but no global catalog server, universal group membership caching can be used to enable caching of logon credentials so that the global catalog does not have to be contacted for subsequent user logons. This feature eliminates the need to retrieve universal group memberships across a WAN link from a global catalog server in a different site. Besides having a global catalog in each geographical site, it is a best practice to enable universal group membership caching in each geographic site.

Domain versus Workgroup

Microsoft offers two main networks: workgroup-based or domain-based. Workgroups (also called peer-to-peer networks) are when computers are connected together directly to each other.

Domains are networks that are controlled by servers that are called domain controllers. Domain controllers are Windows servers that have a copy of a database called Active Directory (AD). Recently Microsoft took domain-based networks a step further by allowing companies to set up a cloud-based version of an Active Directory domain (Azure AD). This means that companies no longer need to maintain and manage their own domain controllers.

By default, a computer is part of a workgroup. A workgroup is usually associated with a peer-to-peer network in which user accounts are decentralized and stored on each individual computer. If several users need to access the computer (while requiring unique usernames and passwords), the administrator will need to create a user account for each user. If those users need to access another stand-alone computer, then the administrator will have to create the same computer accounts and password on that computer as well. As you can see, with multiple computers, this will become a lot of work as the administrator has to keep creating and managing accounts on each individual computer.

A domain is a logical unit of computers that define a security boundary and is usually linked with Microsoft's Active Directory. The security of the domain is generally centralized and controlled by Windows servers acting as domain controllers. As a result, an administrator can manage security much easier for multiple computers while providing better security.

If a computer is added to the domain, a computer account is created to represent the computer. In addition, the information stored on the computer is used to uniquely identify the computer. When these items match, it shows that a computer is who it says it is, which contributes to a more secure work environment.

In a workgroup:

- All computers are peers; no computer has control over another computer.

- Each computer has a set of user accounts. To use any computer in the workgroup, must have an account on that computer.

- There are typically no more than ten to twenty computers.

- All computers must be on the same local network or subnet.

In a domain:

- One or more computers are servers. Administrators use servers to control the security and permissions for all computers on the domain. This makes it easy to make changes because the changes are automatically made to all computers.

- If you have a user account on the domain, you can log on to any computer on the domain without needing an account on that computer.

- There can be hundreds or thousands of computers.

- The computers can be on different local networks.

Adding a Computer to the Domain

Open System Properties and click the Change button. Then select the Domain option and type in the name of the domain. Next, click the OK button. It will prompt you to log in with a domain account that has the ability to add computers to the domain. This is typically a domain administrator or account administrator. After entering the credentials (username and password), a Welcome dialog box appears. Click OK to close the Welcome dialog box. When you close the System Properties dialog box, it will prompt you to reboot the computer.

Remove a Computer from a Domain

Select the workgroup option and type in the name of the workgroup and click OK. If you are removing yourself from the domain, you will be asked for administrative credentials so that it can delete the account from Active Directory. If you don't specify administrative credentials, it will still remove the computer from the domain, but the computer account will still remain within Active Directory.

Defining Functional Levels

In Active Directory, you can have domain controllers running different versions of Windows servers, such as Windows 2008 R2, Windows Server 12, Windows Server 2012 R2, or Windows Server 2016. The *functional level* of a domain or forest depends on which Windows Server operating system versions are running on the domain controllers in that domain or forest. The functional level also controls which advanced features are available in the domain or forest. To get all of the features available with Active Directory, you must have the latest version of the Windows Server operating system, and you have to use the highest forest and domain functional level. Of course, you must take care before migrating to the higher functional level because doing so may close out some legacy features that were only available with the older functional levels. Upgrading to a higher functional level is a one-way process that cannot be reversed. As of Windows Server 2016, there are five available domain functional levels: Windows Server 2003, Windows Server 2008, Windows Server 2008 R2, Windows Server 2012, and Windows Server 2016. If you have multiple domains within a tree, you can upgrade the functional level of a domain without affecting the other domains. Windows Server 2012, Windows Server 2012 R2, and Windows Server

2016 domain controllers do not support the Windows 2000 native mode functional level that was available with Windows Server 2008 R2 and earlier.

Setting the functional level for a domain enables features that affect the entire domain and that domain only. If all domain controllers in a domain are running Windows Server 2016 and the functional level is set to Windows Server 2016, all domain-wide features are available.

Forest functional levels are similar to domain functional levels, except that it affects all domains within the forest. Windows Server 2016 domain controllers support the following forest functional levels: Windows Server 2008, Windows Server 2008 R2, Windows Server 2012, and Windows Server 2016.

When a forest is raised to a functional level, older domain controllers cannot be introduced into the domain. The forest functional level assumes that all domains are raised to the same level before the forest is raised. For example, to raise the forest functional level to Windows Server 2016, you first have to raise the domain functional levels of all domains to Windows Server 2016. Similar to the domain functional level, raising the forest functional level is generally an irreversible procedure.

More Information

For a list of functions available with each domain and forest functional level, visit the following Web sites:

```
https://docs.microsoft.com/en-us/windows-server/identity/ad-ds/windows-
server-2016-functional-levels
```

Microsoft Passport

Microsoft Passport allows users to set up a key-based authentication that allows them to authenticate by using more than just their password (biometrics or PIN numbers). The users would then log on to their systems using a biometric or PIN number that is linked to a certificate or an asymmetrical key pair.

Microsoft Passport allows the user to access applications and website content without the need for a password. It is built on a technology called asymmetric cryptography.

Microsoft Passport works with a Microsoft account, Azure Active Directory account, on-premises Active Directory, and other Windows applications. The user's identity is stored in the device. Thus, a hacker cannot access a user's account from any location if the user's password is compromised.

Windows Hello is integrated with Microsoft Passport; this calls for the hacker to access the user's biometrics as well to intrude upon a user's profile. That is a very hard task for an attacker to accomplish.

Once the user is authenticated using biometrics, Microsoft Passport is unlocked, which then cryptographically authenticates the user to the applications and websites. The device has a Trusted Platform Module (TPM) that generates and protects the private key. Once the keys are generated, Microsoft Passport allows the user to sign in to third-party apps or services without interruptions.

1. The client attempts to connect to a web application using a browser.

2. The browser uses the Passport API to request access to the identity provider (IDP) key for AD. The IDP sends an authentication challenge to the client device.

3. The private key is used to sign the challenge and send it back as a response with the original challenge along with the ID of the key that was used to sign the challenge.

4. The AD then fetches the corresponding public key for the key ID in the response and checks if the signed challenge matches the original unsigned challenge.

5. Once it is verified, the AD returns a session key that is encrypted with the device's public key and an authentication token that is signed using the session key.

6. The device now uses its own private key to decrypt the session key and then uses that key to decrypt the authentication token.

7. This authentication token is then used to gain access to the web application.

Group Nesting

Group nesting is adding a group as a member of another group. For distribution groups, nesting is supported in both mixed mode and native mode. For security groups, nesting is supported only for domains running in native mode.

Nesting in Native Mode

- A domain local group can contain universal groups, global groups, and accounts from any domain or forest. A domain local group can also contain other domain local groups from the same domain that the group belongs to. A domain local group cannot contain other domain local groups from any other domain or forest.

- A global group can contain other global groups and accounts from the same domain that the group belongs to. A global group cannot contain any universal groups, or any global group or account from another domain.

- A universal group can contain other universal groups, global groups, and accounts from any domain within the forest in which this universal group resides.

Nesting in Mixed Mode

Security groups in a mixed-mode domain have the following restrictions:

- A domain local group can contain global groups and accounts from any domain or forest. A domain local group cannot contain any other domain local group.

- A global group can contain accounts from the same domain to which the group belongs. A global group cannot contain any universal groups, any global group, or an account from another domain.

- Universal groups cannot be created in mixed-mode domains because the universal scope is supported only in Windows 2000 native-mode domains.

Default Hidden and Visible Containers

Not all default containers are needed for an administrator's day-to-day activities. Because of that, there are hidden containers. One of the default reasons why there are hidden containers is to avoid the Active Directory Users and Computers console from looking to messy. Additionally, when an administrator begins adding their own OUs, the number of containers could become more chaotic. However, security is the main reason why there are hidden containers in Active Directory.

To make them visible, enable the Advanced Features option from the View menu.

The following are some of the default containers located in Windows Server 2016:

- Computers - a container for computer accounts
- Domain Controllers - a container for domain controllers
- Foreign Security Principals - a container for security identifiers (SID)
- Keys - a container for key objects
- Managed Service Accounts - a container for managed service accounts
- Users - a container for user accounts

Introducing Organizational Units

As mentioned earlier, a single organization might have thousands of users and thousands of computers. With Windows NT, a domain could only handle a limited number of objects before you encountered some performance issues. With later versions of Windows, the size of the domain was dramatically increased. Although you may have required several domains with Windows NT to define your organization, you could now have just one domain to represent a large organization. However, you still need a way to organize and manage the objects within that domain.

Certification Ready?

What is the best way to assign users to manage other users and computers in Active Directory? 3.2

To help organize objects within a domain and minimize the number of domains you require, you can use *organizational units*, commonly known as OUs. OUs can be used to hold users, groups, computers, and other organizational units. See Figure 5.8. An organizational unit can only contain objects that are located in a domain. Although there are no restrictions on how many nested OUs (an OU inside of another OU) you can have, you should strive to design a shallow hierarchy for better performance.

FIGURE 5.8   Active Directory organizational unit

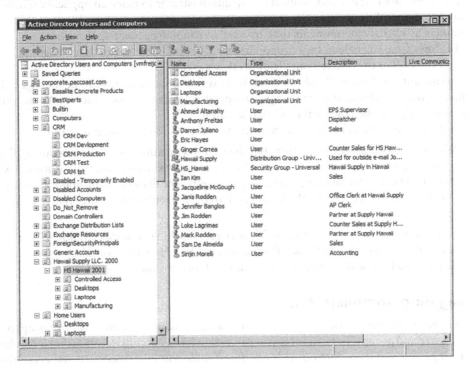

When you first install Active Directory, there are several organizational units already created. They include computers, users, domain controllers, and built-in OUs. Unlike the OUs that you create, these OUs do not allow you to delegate permissions or assign group policies to them. (Group policies will be explained later.) Another OU worth mentioning is the domain controller, which holds the default domain controllers policy.

Containers are objects that can store or hold other objects. They include the forest, tree, domain, and organizational unit. To help manage your objects, you can delegate authority to a container, particularly the domain or organizational unit.

For example, let's say that you have your domain divided by physical location. You can assign a site administrator authoritative control to the OU that represents a physical location so that the user will only have administrative control to the objects within that OU. You can also structure your OUs by function or areas of management. For example, you might create a Sales OU to hold all of your sales users. You might also create a Printers OU to hold all of the printer objects and assign a printer administrator.

Understanding Windows Containers

Windows Containers are independent and isolated environments that run an operating system. These isolated environments allow an administrator to place an application into its own container thus not affecting any other applications or containers. You can think of containers as virtual environments that are used to run independent applications.

Windows Containers load faster than virtual machines and can run as many containers as needed for all of the different applications that are run.

One advantage of using Windows Containers is that the containers can be managed the same way that an administrator manages an operating system. A container works the same way as a newly installed physical or virtual machine.

There are two different types of containers that the Windows Container can use.

- Windows Server Containers - this container allows an administrator to isolate applications so applications can run in their own space and not affect other applications. Windows Containers are smaller, faster, and more efficient than isolating applications. In a Windows Server Container, the kernel is shared between all of the different Windows Containers.

- Hyper-V Containers - these run within a virtual machine, and the Windows Containers don't need to run in a Hyper-V environment. In a Hyper-V Container the container host's kernel is not shared between the other Hyper-V Containers.

Delegating Administration

By delegating administration, you can assign a range of administrative tasks to the appropriate users and groups. For instance, you can assign basic administrative tasks to regular users or groups and leave domain-wide and forest-wide administration to members of the Domain Admins and Enterprise Admins groups. By delegating administration, you allow groups within your organization to take more control of their local network resources. You also help secure your network from accidental or malicious damage by limiting the membership of administrator groups.

You can delegate administrative control to any level of a domain tree by creating organizational units within a domain and delegating administrative control for specific organizational units to particular users or groups.

Delegate Control

To delegate control of an organizational unit, perform the following steps:

1. Open Active Directory Users and Computers.

2. In the console tree, right-click the organizational unit for which you want to delegate control.

3. Click Delegate control to start the Delegation of Control Wizard, and then follow the instructions onscreen.

Looking at Objects

An *object* is a distinct, named set of attributes or characteristics that represent a network resource. Common objects used within Active Directory are computers, users, groups, and printers. Attributes have values that define the specific object. For example, a user could have the first name John, the last name Smith, and the login name as jsmith, all of which identify the user.

Certification Ready?

Why is it important to define users within Active Directory? 3.1

When working with objects, administrators use the names of the objects, such as usernames. However, Active Directory objects are assigned a 128-bit unique number called a globally unique identifier (GUID), sometimes referred to as a security identifier (SID), to uniquely identify an object. Therefore, if a user changes his or her name, you can change his or her username yet he or she will still be able to access all objects and have all of the rights he or she had previously, because these are assigned to the GUID.

GUIDs also provide some security. In particular, if a user is deleted, you cannot create a new user account with the same username and expect to have access to all of the objects and rights the previous user had access to. Thus, if you decide to let someone go within your organization but you plan to replace that person, you can disable the account, hire the new person, rename the user account, change the password, and re-enable the account so that the new person can access all resources and have all of the rights that the previous user had.

The schema of Active Directory defines the format of each object and the attributes or fields within each object. The default schema contains definitions of commonly used objects, such as user accounts, computers, printers, and groups. For example, the schema defines that a user account has the user's first name, last name, and telephone number.

To allow Active Directory to be flexible so that it can support other applications, you can extend the schema to include additional attributes. For example, you could add badge number or employee identification number to the user object. Indeed, when you install some applications, such as Microsoft Exchange, they will extend the schema, usually by adding additional attributes or fields so that the schema can support the application.

Looking at Users

A *user account* enables a user to log on to a computer and domain. As a result, it can be used to prove the identity of a user, and this identity information can then be used to determine what the user can access and what kind of authorization he or she has. It can also be used for auditing so that if there is a security problem in which something was accessed or deleted, the person who accessed or deleted the object can be determined.

On today's Windows networks, there are two types of user accounts:

- Local user accounts

- Domain user accounts

A user account allows users to log on and access resources on the computer in which the account was created. The local user account is stored in the Security Account Manager (SAM) database on the local computer. The only Windows computer that does not have a SAM database is the domain controller. The administrator local user account is the only account that is both created and enabled by default in Windows. Although this account cannot be deleted, it can be renamed.

The only other account created (but not enabled) by default is the guest account. This account was created for the occasional user who needs access to network resources on a low-security network. Use of the guest account is not recommended, and this account is disabled by default.

A domain user account is stored on the domain controller and allows you to gain access to resources within the domain, assuming you have been granted permissions to access those objects. The administrator domain user account is the only account that is created and enabled by default in Windows when you first create a domain. Although the administrator domain user account cannot be deleted, it can be renamed.

When you create a domain user account, you must supply a first name, last name, and user logon name. The user logon name must be unique within the domain. See Figure 5.9. After the user account is created, you can then open the user account properties and configure a person's username, logon hours, telephone numbers, and addresses; which computers the user can log on to; what groups the person is a member of, and so on. You can also specify whether a password expires, whether the password can be changed, and whether the account is disabled. Lastly, in the Profile tab, you can define the user's home directory, logon script, and profile path. See Figure 5.10.

FIGURE 5.9   User Account in Active Directory

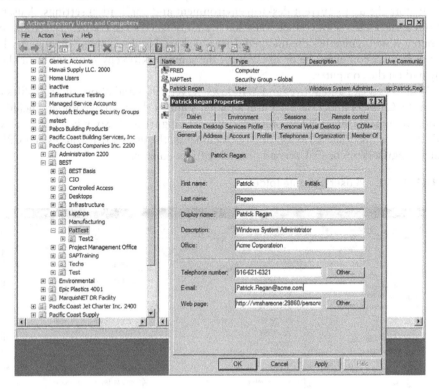

FIGURE 5.10   Profile tab

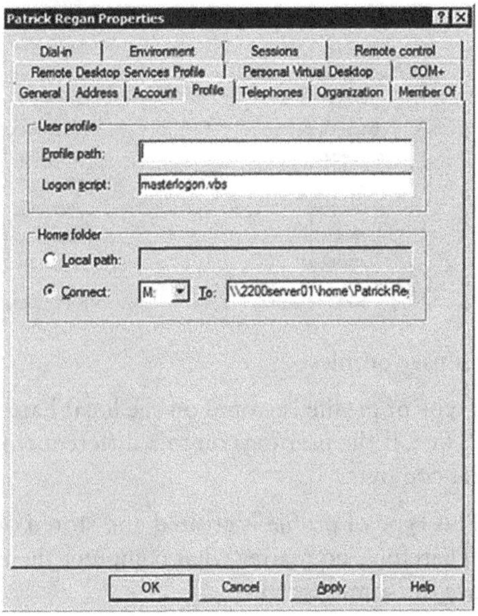

Associated with a user account is the user profile, which is a collection of folders and data that store the user's current desktop environment and application settings. A user profile also records all network connections that are established so that when a user logs on to a computer, it will remember the mapped drives to shared folders. Thus, when a user logs on to a particular computer, he or she will get the same desktop environment he or she previously had on the computer.

For Windows Vista and above, and Windows Server 2008 and above, user profiles are stored in the C:\Users folder. In each user's folder, some of the available folders include Desktop, Documents, Start Menu, and Favorites. See Figure 5.11. So, when ad_patrickreg directly accesses his or her Desktop or My Documents, the user is really accessing C:\Users\ad_patrickreg\Desktop or C:\Users\ad_patrickreg\Documents.

FIGURE 5.11   A user's profile folder

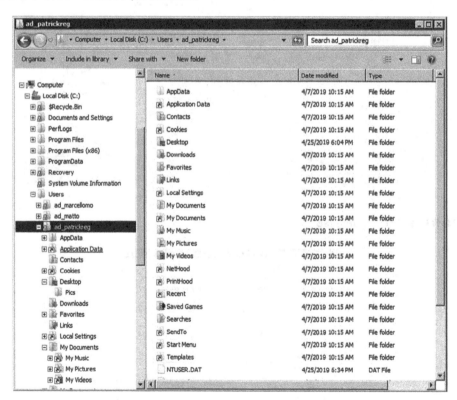

There are three types of user profiles:

Local User Profile   This type of profile is stored on the local hard drive of the computer the user is logging on to. Thus, if the user logs on to a different computer, he or she will get the default settings for that computer.

Roaming User Profile   This type of profile is created and stored on a shared folder on a server over the network. Therefore, no matter what computer the user logs on to within the domain, he or she will have the same settings.

Mandatory User Profile This type of profile is used as a roaming profile in which the settings can be changed but, when the user logs on again, all settings are reset to their default values.

Looking at Computers

Like user accounts, Windows *computer accounts* provide a means for authenticating and auditing a computer's access to a Windows network and access to domain resources. Each Windows computer to which you want to grant access must have a unique computer account. See Figure 5.12. A computer account can also be used for auditing purposes, specifying what system was used when something was accessed.

FIGURE 5.12   Computer account

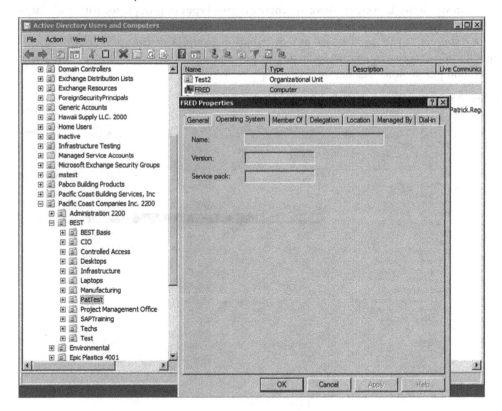

Introducing Groups

A *group* is a collection or list of user accounts or computer accounts. Different from a container, a group does not store user or computer information; rather, it just lists it. The advantage of using groups is that they simplify administration, especially when assigning rights and permissions.

Certification Ready?

How do groups simplify security? 3.1

A group is used to group users and computers together so that when you assign rights and permissions, you assign them to the entire group rather than to each user individually. Users and computers can be members of multiple groups, and in some instances, a group can be assigned to another group.

Comparing Group Types

In Windows Active Directory, there are there are two types of groups: security and distribution. A *security group* is used to assign rights and permissions and gain access to network resources. It can also be used as a distribution group. A *distribution group* is used only for non-security functions, such as distributing email, and it cannot be used to assign rights and permissions. See Figure 5.13.

FIGURE 5.13   Active Directory group

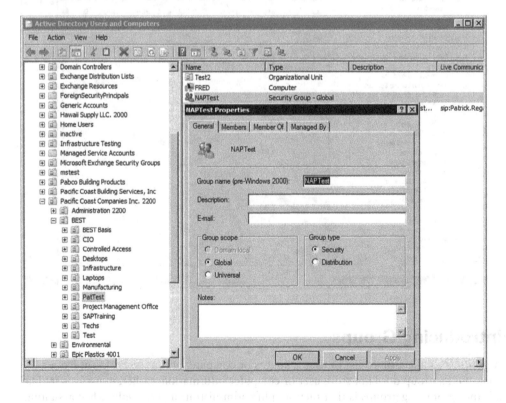

Comparing Group Scopes

Any group, whether a security group or a distribution group, is characterized by a scope that identifies the extent to which the group is applied in the domain tree or forest. The three group scopes (also described in Table 5.2) are as follows:

Domain Local Group   A domain local group contains global groups and universal groups, even though it can also contain user accounts and other domain local groups. It is usually in the domain with the resource to which you want to assign permissions or rights.

Global Group   Global groups can contain user accounts and other global groups. Global groups are designed to be "global" for the domain. After you place user accounts into global groups, the global groups are typically placed into domain local groups or local groups.

Universal Group   This group scope is designed to contain global groups from multiple domains. Universal groups can contain global groups, other universal groups, and user accounts. Because global catalogs replicate universal group membership, you should limit the membership to global groups. This way, if you change a member within a global group, the global catalog will not have to replicate the change.

TABLE 5.2   Group Scopes

Scope	Group can include as members...	Group can be assigned permissions in...	Group scope can be converted to...
Universal	Accounts from any domain within the forest in which the universal group resides; global groups from any domain within the forest in which the universal group resides; universal groups from any domain within the forest in which the universal group resides	Any domain or forest	Domain local Global (as long as no other universal groups exist as members)
Global	Accounts from the same domain as the parent global group; global groups from the same domain as the parent global group	Any domain	Universal (as long as it is not a member of any other global groups)
Domain local	Accounts from any domain; global groups from any domain; universal groups from any domain; domain local groups but only from the same domain as the parent domain local group	Only the same domain as the parent domain local group	Universal (as long as no other domain local groups exist as members)

When assigning rights and permissions, you should always try to arrange your users into groups and assign the rights and permissions to the group instead of the individual users. To effectively manage the use of groups when assigning access to a network resource using global groups and domain local groups, remember the mnemonic AGDLP (Accounts, Global, Domain Local, Permissions):

- Add the user account (A) into the global group (G) in the domain in which the user exists.
- Add the global group (G) from the user domain into the domain local group (DL) in the resource domain.
- Assign permissions (P) on the resource to the domain local group (DL) in its domain.

If you are using universal groups, the mnemonic is expanded to AGUDLP:

- Add the user account (A) into the global group (G) in the domain in which the user exists.
- Add global groups (G) from the user domain into the universal group (U).
- Add universal group (U) to the domain local group (DL).
- Assign permissions (P) on the resource to the domain local group (DL) in its domain.

Looking at Built-in Groups

Similar to the administrator and guest accounts, Windows has default groups called *built-in groups*. These default groups are granted specific rights and permissions to get you started. Various built-in groups are as follows:

Domain Admins   Members of this group can perform administrative tasks on any computer within the domain. The default, the Administrator account, is a member.

Domain Users   Windows automatically adds each new domain user account to the Domain Users group.

Account Operators   Members of this group can create, delete, and modify user accounts and groups.

Backup Operators   Members of this group can backup and restore all domain controllers by using Windows Backup.

Authenticated Users   This group includes all users with a valid user account on the computer or in Active Directory. Use the Authenticated Users group instead of the Everyone group to prevent anonymous access to a resource.

Everyone   This group includes all users who access a computer, even if a particular user does not have a valid account.

Introducing Group Policy

Group Policy is one of the most powerful features of Active Directory that controls the working environment for user accounts and computer accounts. Group Policy provides centralized management and configuration of operating systems, applications, and user settings in an Active Directory environment. For example, you can use Group Policy to specify how often a user has to change his or her password, what the background image on a person's computer is, or whether spell checking is required before a user can send an email.

Certification Ready?

What is Group Policy, and how does it help you manage your network? 3.4

There are literally thousands of settings that can be used to restrict certain actions, make a system more secure, or standardize a working environment. A setting can control a computer registry, NTFS security, audit and security policy, software installation, folder redirection, offline folders, or logon and logoff scripts. *Group Policy* is one of the most powerful features of Active Directory that controls the working environment for user accounts and computer accounts. Group Policy (see Figure 5.14) provides centralized management and configuration of operating systems, applications, and user settings in an Active Directory environment. As each server version is released, Microsoft usually adds additional parameters.

FIGURE 5.14   Group Policy Editor

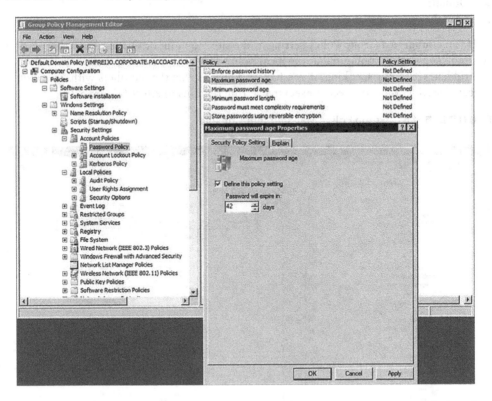

Group Policy objects (GPOs) are collections of user and computer settings including the following:

System Settings   Application settings, desktop appearance, and behavior of system services.

Security Settings   Local computer, domain, and network security settings.

Software Installation Settings   Management of software installation, updates, and removal.

Scripts Settings   Scripts for when a computer starts or shuts down and for when a user logs on and off.

Folder Redirection Settings   Storage for users' folders on the network.

Applying Group Policy

Group Policy can be set locally on a workstation or set at different levels (site, domain, or organizational unit) within Active Directory. Generally speaking, you will not find as many settings locally as you will at the site, domain, or OU level. When group policies are applied, they are applied in the following order:

1. Local

2. Site

3. Domain

4. OU

If you configure a Group Policy setting at the site, domain, or OU level and that setting contradicts a setting configured at the local policy level; the local policy setting will be overridden. Generally speaking, if you have a policy setting that conflicts with a previous executed setting, the more recent executed setting remains in effect (Figure 5.15).

FIGURE 5.15   Group Policy Management Console

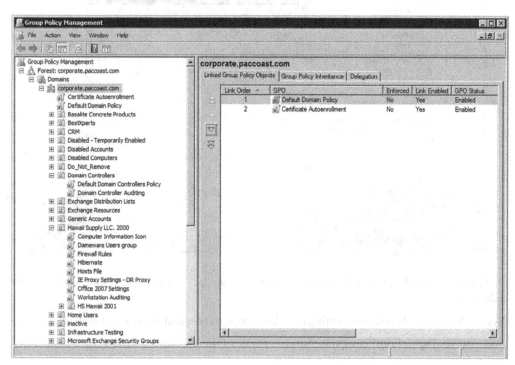

Access the Local Group Policy Editor

You can open the Local Group Policy Editor by using gpedit.msc at a command line or by using the Microsoft Management Console (MMC). To open the Local Group Policy Editor from the command line, perform the following steps:

1. Open MMC. (Click Start, click in the Start Search box, type **mmc**, and then press Enter.)
2. On the File menu, click Add/Remove Snap-in.
3. In the Add or Remove Snap-in dialog box, click Group Policy Object Editor, and then click Add.
4. In the Select Group Policy Object dialog box, click Browse.
5. Click This computer to edit the Local Group Policy object, or click Users to edit Administrator, Non-Administrator, or per-user Local Group Policy objects.
6. Click Finish.

Most times, you only need to access the security settings that you found in the local policy. This can be done by opening the Local Security Policy from Administrative Tools.

Comparing Rights and Permissions

Precisely what a user can or cannot do on a system or to a resource is determined by two things:

- Rights
- Permissions

A *right* authorizes a user to perform certain actions on a computer, such as logging on to a system interactively or backing up files and directories on a system. User rights are assigned through local policies or Active Directory Group Policy. See Figure 5.16.

A *permission* defines the type of access that is granted to an object (an object can be identified with a security identifier) or object attribute. The most common objects assigned permissions are NTFS files and folders, printers, and Active Directory objects. Which users can access an object and what actions those users are authorized to perform are recorded in the access control list (ACL), which lists all users and groups that have access to the object. NTFS and printer permissions will be discussed in the next lesson.

FIGURE 5.16   Group Policy User Rights Assignment

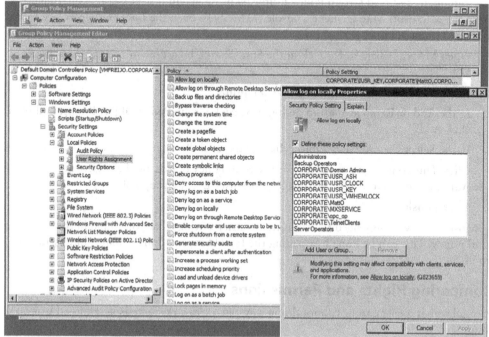

Skill Summary

In this lesson you learned:

- Besides becoming the standard for the Internet, DNS, short for Domain Name System, is a hierarchical client/server-based distributed database management system that translates domain/hosts names to IP addresses.

- A fully qualified domain name (FQDN) describes the exact position of a host within a DNS hierarchy.

- The legacy naming service is Windows Internet Name Service or WINS, which translates from NetBIOS (computer name) to specify a network resource.

- When you share a directory, drive, or printer on a PC running Microsoft Windows or on a Linux machine running Samba, you can access the resource by using the Universal Naming Convention (UNC), also known as Uniform Naming Convention, to specify the location of the resource.

- Dynamic Host Configuration Protocol (DHCP) services automatically assign IP addresses and related parameters (including subnet mask and default gateway and length of the lease) so that a host can immediately communicate on an IP network when it starts.

- The Lightweight Directory Access Protocol, or LDAP, is an application protocol for querying and modifying data using directory services running over TCP/IP.

- Active Directory domains, trees, and forests are logical representations of network organization, which allow you to organize them in the best way to manage them.

- Sites and domain controllers represent the physical structure of a network.

- A site is one or more IP subnets that are connected by a high-speed link, typically defined by a geographical location.

- A domain controller is a Windows server that stores a replica of the account and security information for the domain and defines the domain boundaries.

- A server that is not running as a domain controller is known as a member server.

- To minimize traffic across a WAN link, bridgehead servers perform directory replication between two sites, whereas only two designated domain controllers talk to each other.

- Active Directory uses multimaster replication, which means that there is no master domain controller.

- Because there are certain functions that can only be handled by one domain controller at a time, Active Directory uses Flexible Single Master Operations (FSMO) roles.

- A global catalog holds replicate information of every object in a tree and forest.

- The functional level of a domain or forest controls which advanced features are available in the domain or forest.

- To help organize objects within a domain and minimize the number of domains, you can use organizational units, commonly known as OUs.

- You can delegate administrative control to any level of a domain tree by creating organizational units within a domain and delegating administrative control for specific organizational units to particular users or groups.

- A user account enables a user to log on to a computer and domain. As a result, it can used to prove the identity of a user, and this information can then be used to determine what a user can access and what kind of access they will have (authorization).

- Windows computer accounts provide a means for authenticating and auditing a computer's access to a Windows network and to domain resources.

- A group is a collection of user accounts or computer accounts.

- Group Policy provides the centralized management and configuration of operating systems, applications, and user settings in an Active Directory environment.

- A right authorizes a user to perform certain actions on a computer.

- A permission defines the type of access that is granted to an object (an object can be identified with a security identifier) or object attribute.

Knowledge Assessment

Fill in the Blank

1. The file that is used to resolve hostnames to IP addresses is _____.

2. The resource record used in DNS to resolve IP address to hostnames is _____.

3. The _____ automatically assigns IP addresses and other IP configuration to a host.

4. _____ is a popular directory service with objects in a logical hierarchical manner.

5. The _____ are roles that provide certain functions that can only be handled by one domain controller.

6. A(n) _____ is used to organize the objects within a domain.

7. Printers, users, and computers are examples of _____ in Active Directory.

8. The local security database found on a member server is known as the _____.

9. A collection or list of users is known as _____.

10. The _____ built-in group is used to create, delete, and modify user accounts and groups.

Multiple Choice

1. The primary naming service used in Windows is _____.
   A. AD
   B. WINS
   C. DNS
   D. DHCP

2. What is the resource record that translates from hostname to IP address in DNS?
   A. PTR
   B. H
   C. IP
   D. A

3. _____ is a legacy naming system used to translate Computer Names/NetBIOS names to IP addresses.
   A. AD
   B. WINS

C. DNS

D. DHCP

4. What is the master time server?

   A. Schema Master

   B. Domain Naming Master

   C. PDC Emulator

   D. RID Master

5. What holds replica information of every object in a tree and forest?

   A. Infrastructure Master

   B. Schema Master

   C. Global Catalog

   D. PDC Emulator

6. Which group scope is meant to be used to assign permissions to a local resource?

   A. Distribution group

   B. Domain local

   C. Global

   D. Captured

7. Which group scope can contain global groups from multiple domains?

   A. Emulation

   B. Domain local

   C. Global

   D. Universal

8. What can be used to specify how many times a user can enter a login with an incorrect password before the account is disabled?

   A. User profile

   B. Group policy

   C. Software policy

   D. User account collection

9. To which of the following can a group policy not be directly applied?

   A. Group

   B. Site

   C. Domain

   D. OU

10. What authorizes a user to perform certain actions on a computer?

    A. Permission

    B. UNC

    C. Right

    D. Task

True/False

1. A collection is two or more trees.

2. A site and domain controllers are the physical aspects of the network.

3. A member server is running Active Directory domain services.

4. Higher domain and forest functional levels will enhance the functionality of Active Directory.

5. Active Directory is closely tied to DNS.

Competency Assessment

Scenario 5-1: Designing Active Directory

You have ten sites throughout the country and five major departments. How would you design your Active Directory structure?

Scenario 5-2: Designing AD Physical Structure

How do you define how the domain controllers will replicate data to the other domain controllers?

Proficiency Assessment

Scenario 5-3: Installing Active Directory

Install Active Directory services and promote your computer to a domain controller with the domain name of domain*xx* where *xx* is your student number. If you do not have a student number, use 01.

Scenario 5-4: Managing a Domain

Next, create three users in each OU. Then create a group in each OU that contains the members of the OU. Create a user called JSmith in the Engineering OU. Add JSmith to the Engineers group.

 Real World Scenario

Workplace Ready: User Administrator and Service Accounts

Active Directory is a major part of many corporations and is central to authentication, authorization, and auditing. However, you must sometimes think a bit out of the box to get everything possible out of Active Directory, including making your network as secure as you can.

Running your system as an administrator gives you great power and responsibility. Because you have access to so much, you can accidentally or unknowingly cause problems. For example, if your system is infected with malware, such as a virus, this malware can spread to other computers because you have permission to access those computers. As a safety precaution, you should consider creating two accounts for administrators. The "normal" user account should be used for performing day-to-day tasks, such as accessing a person's personal files, checking email, or running reports. The "administrator" account should be used for accessing servers and applications that need to be managed or reconfigured. You can even login as the "normal" account and temporarily switch your context by executing the runas command at the command prompt, using the run option, or right-clicking an executable and selecting Run as Administrator.

Some applications and services need to run as administrator or with administrative permissions. Therefore, you can create a user account and assign the minimum permissions needed for the application to run properly. As a side note, it is not recommended that you use "normal" user accounts to run application or services because people leave from time to time. If you disable an account that an application or service is running, the application or service will fail to run.

Lesson 6

File and Print Services

Key Terms

administrative shares	NTFS permissions
auditing	owner
driver deployment	print device
effective permissions	print job
Encrypted File System (EFS)	printer
encryption	printer permissions
explicit permission	printer pools
inherited permission	share permission
Internet printing	shared folder
local printers	web printing
network printers	web management

 Real World Scenario

Lesson 6 Case

Say you have multiple servers running Windows Server 2016. You want to centralize your document storage and printing so that users can easily access files while providing an efficient way to back up data files. In addition, you want to buy two large, fast color printers that will be centrally located to handle many large print jobs.

Introducing NTFS

In Lesson 3, you learned that NTFS is the preferred file system in part because it supports much larger hard disks and a higher level of reliability. In addition, NTFS offers better security through permissions and encryption.

Certification Ready

Why is NTFS the preferred file system? 2.4

In this lesson, a permission is defined as the type of access that is granted to an object, such as NTFS files and folders. When files and folders are created on an NTFS volume, a security descriptor known as an Access Control List (ACL) is created. This descriptor includes information that controls which users and groups can access the file or folder, as well as what type of access is granted to particular users and groups. Each assignment of permissions to a user or group is represented as an access control entry (ACE).

NTFS permissions are managed using Windows Explorer (explorer.exe).

Setting NTFS Permissions

NTFS permissions allow you to control which users and groups can gain access to files and folders on an NTFS volume. The advantage of NTFS permissions is that they affect local users as well as network users.

Usually, when assigning NTFS permissions, you would assign the following standard permissions:

Full Control This is permission to read, write, modify, and execute files in a folder; change attributes and permissions; and take ownership of a folder or the files within it.

Modify This is permission to read, write, modify, and execute files in a folder, as well as change attributes of the folder or the files within it.

Read & Execute This is permission to display a folder's contents; display the data, attributes, owner, and permissions for files within the folder; and run files within the folder.

List Folder Contents This is permission to display a folder's contents; display the data, attributes, owner, and permissions for files within the folder; and run files within the folder.

Read This is permission to display a file's data, attributes, owner, and permissions.

Write This is permission to write to a file, append to the file, and read or change the file's attributes.

While List Folder Contents and Read & Execute appear to have the same special permissions, these permissions are inherited differently. List Folder Contents is inherited by folders but not files, while Read & Execute is inherited by both files and folders.

To manage NTFS permissions, right-click a drive, folder, or file and select Properties; then select the Security tab. As shown in Figure 6.1, you should see the group and users who have been given NTFS permissions and their respective standard NTFS permissions. To change the permissions, click the Edit button.

FIGURE 6.1   NTFS permissions

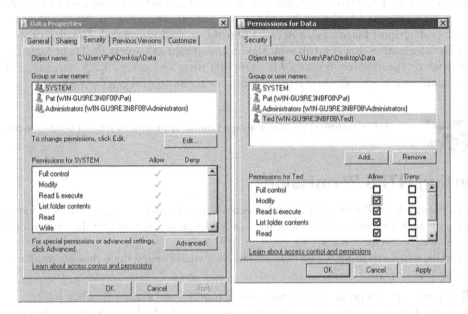

Each of the standard permissions consists of a logical group of special permissions. The available special permissions are as follows:

Traverse Folder/Execute File   Traverse folder allows or denies moving through folders to reach other files or folders, even if the user has no permissions for the traversed folders. By default, the Everyone group is granted the Bypass traverse checking user right. (This applies to folders only.) Execute file allows or denies running program files. (This applies to files only.) Setting the Traverse folder permission on a folder does not automatically set the Execute file permission on all files within that folder.

List Folder/Read Data   List folder allows or denies viewing filenames and subfolder names within a folder. List folder affects the contents of that folder only and does not affect whether the folder you are setting the permission on will be listed. (This applies to folders only.) Read data allows or denies viewing data in files. (This applies to files only.)

Read Attributes   Read attributes allows or denies viewing the attributes of a file or folder, such as read-only and hidden.

Read Extended Attributes   This permission allows or denies viewing the extended attributes of a file or folder. Extended attributes are defined by programs and may vary by program.

Create Files/Write Data   Create files allows or denies creating files within a folder. (This applies to folders only.) Write data allows or denies making changes to a file and overwriting existing content. (This applies to files only.)

Create Folders/Append Data   Create folders allows or denies creating folders within a folder. (This applies to folders only.) Append data allows or denies making changes to the end of a file but not changing, deleting, or overwriting existing data. (This applies to files only.)

Write Attributes   Write attributes allows or denies changing the attributes of a file or folder, such as read-only or hidden. The Write attributes permission does not imply creating or deleting files or folders; it only includes the permission to make changes to the attributes of a file or folder. To allow (or deny) create or delete operations, see Create files/Write data, Create folders/Append data, Delete subfolders and files, and Delete.

Write Extended Attributes   This permission allows or denies changing the extended attributes of a file or folder. Extended attributes are defined by programs and may vary by program. The Write extended attributes permission does not imply creating or deleting files or folders; it only includes the permission to make changes to the attributes of a file or folder. To allow (or deny) create or delete operations, see Create folders/Append data, Delete subfolders and files, and Delete.

Delete Subfolders and Files   This permission allows or denies deleting subfolders and files, even if the Delete permission has not been granted on the subfolder or file.

Delete   Delete allows or denies deleting the file or folder. If you do not have Delete permission on a file or folder, you can still delete it if you have been granted Delete subfolders and files permission on the parent folder.

Read Permissions   This allows or denies reading the permissions of a file or folder, such as full control, read, and write.

Change Permissions   This allows or denies changing the permissions of a file or folder, such as full control, read, and write.

Take Ownership   This permission allows or denies taking ownership of a file or folder. The owner of a file or folder can always change permissions on it, regardless of any existing permissions on the file or folder.

Synchronize   Synchronize allows or denies different threads to wait on the handle for a file or folder and synchronize with another thread that may signal it. This permission applies only to multithreaded, multiprocess programs.

Table 6.1 shows the special permissions assigned to each standard NTFS permission. If for some reason you need more granular control, you can assign special permissions. To assign special permissions, right-click a drive, folder, or file, click on Properties, and select the Security tab. Then click the Advanced button to open the Advanced Security Settings, where you can click Add, Edit, or Remove buttons, click the Change Permissions button, and click the Add, Edit, or Remove button. See Figure 6.2.

TABLE 6.1 NTFS permissions

Special Permissions	Full Control	Modify	Read & Execute	List Folder Contents (folders only)	Read	Write
Traverse folder/Execute file	x	x	x	X		
List folder/Read data	x	x	x	X	x	
Read attributes	x	x	x	X	x	
Read extended attributes	x	x	x	X	x	
Create files/Write data	x	x				x
Create folders/Append data	x	x				x
Write attributes	x	x				x
Write extended attributes	x	x				x
Delete subfolders and files	x					
Delete	x	x				
Read permissions	x	x	x	x	x	x
Change permissions	x					
Take ownership	x					
Synchronize	x	x	x	x	x	x

Groups or users that are granted full control permission on a folder can delete any files in that folder regardless of the permissions protecting the file. In addition, the List folder contents permission is inherited by folders but not files, and it should only appear when you view folder permissions. In Windows Server 2016, the Everyone group does not include the Anonymous Logon group by default, so permissions applied to the Everyone group do not affect the Anonymous Logon group.

To simplify administration, you can grant permissions using groups. By assigning NTFS permissions to a group, you are granting permissions to one or more people simultaneously, reducing the number of entries in each access list, as well as the amount of effort required to grant multiple people access to certain files or folders.

FIGURE 6.2   Advanced Security Settings

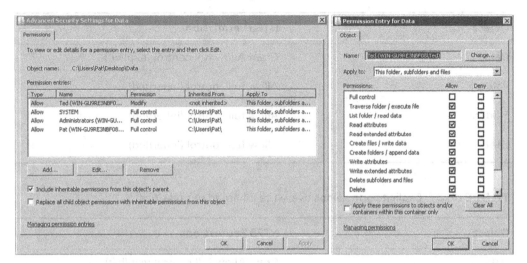

Looking at Effective NTFS Permissions

The folder/file structure on an NTFS drive can be complicated, with many folders and nested folders. In addition, because you can assign permissions to groups and at different levels on an NTFS volume, figuring out the effective permissions of a particular folder or file for a particular user can be tricky.

There are two types of permissions used in NTFS:

Explicit Permissions   Permissions granted directly to a file or folder.

Inherited Permissions   Permissions that are granted to a folder (parent object or container) that flow into a child objects (subfolders or files inside the parent folder).

When assigning permissions to a folder, by default, the permissions apply to both the folder and the subfolders and files within it. To stop permissions from being inherited, you can select the "Replace all existing inheritable permissions on all descendants with inheritable permissions from this object" check box in the Advanced Security Settings dialog box. You will then be asked whether you are sure you want to proceed. You can also clear the "Allow inheritable permissions from parent to propagate to this object" check box. When this check box is clear, Windows will respond with a Security dialog box. When you click the Copy button, the explicit permission will be copied from the parent folder to the subfolder or file. You can then change the subfolder's or file's explicit permissions. If you click the Remove button, you will remove the inherited permission altogether.

By default, any objects within a folder inherit the permissions from that folder when they are created (Table 6.2). However, explicit permissions take precedence over inherited permissions (Table 6.3). So, if you grant different permissions at a lower level, the lower-level permissions take precedence.

TABLE 6.2   Inherited permissions

Object	NTFS Permissions
Data	Grant Allow full control (explicit)
Folder1	Allow full control (inherited)
Folder2	Allow full control (inherited)
File1	Allow full control (inherited)

TABLE 6.3   Explicit permissions overwrite inherited permissions

Object	NTFS Permissions
Data	Grant Allow full control (explicit)
Folder1	Allow read (explicit)
Folder2	Allow read (inherited)
File1	Allow read (inherited)

For example, say you have a folder called Data. Within the Data folder, you have Folder1, and within Folder1, you have Folder2. If you grant Allow full control to a user account, the Allow full control permission will flow down to the subfolders and files within the Data folder.

In comparison, if you grant Allow full control on the Data folder to a user account and you grant Allow read permission to Folder1, the Allow read permission will overwrite the inherited permissions and will then flow down to Folder2 and File1.

If a user has access to a file, he or she will still be able to gain access to the file even if he or she does not have access to the folder containing the file. Of course, because the user doesn't have access to the folder, the user cannot navigate or browse through the folder to get to the file. Therefore, the user will have to use the universal naming convention (UNC) or local path to open the file.

When you view permissions, they will be one of the following:

Checked   Here, permissions are explicitly assigned.

Cleared (Unchecked)   Here, no permissions are assigned.

Shaded   Here, permissions are granted through inheritance from a parent folder.

Besides granting the Allow permissions, you can also grant the Deny permission. The Deny permission always overrides other permissions that have been granted, including when a user or group has been given Full control. For example, if a group has been granted Read and write permission yet one person within the group has been denied the Write permission, that user's effective rights would be the Read permission.

When you combine applying Deny versus Allowed with explicit versus inherited permissions, the hierarchy of precedence of permission is as follows:

1. Explicit Deny

2. Explicit Allow

3. Inherited Deny

4. Inherited Allow

Because users can be members of several groups, it is possible for them to have several sets of explicit permissions for a particular folder or file. When this occurs, the permissions are combined to form the *effective permissions*, which are the actual permissions when logging in and accessing a file or folder. These consist of explicit permissions plus any inherited permissions.

When you calculate effective permissions, you must first calculate the explicit and inherited permissions for an individual or group and then combine them. When combining user and group permissions for NTFS security, the effective permission is the cumulative permission. The only exception is that Deny permissions always apply.

For example, say you have a folder called Data. Within the Data folder, you have Folder1, and within Folder1, you have Folder2. If User 1 is a member of Group 1 and Group 2 and you assign the Allow write permission to the Data folder to User 1, the Allow read permission to Folder1 to Group 1, and the Allow modify permission to Folder2 to Group 2, then User 1's effective permissions would be as shown in Table 6.4.

TABLE 6.4   Calculating effective permissions

Object	User 1 NTFS Permissions	Group 1 Permissions	Group 2 Permissions	Effective Permissions
Data	Allow write (explicit)			Allow write
Folder1	Allow write (inherited)	Allow read (explicit)		Allow read and write
Folder2	Allow write (inherited)	Allow read (inherited)	Allow modify* (explicit)	Allow modify*
File1	Allow write (inherited)	Allow read (inherited)	Allow modify* (inherited)	Allow modify*

*The Modify permission includes the Read and write permissions.

As another example, say you have a folder called Data. Within the Data folder, you have Folder1, and within Folder1, you have Folder2. If User 1 is a member of Group 1 and Group 2 and you assign the Allow write permission to the Data folder to User 1, the Allow read permission to Folder1 to Group 1, and the Deny modify permission to Folder2 to Group 2, User 1's effective permissions would be as shown in Table 6.5.

TABLE 6.5   Effective permissions affected by Deny permissions

Object	User 1 NTFS Permissions	Group 1 Permissions	Group 2 Permissions	Effective Permissions
Data	Allow write (explicit)			Allow write
Folder1	Allow write (inherited)	Allow read (explicit)		Allow read and write
Folder2	Allow write (inherited)	Allow read (inherited)	Deny modify (explicit)	Deny modify
File1	Allow write (inherited)	Allow read (inherited)	Deny modify (inherited)	Deny modify

View NTFS Effective Permissions

To view the NTFS effective permissions for a file or folder, perform the following steps:

1. Right-click the file or folder and select Properties.
2. Select the Security tab.
3. Click the Advanced button.
4. Click the Effective Permissions tab.
5. Click the Select a user option and type in the name of the user or group you want to view. Click the OK button.
6. Click the View effective access button, as shown in Figure 6.3.

FIGURE 6.3   NTFS Effective Permissions tab

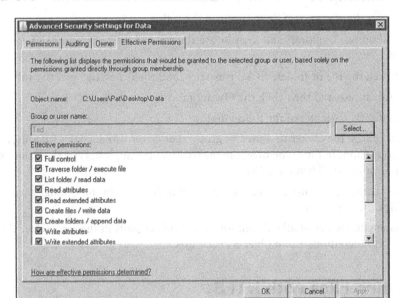

Copying and Moving Files

When you move or copy files from one location to another, you need to understand what happens to the files' NTFS permissions.

When copying and moving files, the following three scenarios can result:

- If a folder or file is copied, the new folder or file will automatically acquire the permissions of the drive or folder to which it is being copied.

- If a folder or file is moved within the same volume, the folder or file will retain the same permissions that were already assigned.

- If a folder or file is moved from one volume to another volume, the folder or file will automatically acquire the permissions of the drive to which it is being moved.

Looking at Folder and File Owners

The *owner* of an object controls how permissions are set on the object and to whom permissions are granted. If for some reason you have been denied access to a file or folder, you need to reset the permissions by taking ownership of the file or folder and modifying the permissions. All administrators automatically have the Take ownership permission of all NTFS objects.

Take Ownership of a File or Folder

To take ownership of a file or folder, perform the following steps:

1. Open Windows Explorer, and then locate the file or folder you want to take ownership of.

2. Right-click the file or folder, click Properties, and then click the Security tab.

3. Click Advanced, and then click the Owner tab.

4. Click Edit, then do *one* of the following:

    ▪ To change the owner to a user or group that *is not* listed: click Other users and groups and, in Enter the object name to select (examples), type the name of the user or group. Then click OK.

    ▪ To change the owner to a user or group that *is* listed: in the Change owner to box, click the new owner.

5. To change the owner of all subcontainers and objects within the tree, select the Replace owner on subcontainers and objects check box.

Encrypting Files with NTFS

Encryption is the process of converting data into a format that cannot be read by another user. Once a user has encrypted a file, it automatically remains encrypted when stored on disk. Decryption is the process of converting data from an encrypted format back to its original format. Once a user has decrypted a file, the file remains decrypted when stored on disk.

If a hard drive were stolen from a system, the thief could install the hard drive on a Windows system for which he or she is an administrator. As an administrator, the thief could then take ownership and access every file and folder on the disk. This is one reason why your servers must have physical security. To help protect your data in situations like this one, you can use encryption.

Encrypting File System (EFS) is a core file encryption technology used to store encrypted files on NTFS file system volumes. Encrypted files cannot be used unless a user has access to the keys required to decrypt the information. After a file has been encrypted, you do not have to manually decrypt that file before you can use it. Rather, once you encrypt a file or folder, you can work with that file or folder just as you would with any other file or folder.

Encryption can also be used to protect data on laptops, which have a much greater chance of being stolen because they are mobile devices. On Windows 10 and Windows Server 2016, EFS can be used to encrypt individual folders or files, and BitLocker can be used to encrypt entire volumes.

Encrypt a Folder or File Using EFS

To encrypt a folder or file, perform the following actions:

1. Right-click the folder or file you want to encrypt, and then click Properties.

2. Click the General tab. Next, click Advanced.

3. Select the Encrypt contents to secure data check box (as shown in Figure 6.4), click OK, and then click OK again.

FIGURE 6.4   Encrypting content using EFS

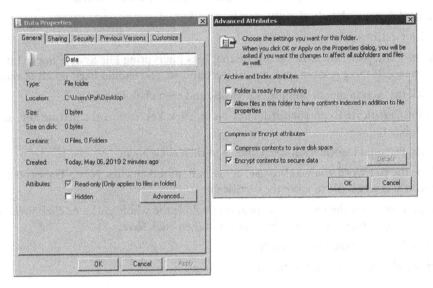

   You cannot encrypt a file with EFS while compressing a file with NTFS. You can only do one or the other.

Decrypt a Folder or File

To decrypt a folder or file, perform the following actions:

1. Right-click the folder or file you want to decrypt, and then click Properties.

2. Click the General tab. Next, click Advanced.

3. Clear the Encrypt contents to secure data check box, click OK, and then click OK again.

The first time you encrypt a folder or file, an encryption certificate is automatically created. If your certificate and key are lost or damaged and you don't have a backup, you won't be able to use the files that you have encrypted. Therefore, you should back up your encryption certificate.

Back Up EFS Certificate

To back up your EFS certificate, perform the following actions:

1. Execute the certmgr.msc command. If you are prompted for an administrator password or confirmation, type your password or provide confirmation.

2. In the left pane, double-click Personal.

3. Click Certificates.

4. In the main pane, click the certificate that lists Encrypting File System under Intended Purposes. If there is more than one EFS certificate, you should back up all of them.

5. Click the Action menu, point to All Tasks, and then click Export.

6. In the Certificate Export wizard, click Next, click Yes, export the private key; and then click Next.

7. Click Personal Information Exchange, and then click Next.

8. Type the password you want to use, confirm it, and then click Next. The export process will create a file to store the certificate.

9. Type a name for the file and the location (include the whole path), or click Browse, navigate to a location, type a filename, and then click Save.

10. Click Next, and then click Finish.

You should then place the certificate in a safe place.

Sharing Drives and Folders

Most users are not going to log onto a server directly to access their data files. Instead, a drive or folder will be shared (known as a *shared folder*), and they will access the data files over a network. To help protect against unauthorized drive or folder access, you should use share permissions along with NTFS permissions (assuming the shared folder is on an NTFS volume). When a user needs to access a network share, he or she will use the UNC, which is \\servername\sharename.

Certification Ready

How do you make a folder available to others over a network? 2.4

Share a Folder

To share a drive or folder, perform these steps:

1. In Windows Server 2016, right-click the drive or folder, select Properties and select the Sharing tab, and then click the Advanced Sharing button. Then follow these steps:

2. Select Share this folder.

3. Type in the name of the shared folder.

4. If necessary, specify the maximum number of people that can access the shared folder at the same time.

5. Click the Permissions button.

6. By default, Everyone is given the Allow read shared permission. You can then remove Everyone, expand the Read shared permission, or add additional people.

7. After users and groups have been added with the proper permissions (as shown in Figure 6.5), click the OK button to close the Permissions dialog box.

8. Click OK to close the Properties dialog box.

FIGURE 6.5   Sharing a folder

The *share permissions* that are available are as follows:

Full Control   Users who are allowed this permission have Read and Change permissions, as well as additional capabilities to change file and folder permissions and take ownership of files and folders.

Change   Users who are allowed this permission have Read permission and the additional capability to create files and subfolders, modify files, change attributes on files and subfolders, and delete files and subfolders.

Read   Users with this permission can view file and subfolder names, access the subfolders of the share, read file data and attributes, and run program files.

As with NTFS, you can allow or deny each share permission. To simplify managing share and NTFS permissions, Microsoft recommends giving Everyone Full control at the share level, then controlling access using NTFS permissions. In addition, because a user can be member of several groups, it is possible for a particular user to have several sets of permissions to a shared drive or folder. The effective share permissions are a combination of the user's permissions and the permissions of all groups of which the user is a member.

When a person logs onto the server and accesses files and folders without using the UNC, only the NTFS permissions apply, not the share permissions. When a person accesses a shared folder using the UNC, you must combine the NTFS and share permissions to see what a user can do. To figure overall access, first calculate the effective NTFS permissions. Then determine the effective shared permissions. Finally, apply the more-restrictive permissions between the NTFS and shared permissions.

Network Discovery and Browsing

In Windows Server 2003, you need only two services to provide and access shared folders. The Workstation service allows you to access shared folders and printers, and the Server service allows you to provide shared folders and printers. In Windows Server 2016, Network Discovery is turned off by default. To browse the network, you must first enable Network Discovery from the Control Panel in the Network and Sharing Center ➤ Advanced Sharing settings.

When you use servers, you should only enable those services that you need to reduce the surface area of the server, which reduces the ability to exploit vulnerabilities. Therefore, to provide services on a network, the server should be discoverable on the network.

Enable Network Discovery

To enable network discovery, perform these actions:

1. Open the Network and Sharing Center.
2. Click Change advanced sharing settings.
3. Select Turn on network discovery. See Figure 6.6.
4. Click the Save changes button.

FIGURE 6.6 Network discovery

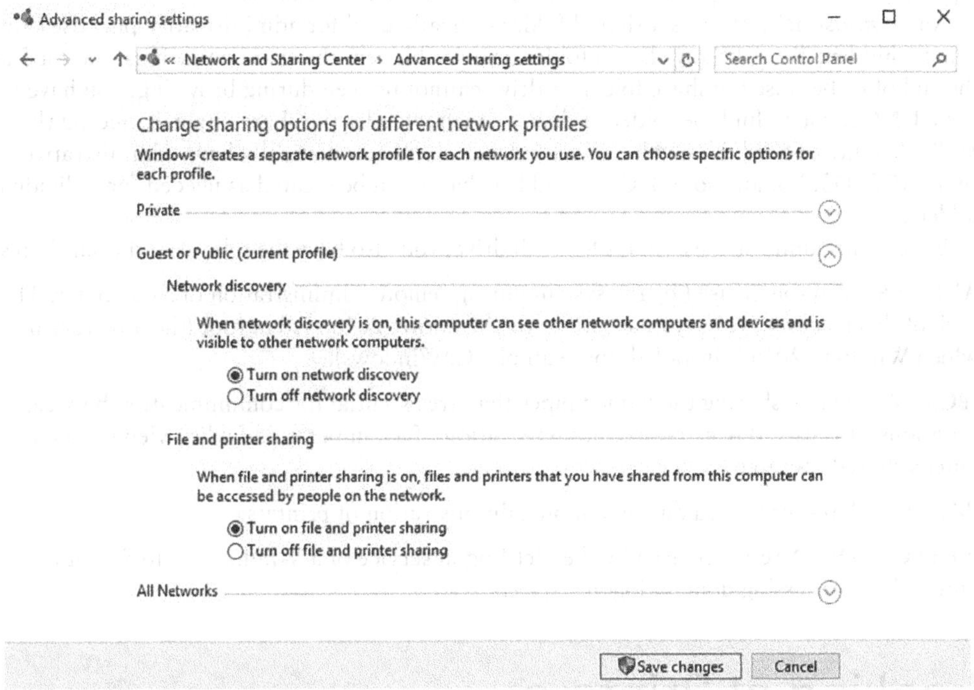

The network services configurable under advanced sharing settings are as follows:

Network Discovery   Allows this computer to see other network computers and devices and be visible to other network computers.

File and Printer Sharing   Allows files and printers that you have shared from this computer to be accessed by people on the network.

Public Folder Sharing   Allows people on the network to access files in the public folder.

Media Streaming   Allows people and devices on the network to access pictures, music, and videos on the computer. In addition, this permits the computer to find media on the network.

Looking at Special and Administrative Shares

In Windows, there are several special shared folders that are automatically created by Windows for administrative and system use. Different from regular shares, these shares do not show when a user browses computer resources using Network Neighborhood, My Network Place, or similar software. In most cases, special shared folders should not be deleted or modified. For Windows Servers, only members of the Administrators, Backup Operators, and Server Operators groups can connect to these shares.

An *administrative share* is a shared folder typically used for administrative purposes and usually hidden. To make any shared folder or drive hidden, the share name must have a $ at the end of it. Because the share folder or drive cannot be seen during browsing, you have to use a UNC name to find the folder or drive, which includes the share name (including the $). By default, all hard drive volumes with drive letters automatically have administrative shares (C$, D$, E$, and so on). Other hidden shares can be created as needed for individual folders.

Besides the administrative shares for each drive, you also have the following special shares:

ADMIN$ A resource used by the system during remote administration of a computer. The path of this resource is always the path to the Windows 2016 system root (the directory in which Windows 2016 is installed; for example, C:\Windows).

IPC$ A resource sharing the named pipes that are essential for communication between programs. It is used during remote administration of a computer and when viewing a computer's shared resources.

PRINT$ A resource used during remote administration of printers.

NETLOGON   A resource used by the Net Logon service of a Windows 2016 Server computer while processing domain logon requests.

Looking at Printers

One basic network services is network printing, in which multiple users can share the same printer. This is a cost-effective solution when you have multiple employees in different locations.

Certification Ready

How do you limit printing to expensive printers? 2.4

As an administrator, you can install two types of printers: local and network. Today, most local printers are connected using USB ports, although some legacy printers may use parallel or serial ports. Network printers can be shared local printers or printers that connect directly to a network with built-in network cards or expandable jet-direct cards.

When you install a physical printer, which Microsoft refers to as a *print device*, you must first connect the printer and turn it on. Next, you need to create a logical printer

(Microsoft refers to this as the *printer*), which will provide a software interface between the print device and the applications. When you create the printer, you also load a print driver that acts as a translator for Windows and the programs running on Windows so that they do not have to worry about the specifics of the printer's hardware and printer language.

When you print a document in Windows, the printer uses the logical printer and printer driver to format the document into a form that is understood by the printer, including rendering it into a printer language such as HP's Printer Control Language or Adobe's Postscript to create an enhanced metafile (EMF). The *print job* is then sent to the local spooler, which provides background printing, allowing you to print and queue additional documents while your first document is being printed.

If a print job is being sent to the local print device, it will temporarily save it to the local hard drive's spool file. When the printer is available, it will then send the print job to the local print device. If Windows determines that the job is for a network print device, Windows sends the job to the print server's spooler. The print server's spooler will save it to the print server's hard drive spool file. Then, when the network print device becomes available, the job will print on the network print device.

Installing Printers

If you have the correct permissions to add a local printer or a remote shared printer, you can use the Add Printer Wizard to install the printer. After the printer is installed, it will appear in the Devices and Printers folder as well as in the Device Manager.

Add a Local Printer

To add a local printer to a Windows Server 2016, perform these actions:

1. Right-click the Start button, and click Control Panel.

2. Under Hardware and Sound, click View Devices and Printers.

3. To start the Add Printer Wizard, click Add a printer.

4. Click The printer that I want isn't listed.

5. Select Add a Local Printer or network printer with manual settings and click Next.

6. When the Add Printer dialog box appears, specify the port to which the printer is connected. See Figure 6.7. If the port already exists, such as an LPT1 or a network port specified by an IP address, select the port from the Use an existing port drop-down list. If the port does not exist, click Create a New Port, select Standard TCP/IP Port, and click Next. For the device type, you can select either Auto detect, TCP/IP device, or Web services device. Then specify the IP address or DNS name of the printer and the Port Name. If you type the address in hostname or IP address box, it will populate the IP address in the port name. It will then try to communicate with the printer using the address you specified.

FIGURE 6.7   Adding a local printer

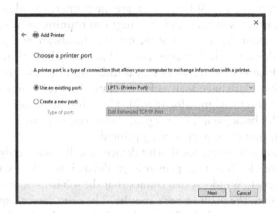

7. If Plug and Play does not detect and install the correct printer automatically, you will be asked to specify the printer driver (printer manufacturer and printer model). If the printer is not listed, you will have to use the Have Disk option.

8. When the Type a Printer Name dialog box appears, specify the name of the printer. If you want this to be the default printer for the system, select the Set as the default printer option. Click the Next button.

9. In the Printer Sharing dialog box, specify the share name. You can also specify the Location or Comments. Although Windows Server 2016 supports long printer names and share names (including spaces and special characters), it is best to keep names short, simple, and descriptive. The entire qualified name, including the server name (for example, \\Server1\HP4100N-1), should be 32 characters or fewer.

10. When the printer is successfully added, you can print the standard Windows test page by clicking the Print a test page button. Click the Finish button.

The TCP/IP printer port uses host port 9100 to communicate.

Windows Servers can provide a driver to the clients if the driver is loaded on the server. For example, because Windows Server 2016 is only available in 64-bit versions, it will have a 64-bit print driver so that the server can print to the printer. However, most computers used within organizations today will most likely be 32-bit clients that need to use 32-bit print drivers. Therefore, you would load both 64-bit and 32-bit print drivers on the server so that it can hand out either driver as needed.

Add Additional Print Drivers

To add additional print drivers in Windows Server 2016, perform these steps:

1. Open Devices and Printers.
2. Click the Print Server Properties button.
3. Select the Drivers tab.
4. Click the Change Driver Settings.
5. Click the Add button. See Figure 6.8.

FIGURE 6.8   Add Printer Driver Wizard

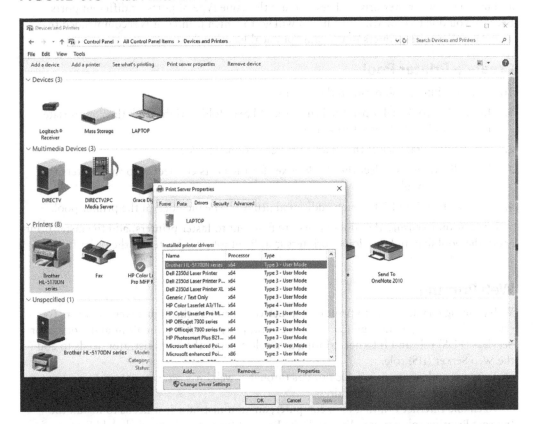

6. When the Welcome to the Add Printer Driver Wizard screen appears, click the Next button.
7. Select the appropriate processor and operating system drivers and click the Next button.
8. If necessary, provide a path for the printer driver and click the OK button.
9. When the wizard is complete, click the Finish button.

You can also use group policies to install and configure printers.

Network printers are usually used by more than one user. If you have a high volume of print jobs, the printer can become congested and users will have to wait for the documents to print. Either you can purchase a faster printer or you can create a group of printers called a printer pool that acts as a single virtual printer with a single print queue. Users print to a single printer, and the print jobs are distributed among the printers within the pool.

To create a printer pool, you must have two or more printers that are the same model and use the same printer driver. They can use the same type of ports or different ports. Because you don't know which print job will go to which printer, it is recommended that you place all pooled printers in the same physical location.

Create a Printer Pool

To create a printer pool, perform these steps:

1. In the Control Panel, open the Printers and Faxes folder, right-click the appropriate printer, and click Printer Properties.

2. On the Ports tab, select the Enable printer pooling check box.

3. In the list of ports, select the check boxes for the ports connected to the printers that you want to pool.

4. Repeat steps 2 and 3 for each additional printer to be included in the printer pool.

If you want to ensure that documents are first sent to faster printers, add the faster printers to the pool first and the slower printers last. Print jobs are routed in the order in which you create the ports.

Web Printing

Web printing enables users to print files to network printers through a web browser. To set up web printing in an organization's network, prior to adding the Print and Document Services (PDS) role and Internet Printing as a role service, the administrator needs to add the Web Server (IIS) role.

To access and manage available printers through a web browser, enter http://servername/printers in the browser's web address.

To enable Internet Printing on a computer, an administrator just needs to install the Internet Printing role service. To install the Internet Printing Client, click Add Features in Server Manager, select the Internet Printing Client check box, and then click OK.

Web Management

Web printing or Internet Printing role services enables web printing management. Through the web browser, users can manage print jobs in a similar way to the traditional method of managing print jobs.

To manage printers through a web interface, enter http://servername/printers in the browser's address bar and then select the printer.

Configure Print Server and Network Printer on Windows Server 2016

After successfully installing the role, can start the configure it.

1. From the dashboard, click Tools, and from the drop-list, click on Print Management.

2. From the left pane, click the server and then right-click and select Add Printer.

3. Select "TCP/IP or Web Service Printer by IP address or Hostname" option, click Next to continue as shown.

4. Now enter IP address or the hostname of the printer, and then click Next.

5. Select "Install a new driver" to get the latest driver for the printer and click Next.

6. Select the printer driver, or if you have the required files for its driver, click "Have disk…", for me I will select the driver from the drivers already on my Windows server, and then click Next.

7. Now if you want to share your printer, check "Share Printer." If not, uncheck it and click Next.

8. This page of the installation will confirm the printer details; if it's correct, click Next.

9. Now the printer driver is installed, you can test it by checking the "Print test page," and once Finish is clicked, a test page will be printed.

Looking at Printer Properties

With most printers, you have a wide range of options. Although these options vary from printer to printer, they are easily accessible by right-clicking the printer in the Devices and Printers folder and selecting Printer Properties.

When you open Printer Properties (Figure 6.9), you will find the following options:

General Tab Allows you to configure the printer name, location, and comments and to print a test page. In addition, if you click the Printing Preferences button on the General tab, the default paper size, paper tray, print quality/resolution, pages per sheet, print order (such as front to back or back to front), and number of copies will display. The actual options that are available will vary depending on your printer.

Sharing Tab Allows you to share a printer. You can also publish the printer in Active Directory if you choose the List in the directory option. Because a printer on a server can be used by other clients connected to the network, you can add additional drivers by clicking the Additional Drivers button.

Ports Tab Allows you to specify which port (physical or TCP/IP) the printer will use, as well as to create new TCP/IP ports.

Advanced Tab   Allows you to configure the driver to use with the printer, the priority of the printer, when the printer is available, and how print jobs are spooled.

Color Management Tab   Allows you to specify the color management profiles used for displaying images on the monitor, editing and saving RGB images, saving and printing CMYK images, and settings for color space conversion.

Security Tab   Allows you to specify the permissions for the printer.

Device Settings Tab   Allows you to configure the trays, font substitution, and other hardware settings.

FIGURE 6.9   Printer Properties

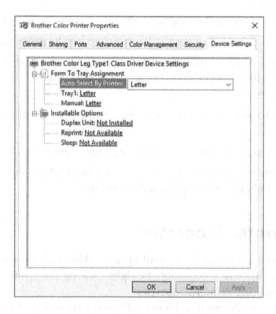

Setting Printer Permissions

Printers are considered objects. Therefore, as with NTFS files and folders, you can assign permissions to a printer so that you can specify who can use the printer, who can manage the printer, and who can manage the print jobs.

Windows Server 2016 provides three levels of *printer permissions* (Figure 6.10):

Print   Allows users to send documents to the printer.

Manage this Printer   Allows users to modify printer settings and configurations, including the ACL itself.

Manage Documents   Provides the ability to cancel, pause, resume, or restart a print job.

FIGURE 6.10   Printer permissions

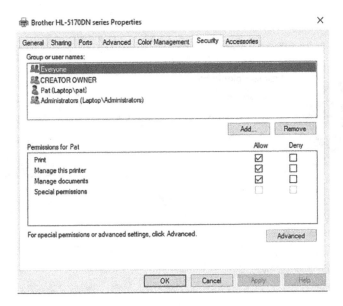

By default, the Print permission is assigned to the Everyone group. If you need to restrict who can print to the printer, you will need to remove the Everyone group and add another group or user and assign the Allow print permission to the user or group. Of course, it is still recommended that you use groups instead of users. As with file permissions, you can also deny print permissions.

Managing the Print Jobs

The print spooler is an executable file that manages the printing process, which includes retrieving the location of the correct print driver, loading the driver, creating the individual print jobs, and scheduling the print jobs for printing.

On occasion, a print job may have been sent that was not intended, or you may decide it is not necessary to print a job. Therefore, you need to delete the print job from the print queue.

View the Print Queue

To view the print queue, perform these steps:

1. Open the Devices and Printers folder.

2. Double-click the printers for which you want to view the print jobs waiting to print. See Figure 6.11.

FIGURE 6.11   Viewing the print queue

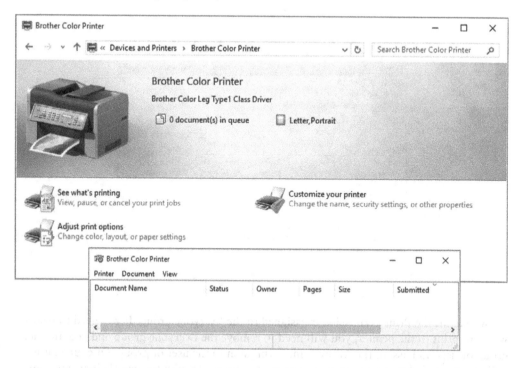

The print queue shows information about a document, such as print status, owner, and number of pages to be printed. To pause a document, open the print queue, right-click the document you want to pause, and select the Pause option. If you want to stop printing the document, right-click the document that you want to stop printing and select the Cancel option. You can cancel the printing of more than one document by holding down the Ctrl key and clicking each document that you want to cancel.

By default, all users can pause, resume, restart, and cancel their own documents. To manage documents that are printed by other users; however, you must have the Allow manage documents permissions.

When the print device is available, the spooler retrieves the next print job and sends it to the print device. By default, the spool folder is located at C:\Windows\\System32\Spool\ Printers. If you have a server that handles a large number of print jobs or several large print jobs, make sure the drive where the spool folder is has sufficient disk space.

Change the Location of the Spool Folder

To change the location of the spool folder in Windows Server 2016, perform these steps:

1. Open the Devices and Printers folder.

2. Click a printer and select the Print server properties.

3. Click the Advanced tab.

4. Specify the new location and click the OK button.

On occasion, the print spooler may freeze or become unresponsive. You can restart the print spooler by following these steps:

1. Open the Services console located in Administrative Tools.

2. Right-click Print Spooler, and select Restart.

You can also stop and start the service.

Enabling Auditing

Security can be divided into three areas. Authentication is used to prove the identity of a user. Authorization gives access to the user that was authenticated. To complete the security picture, you need to enable *auditing* so that you can have a record of the users who have logged in and what the user accessed or tried to access.

Certification Ready

What are the steps in enabling auditing for an NTFS folder? 2.4

It is important that you protect your information and service resources from people who should not have access to them and at the same time make those resources available to authorized users. Along with authentication and authorization, you can also enable auditing to that you can have a record of:

- Who has successfully logged in
- Who has attempted to log in but failed
- Who has changed accounts in Active Directory
- Who has access or changed certain files
- Who has used a certain printer
- Who restarted a system
- Who has made some system changes

Auditing is not enabled by default. To enable auditing, you specify what types of system events to audit using Group Policy or the local security policy (Security Settings\Local Policies\Audit Policy). See Figure 6.12. Table 6.6 shows the basic events to audit that are available in Windows Server 2003 and higher. However, with Windows Server 2016, you can use Advanced Audit Policy Configuration for more granular control. After you enable logging, you then open the Event Viewer security logs to view the security events.

FIGURE 6.12 Audit events in the local security policy

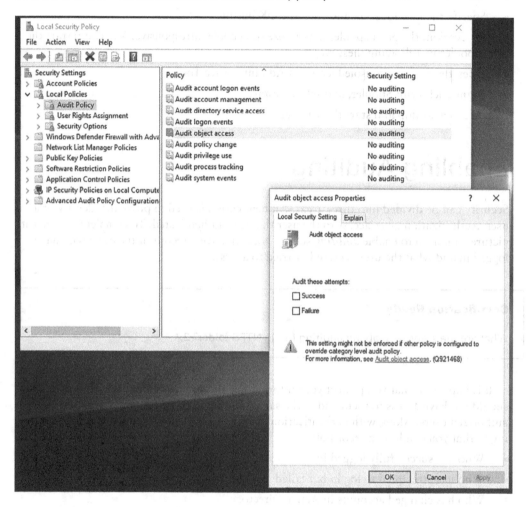

TABLE 6.6 Audit events

Event	Explanation
Account logon events	Determines whether the OS audits each time the computer validates an account's credentials, such as account login.
Account management	Determines whether to audit each event of account management on a computer including changing passwords and creating or deleting user accounts.

Event	Explanation
Directory service access	Determines whether the OS audits user attempts to access Active Directory objects.
Logon events	Determines where the OS audits each instance of a user attempting to log on to or log off his or her computer.
Object access	Determines whether the OS audits user attempts to access non-Active Directory objects including NTFS files and folders and printers.
Policy change	Determines whether the OS audits each instance of an attempt to change user rights assignments, auditing policy, account policy, or trust policy.
Privilege use	Determines whether to audit each instance of a user exercising a user right.
Process tracking	Determines whether the OS audits process-related events such as process creation, process termination, handle duplication, and indirect object access. This is usually used for troubleshooting.
System events	Determines whether the OS audits if the system time is changed, if the system is started or shut down, if there is an attempt to load extensible authentication components, if there is a loss of auditing events due to auditing system failure, and if the security log is exceeding a configurable warning threshold level.

To audit NTFS files, NTFS folders, and printers is a two-step process. You must first enable Object Access using Group Policy. Then you must specify which objects you want to audit.

 Enabling auditing of successful events can affect server performance, in particular for busy folders.

Audit Files and Folders

To audit files and folders, perform these steps:

1. Open Windows Explorer.
2. Right-click the file or folder that you want to audit, click Properties, and then click the Security tab.
3. Click Advanced.

4. In the Advanced Security Settings for <object> dialog box, click the Auditing tab.

5. Do *one* of the following:

- To set up auditing for a new user or group, click Add. In Enter the object name to select, type the name of the user or group that you want, and then click OK. See Figure 6.13.

- To remove auditing for an existing group or user, click the group or username, click Remove, click OK, and then skip the rest of this procedure.

- To view or change auditing for an existing group or user, click its name, and then click Edit.

FIGURE 6.13 Auditing an NTFS folder

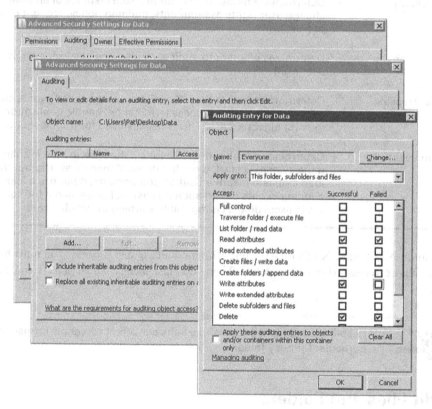

6. In the Apply onto box, click the location where you want auditing to take place.

7. In the Access box, indicate what actions you want to audit by selecting the appropriate check boxes:

- To audit successful events, select the Successful check box.

- To stop auditing successful events, clear the Successful check box.

- To audit unsuccessful events, select the Failed check box.
- To stop auditing unsuccessful events, clear the Failed check box.
- To stop auditing all events, click Clear All.

8. If you want to prevent subsequent files and subfolders of the original object from inheriting these audit entries, select the "Apply these auditing entries to objects and/or containers within this container only" check box.

9. Click OK to close the Advanced Security Settings dialog box.

10. Click OK to close the Properties dialog box.

Audit Printing

To audit printing in Windows Server 2016, perform these steps:

1. Right-click the printer in Devices and Printers, and select Printer Properties.

2. Select the Security tab, and click the Advanced button.

3. Select the Auditing tab.

4. Click the Add button and

   - To set up auditing for a new user or group, click Add. In Enter the object name to select, type the name of the user or group that you want, and then click OK.
   - To remove auditing for an existing group or user, click the group or username, click Remove, click OK, and then skip the rest of this procedure.
   - To view or change auditing for an existing group or user, click its name, and then click Edit.

5. Click OK to close the Advanced Security Settings dialog box.

6. Click OK to close the Properties dialog box.

Because the security log is limited in size, select only those objects that you need to audit and consider the amount of disk space that the security log will need. The maximum size of the security log is defined in Event Viewer by right-clicking Security Log and selecting the Properties option.

Skill Summary

In this lesson you learned:

- NTFS permissions allow you to control which users and groups can gain access to files and folders on an NTFS volume.
- Each of the standard permissions consists of a logical group of special permissions.
- Explicit permissions are permissions granted directly to the file or folder.

- Inherited permissions are permissions that are granted to a folder (parent object or container) and that flow into child objects (subfolders or files inside the parent folder).

- The deny permission always overrides the permissions that have been granted, including when a user or group has been given the full control permission.

- Effective permissions are the actual permissions when logging in and accessing a file or folder. They consist of explicit permissions plus any inherited permissions as a user or from any groups that user is a member of.

- If a file or folder is copied, the new file or folder automatically acquires the permissions of the drive or folder to which it is being copied.

- If a file or folder is moved within the same volume, the file or folder retains the same permissions that were already assigned to it.

- If a file or folder is moved from one volume to another volume, it automatically acquires the permissions of the drive or folder to which it is being copied.

- The owner of the object controls how permissions are set on the object and to whom permissions are granted.

- If for some reason, you have been denied access to a file or folder, you need to reset the permissions by taking ownership of a file or folder and modifying the permissions.

- Encryption is the process of converting data into a format that cannot be read by another user.

- Encrypting File System (EFS) is a core file encryption technology used to store encrypted files on NTFS file system volumes.

- Most users are not going to log on to a server directly to access their data files. Instead, a drive or folder will be shared (known as a shared folder), and they will access the data files over the network.

- Like NTFS, you can allow or deny each share permission.

- To simplify managing share and NTFS permissions, Microsoft recommends giving everyone full control, and then controlling access using NTFS permissions.

- An administrative share is a shared folder typically used for administrative purposes.

- Microsoft refers to the printer itself as a print device.

- A printer in Windows is a logical printer, which will provide a software interface between the print device and applications.

- A printer pools to act as a single virtual printer with a single print queue, but it contains two or more physical printers.

- Since printers are considered objects, you can assign permissions to a printer. You can specify who can use the printer, who can manage the printer, and who can manage the print jobs.

- By default, the print permission is assigned to the Everyone group.
- The print queue shows information about a document such as print status, owner, and number of pages to be printed.
- Auditing provides a record of the users that have logged in and what the user accessed or tried to access.
- Auditing is not enabled by default. To enable auditing, you specify what types of system events to audit using group policies or the local security policy.
- To audit NTFS files, NTFS folders, and printers is a two-step process. You must first enable Object Access using group policies. Then you must specify which objects you want to audit.

Knowledge Assessment

Fill in the Blank

1. To print to a printer, you need the _____ permission.

2. The NTFS special permission that allows you to move through a folder to reach lower files or folders is _____.

3. The Windows component that allows you to manage shares and NTFS permissions is _____.

4. Permissions that flow from a parent object to a child object are called _____.

5. The _____ are the actual permissions when a user logs in and accesses a file or folder.

6. The encrypting technology included in NTFS is _____.

7. For Windows Server 2016 to be seen on the network, you must enable _____.

8. A(n) _____ share is not seen when browsed.

9. When some has removed all users from a folder, you can _____ of the folder.

10. The default location of the spool folder is _____.

Multiple Choice

1. What is the standard NTFS permission needed to change attributes of a NTFS folder?
   A. Write
   B. Read
   C. Modify
   D. Fully Control

2. Which permission takes precedence?
   A. Explicit deny
   B. Explicit allow
   C. Inherited deny
   D. Inherited allow

3. Which of the following is NOT a share permission?
   A. Full Control
   B. Write
   C. Change
   D. Read

4. TCP/IP printers use port _____
   A. 443
   B. 23
   C. 9100
   D. 3000

5. What is a single virtual printer with a single print queue that consist of two or more printers?
   A. Print collection
   B. Direct printers
   C. Printer group
   D. Printer pool

6. What symbol makes an administrative share not seen when browsed?
   A. #
   B. *
   C. !
   D. $

7. When enabling Internet Printing, you need to install _____.
   A. DFS
   B. IIS
   C. GPO Manager
   D. Task Manager

8. What is the minimum share permission that allows you to change file and folder permissions?
   A. Full Control
   B. Change
   C. Read
   D. Manage

9. When you copy files from one folder to another folder within the same volume, you get the
   _____.

   A. Same permissions as the source

   B. Same permissions as the target

   C. No permissions are set

   D. Everyone has full permission

10. You are an administrator on a computer. Unfortunately, there is a folder that you cannot access because you have do not have permissions to the folder. What can you do?

   A. Take ownership of the folder.

   B. Delete the folder and re-create it.

   C. Turn off the deny attribute.

   D. Grant the allow everyone full permission.

True/False

1. If full control is assigned to a parent object for a user, the full control permission will over-write explicit permissions at a child object.

2. To see who accesses a file over time, you only have to turn on object access audit events.

3. When you are looking at NTFS permissions that are grayed out, it means that you don't have the permissions needed to modify the NTFS permissions.

4. You can encrypt and compress a file within NTFS at the same time.

5. When calculating the NTFS and share permissions, you would apply the more restrictive permissions between the NTFS and shared permission.

Competency Assessment

Scenario 6-1: Creating a Shared Folder

You have a Data folder that you need to share so that all managers have access and can make changes, but no one else can access it. What should you do to set this folder up?

Scenario 6-2: Auditing the Managers folder

You just created a Data folder for your Managers, and you need to verify that it is not getting accessed by anyone who is not supposed to access the files and if someone deletes or makes changes to a system. What should you do?

Proficiency Assessment

Scenario 6-3: Managing a Folder

1. Create a Data folder. In the Data folder, create a Manager folder and Sales folder.
2. Share the Data folder and assign Everyone Allow Full Control.
3. Modify the NTFS permissions for the Manager folder so that only the Managers group and Administrators group have access to the Managers folder. Grant Allow Modify NTFS permission to the Manager group.
4. Modify the NTFS permissions for the Sales folder so that only the Sales and Managers groups and Administrators groups have access to the Managers folder. Grant Allow Modify NTFS permission to the Manager and Sales group.

Scenario 6-4: Manage Printers

1. Install a local printer to your server.
2. Share the printer.
3. Configure the permissions so that the Managers group is the only group that can print to the printer.

🌐 Real World Scenario

Workplace Ready: Distributed File Systems

Distributed File Systems (DFS) is an extension of file services. DFS namespaces allows you to create a share of shares. It allows you to take multiple shared folders and place them under a single shared folder even if the shared folders exist among multiple servers, making it easier for users to find and access those shares.

DFS replication uses File Replication Service (FRS) to duplicate a share folder between two computers. You can use it as a redundancy to provide access to those files when one of the servers is no longer accessible. You can also use it to centralize files that may be spread out between sites so that you can back them up more easily.

Lesson 7

Popular Windows Network Services and Applications

Key Terms

application	Secure Sockets Layer (SSL)
application pool	Simple Mail Transfer Protocol (SMTP)
digital certificate	snapshot
File Transfer Protocol (FTP)	virtual directory
HyperText Markup Language (HTML)	virtual machine
hypervisor	virtual private network (VPN)
Internet Information Services (IIS)	virtual-to-physical (V2P) conversion
nested virtualization	web server
physical-to-virtual (P2V) conversion	web services
Remote Assistance	World Wide Web (WWW)
Remote Desktop Services	

 Real World Scenario

Lesson 7 Case

You have installed several servers running Windows Server 2016 to form a new network, and you have set up Active Directory and DNS. Now you need to install a web server that will host HR forms. Therefore, you are ready to take one of your computers running Windows Server 2016 and configure it as a web server. You also need an FTP server to provide files to users throughout your organization. However, you want to keep the two servers isolated while minimizing cost. Therefore, you decide to install Hyper-V to create a virtual server for the web server and a virtual server for the FTP server.

Introducing the Web Server

The Internet is a global WAN consisting of interconnected networks that use the Internet Protocol Suite (TCP/IP). It is a network of networks that consists of millions of computers, including home, corporation, public, academic, and government computers. The Internet allows users to access a vast array of information resources and services, including web servers that make up the World Wide Web (WWW) and support sending and receiving email. It has also changed the newspaper publishing industry as Web sites, blogging, and web feeds have grown in popularity and newspaper circulation has declined. Lastly, streaming media, Voice over Internet Protocol (VoIP), and IPTV have become common.

Certification Ready

How do you create a web server on Windows server? 2.2

The *World Wide Web* is a system of interlinked hypertext documents known as web pages that can be viewed with a web browser such as Internet Explorer. Web pages may contain text, images, videos, and other multimedia that you can navigate between by using hyperlinks, and they are usually found by using a search engine such as Bing or Google.

 Because Web sites using HTML have become common on the Internet and it is readily available on any computer with a browser, this technology is often used within an organization to access internal applications.

HTML, which stands for *HyperText Markup Language*, is the predominant markup language interpreted by browsers for web pages. It may include text, headings, paragraphs, lists, and hyperlinks. It can also contain embedded objects such as images and videos. It is flexible enough to include scripts and other languages such as JavaScript.

Traditional web pages consisted of static pages that do not change content without being manually changed. Active Server Pages (ASP) is a technology that enables you to make dynamic and interactive web pages. Instead of using .htm or .html, ASP pages use the .asp extension. The default scripting language used for writing ASP is VBScript, although you can use other scripting languages like JScript (Microsoft's version of JavaScript).

When you view web pages, you are connecting to the *web server* using TCP port 80. However, the content is not encrypted and could be read by anyone who can access the data stream. Since personal information can be sent over the Internet, including credit card numbers, a supplemental protocol was developed called SSL. SSL, short for *Secure Sockets Layer*, uses TCP port 443, which uses a digital certificate to encrypt the packet so that it cannot be read by anyone else except the source and target. When you are using SSL, the browser URL starts with https (e.g., https://www.acme.com).

Another traditional service provided over the Internet is FTP. *File Transfer Protocol (FTP)* is a standard network protocol used to transfer a file from one host to another over a TCP/IP-based network. Different from HTTP, it uses two TCP ports to operate—ports 20 and 21. FTP can be used with user-based password authentication or with anonymous user access. Unfortunately, the username, password, and data transfers are sent unencrypted. Therefore, when encryption is needed, you should use SFTP (SSH File Transfer Protocol), or FTPS (FTP over SSL), which adds SSL or TLS encryption.

For emails to travel over the Internet, email servers (or any server or client that sends email directly out) use *Simple Mail Transfer Protocol (SMTP)* as an outgoing mail transport. SMTP uses TCP port 25.

Managing Web Sites with IIS

Microsoft's web server/application server is *Internet Information Services (IIS)*. Windows Server 2016 includes IIS 10, which supports FTP, FTPS, SMTP, and HTTP/HTTPS.

Install IIS in Windows Server 2016

To install IIS in Windows Server 2016:

1. Click Start, and click Server Manager.
2. Open the Manage menu, click Add Roles and Features.
3. In the Add Roles and Features Wizard on the Before You Begin page, click Next.
4. In the Installation Type page, click Next.
5. On the Server Selection page, click Next.
6. On the Server Roles page, select Web Services. When you are asked to add features, click the Add Features button. Click Next.
7. On the Features page, click Next.
8. On the Web Server Role (IIS) page, click Next.
9. On the Role Services page, select the additional role services (as shown in Figure 7.1). Click Next.
10. On the Confirmation page, click Install.
11. When the installation is completed, click Close.

FIGURE 7.1   Selecting web server role services

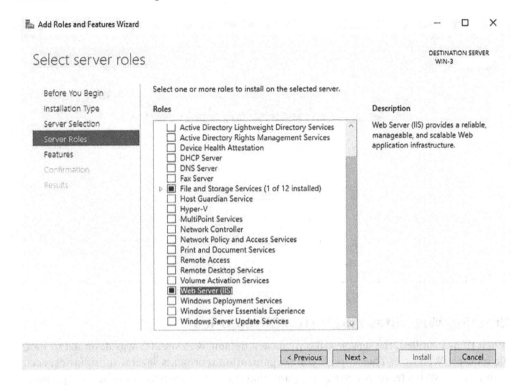

To open IIS manager, you use one of the following methods:

- Start ➤ Windows Administrative Tools ➤ Internet Information Services (IIS) Services
- Using Server Manager, open the Tools menu and select Internet Information Services (IIS) Manager.

The Internet Information Services (IIS) Manager is shown in Figure 7.2.

FIGURE 7.2 IIS Manager

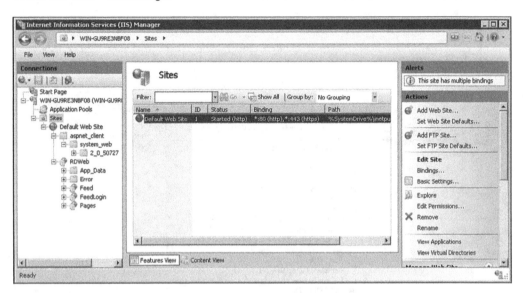

Creating Web Sites and Virtual Directories

When IIS is installed, the server will only have a default Web site. IIS was designed to handle multiple Web sites. Therefore, if your organization represents several subsidiaries, each with its own Web site, or you are a company that hosts web services for other companies, you would create multiple sites within IIS.

Create a Web Site

To create additional Web sites:

1. Open IIS Manager.

2. In the Connections pane, right-click the Sites node in the tree, and then click Add Website.

3. In the Add Web Site dialog box, type a friendly name for your Web site in the Web site name box.

4. Click Select if you want to select a different application pool than the one listed in the Application Pool box. In the Select Application Pool dialog box, select an application pool from the Application Pool list and then click OK. Application pools will be discussed a little bit later.

5. In the Physical path box, type the physical path of the Web site's folder, or click the browse button (...) to navigate to the file system to find the folder.

6. If the physical path that you entered in step 5 is to a remote share, click Connect to specify credentials that have permission to access the path. If you do not use specific credentials, select the Application user (pass-thru authentication) option in the Connect As dialog box.

7. Select the protocol for the Web site from the Type list.

8. The default value in the IP address box is All Unassigned. If you must specify a static IP address for the Web site, type the IP address in the IP address box.

9. Type a port number in the Port text box.

10. Optionally, type a host header name for the Web site in the Host Header box as shown in Figure 7.3.

FIGURE 7.3 Adding a website

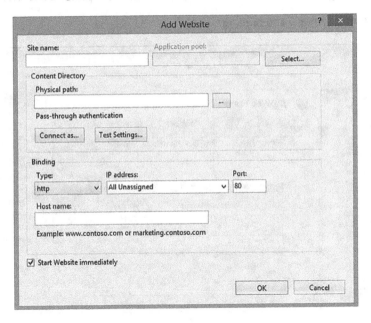

11. If you do not have to make any changes to the site and you want the Web site to be immediately available, select the "Start Web site immediately" check box.

12. Click OK.

The default Web site is made to respond to all IP addresses assigned to server port 80. In addition, the web server will respond to any name that corresponds to one of the IP addresses of the web server.

To support multiple Web sites, you can assign additional IP addresses and assign a Web site to each IP address. You can also define a different port instead of port 80 or 443.

When a user tries to access http://TestWebSite.com, they are really accessing http://TestWebSite.com:80. The :80 means port 80. If you want to make a Web site to respond to port 8080, you would then access the Web site by specifying http://TestWebSite.com:8080.

One method that allows you to share the same IP address and port is to use host headers, which are used to specify a name that the Web site will respond to rather than all names that point to the address.

To configure the IP address, port, and name a Web site will respond to, you need to configure the site binding. To change the site bindings, right-click the site in IIS Manager and select Edit Bindings. To change the binding, click the binding you want to change and click the Edit button. To add a new binding, click the Add button. See Figure 7.4. If you want the Web site to respond to two different names such as www.acme.com and acme.com, you need to add two bindings. If you want to use SSL, you will have to specify a SSL certificate.

FIGURE 7.4   Adding a site binding

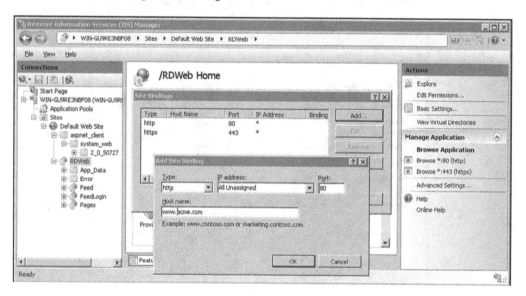

When you create a Web site, you specify a folder that represents the root of the Web site. Within that folder, you can create subfolders. For example, you have a Web site for acme.com. When you access http://TestWebSite.com, it goes to the root of the folder to access the default web pages. You can then create a subfolder called sales. Type in a URL similar to http://TestWebSite.com/sales or click on a hyperlink on the home page that points to the http://TestWebSite.com/sales folder and execute a default web page in the sales folder.

A *virtual directory* is a directory used in a Web site that corresponds to a physical directory elsewhere on the server, on another server, or on a Web site. This allows you to reuse the same folder for multiple sites or to connect to content without physically moving it.

Add a Virtual Directory

To add a virtual directory within your Web site:

1. Open IIS Manager.

2. In the Connections pane, expand the Sites node in the tree and click to select the site in which you want to create a virtual directory.

3. In the Actions pane, click View Virtual Directories.

4. On the Virtual Directories page in the Actions pane, click Add Virtual Directory.

5. In the Add Virtual Directory dialog box, type a name in the Alias text box. This alias is used to access the content from a URL.

6. In the Physical path text box, type the physical path of the content folder or click Browse to navigate through the file system to find the folder.

7. Optionally, click Connect As to specify credentials that have permission to access the physical path. If you do not use specific credentials, select the Application user (pass-thru authentication) option in the Connect As dialog box.

8. Optionally, click Test Settings to verify the settings that you specified for the virtual directory.

9. Click OK.

Exploring Applications and Application Pools

An *application* is a grouping of content on a Web site that is defined at the root level or in a separate folder that has specific properties, such as the application pool in which the application runs and the permissions that are granted on the folder. Each site must have at least one application named the root application or default application.

An *application pool* is a set of resources (a worker process or a set of worker processes) used by a Web site or application that defines the memory boundaries for the Web site. Forcing each application to have its own application pool ensures that one Web site does not interfere with another Web site on the same server, which ensures application performance and improved application availability. Therefore, if one application has a memory leak or crashes, it will not affect the other sites.

Create an Application in IIS

To create an application:

1. Open IIS Manager.

2. In the Connections Pane, expand the Sites node.

3. Right-click the site for which you want to create an application and click Add Application.

4. In the Alias box, type a value for the application URL, such as sales.

5. Click Select if you want to select a different application pool than the one listed in the Application Pool box. In the Select Application Pool dialog box, select an application pool from the Application Pool List and click OK.

6. In the Physical Path box, type the physical path of the application's folder or click Browse to navigate the file system to find the folder.

7. Optionally, click Connect As to specify credentials that have permission to access the physical path. If you do not use specific credentials, select the Application user (pass-thru authentication) option in the Connect As dialog box.

8. Optionally, click Test Settings to verify the settings that you specified for the application.

9. Click OK.

Create an Application Pool

To create an application pool:

1. Open IIS Manager.

2. In the Connections pane, expand the server node and click Application Pools.

3. On the Application Pools page in the Actions pane, click Add Application Pool.

4. On the Add Application Pool dialog box, type a friendly name for the application pool in the Name box.

5. From the .NET Framework version list, select the version of the .NET Framework required by your managed applications, modules, and handlers, or select No Managed Code if the applications that you run in this application pool do not require the .NET Framework.

6. From the Managed pipeline mode list, select **one** of the following options:
    ▪ Integrated if you want to use the integrated IIS and ASP.NET request-processing pipeline.
    ▪ Classic if you want to use IIS and ASP.NET request-processing modes separately. In classic mode, managed code is processed using Aspnet_isapi.dll instead of the IIS 7 integrated pipeline.

7. Select Start application pool immediately to start the application pool whenever the WWW service is started. By default, this is selected.

8. Click OK.

Change an Application Pool

To change an application pool for an application:

1. Open IIS Manager.

2. In the Connections pane, expand the server node and click Application Pools.

3. On the Application Pools page, select the application pool that contains the application that you want to change.

4. In the Actions pane, click View Applications.

5. Select the application whose application pool you want to change and click Change Application Pool in the Actions pane.

6. In the Select Application Pool dialog box, select an application pool from the Application pool list and click OK.

If you have a problematic application and you cannot easily correct the code that causes the problems, you can limit the extent of these problems by periodically recycling the worker process that services the application.

Recycle a Worker Process Manually

To manually recycle a worker process:

1. Open IIS Manager.

2. In the Connections pane, expand the server node and click Application Pools.

3. On the Application Pools page, select the application pool you want to recycle immediately.

4. In the Actions pane, click Recycle and then click Yes.

Rather than manually recycling a worker process, you can choose to configure an application pool to recycle at a scheduled time.

Configure an Application Pool to Recycle at a Scheduled Time

To configure an application pool to recycle at a scheduled time:

1. Open IIS Manager.

2. In the Connections pane, expand the server node and click Application Pools.

3. On the Application Pools page, select an application pool and click Recycling in the Actions pane.

4. Select Specific time(s) and, in the corresponding box, type a time at which you want the application pool to recycle daily. For example, type 11:30 AM or 11:30 PM. You can also specify time intervals such as every 60 minutes.

5. Click Next, select the events that should be logged when an application pool recycles, and click Finish.

Exploring Default Documents and Directory Listings

By default, when you type in a Web site's URL such as http://acme.com, it will go to the root folder designed for acme.com and first look for one of the following files:

1. Default.htm

2. Default.asp

3. Index.htm

4. Index.html

5. Isstart.htm

6. Default.aspx

The Default Documents feature allows you to configure the list of default documents that will automatically be presented to a browser if a document is not specified, such as `http://TestWebSite.com/start.html`. Therefore, it will first look for `http://TestWebSite.com/default.htm`. If it does not find default.htm, it will then try `http://TestWebSite.com/default.asp`, and so on. You can change the order of default documents or add additional default documents by clicking the Web site or folder and double-clicking Default Document under IIS in the left pane. To change the order, click the file you want to change and click the Move Up or Move Down arrows in the Actions pane. If you want to add a new default document, click the Add option in the Actions pane.

In some instances, you may just want to provide a directory listing of files so that users can quickly download those files. Use the Directory Browsing feature page to modify the content settings for browsing a directory on the web server. When you configure directory browsing, all subdirectories use the same settings unless you override them at a lower level.

Using IIS Security

Since Web sites are designed to provide information, some of which may be sensitive, there will be times when you have to protect that data. You can protect it by limiting who can access the Web site, by specifying how users authenticate, and/or by encrypting the content when a request is made.

You can grant or deny specific computers, groups of computers, or domains access to sites, applications, directories, or files on your server by using authorization rules.

View URL Authorization Rules

To view the URL authorization rules using IIS Manager:

1. Open IIS Manager and navigate to the level you want to manage.
2. In Features View, double-click Authorization Rules.

Create a New Authorization Rule

To create a new authorization rule using IIS Manager:

1. Open IIS Manager and navigate to the level you want to manage.
2. In Features View, double-click Authorization Rules.
3. In the Actions pane, click Add Allow Rule.
4. In the Add Allow Authorization Rule dialog box, select **one** of the following types of access:

    All users: Specifies that all users, whether they are anonymous or identified, can access the content.

    All anonymous users: Specifies that anonymous users can access the content.

    Specified roles or user groups: Specifies that only members of certain roles or user groups can access the content. Type the role or user group in the text box.

    Specified users: Specifies that only certain users can access the content. Type the user IDs in the text box.

5. Optionally, check "Apply this rule to specific verbs" if you want to further stipulate that the users, roles, or groups allowed to access the content can only use a specific list of HTTP verbs or actions. Type those verbs in the text box.

6. Click OK.

To create a Deny Rule, select Add Deny Rule instead of selecting Add Allow Rule.

Limit Access to Web Site by Address and Domain

To limit access to the Web site by IPv4 address and domain:

1. Open IIS Manager and navigate to the level you want to manage.

2. In Features View, double-click IPv4 Address and Domain Restrictions.

3. In the Actions pane, click Add Allow Entry.

4. In the Add Allow Restriction Rule dialog box, select Specific IPv4 address, IPv4 address range, or Domain name, add the IPv4 address, range, mask, or domain name, and click OK.

Use the Edit IP and Domain Restrictions dialog box to define access restrictions for unspecified clients or to enable domain name restrictions for all rules.

Authentication is used to confirm the identity of clients who request access to your sites and applications. IIS 10.0 supports the following forms of authentication:

Anonymous Allows access without providing a username and password.

ASP.NET Impersonation Allows you to run ASP.NET applications under a context other than the default ASP.NET account.

Basic Authentication Requires that users provide a valid username and password to gain access to content. Since basic authentication transmits passwords across the network in clear text, you should use it with a digital certificate to encrypt usernames and passwords being sent over the network.

Digest Authentication Uses a Windows domain controller to authenticate users who request access to content on your server.

Forms Authentication Uses client-side redirection to forward unauthenticated users to an HTML form where they can enter their credentials, which are usually a username and password.

Windows Authentication Uses NTLM or Kerberos protocols to authenticate clients.

AD Client Certificate Authentication Allows you to use the Active Directory service features to map users to client certificates for authentication.

To configure authentication for a Web site, application, or virtual folder, click the site, application, or virtual folder and double-click Authentication. The default setting for Windows authentication is Negotiate. This setting means that the client can select the appropriate security support provider.

Exploring Secure Sockets Layer and Digital Certificates

When you use SSL to encrypt web traffic, you are using asymmetric encryption, which involves a private key and a public key. The public key is provided to anyone who wants to access the web server, and the private key is kept secret, usually by the web server that you are trying to protect. The public key is used to encrypt data, which only the private key can decrypt.

To enable SSL, you must obtain and install a valid server certificate on the web server from a recognized certificate authority (CA) or use a self-signed certificate. The CA can be your internal Windows domain or a trusted third-party public CA such as Entrust or Verisign. While the self-signed certificate is not a trusted certificate, it can still be used for troubleshooting, testing, or application development.

When you visit an SSL Web site using Internet Explorer, you will notice a lock icon at the top of the IE window. To view the *digital certificate*, click the lock and select View Certificates. The most common type of digital certificate is the X.509 digital certificate. See Figure 7.5.

FIGURE 7.5 Digital certificate

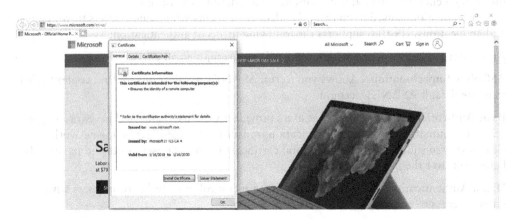

Acquire a Digital Certificate

To acquire a digital certificate using IIS 10:

1. Request an Internet server certificate from the IIS server. To request an Internet server certificate, click the server from within IIS Manager and double-click Server Certificates in Features View. Then click Create Certificate Request from the Actions Pane.

2. Send the generated certificate request to the CA, usually using the vendor's Web site.

3. Receive a digital certificate from the CA and install it on the IIS server. Again, open IIS Manage, double-click the server from within IIS Manager, and double-click Server Certificates in Features View. Then select the Complete Certificate Request.

4. On the Distinguished Name Properties page of the Request Certificate Wizard, type the following information and click Next.

   - In the Common name text box, type a name for the certificate.

   - In the Organization text box, type the name of the organization in which the certificate will be used.

   - In the Organizational unit text box, type the name of the organizational unit in the organization in which the certificate will be used.

   - In the City/locality text box, type the unabbreviated name of the city or locality where your organization or organizational unit is located.

   - In the State/province text box, type the unabbreviated name of the state or province where your organization or organizational unit is located.

   - In the Country/region text box, type the name of the country or region where your organization or organizational unit is located.

5. On the Cryptographic Service Provider Properties page, select either Microsoft RSA SChannel Cryptographic Provider or Microsoft DH SChannel Cryptographic Provider from the Cryptographic service provider drop-down list. By default, IIS 7 uses the Microsoft RSA SChannel Cryptographic Provider.

6. In the Bit length drop-down list, select a bit length that can be used by the provider. By default, the RSA SChannel provider uses a bit length of 1024. The DH SChannel provider uses a bit length of 512. A longer bit length is more secure, but it can affect performance.

7. Click Next.

8. On the File Name page, type a filename in the "Specify a file name for the certificate request text" box, or click the browse button (...) to locate a file, and click Finish.

9. Send the certificate request to a public CA.

From time to time, you may need to import and export digital certificates. The common formats used today are:

X509 format (.cer and .crt file extensions for Windows) A widely supported digital certificate that represents the individual certificate.

Cryptographic Message Syntax—PKCS #7 Format (.p7b file extension for Windows) Used to export the complete chain of digital certificates.

Personal Information Exchange Syntax—PKCS #12 Format (.pfx and .p12 file extensions for Windows) Used for exporting the public/private key pair.

Certificate Signing Request (CSR) Syntax—PKCS #10 Format Used in generating signed requests to trusted certificate signing authorities.

If you have a farm that consists of multiple web servers, you need to install the digital certificate from the first server and then export the digital certificate to a .pfx format to copy the public and private key to the other servers. Therefore, you will need to export the key from the first server and import to the other servers.

Export a Digital Certificate

To export a digital certificate:

1. Open IIS Manager and navigate to the level you want to manage.
2. In the Features View, double-click Server Certificates.
3. In the Actions pane, click Export.
4. In the Export dialog box, type a filename in the Export to box or click the browse button to navigate to the name of a file in which to store the certificate for exporting.
5. Type a password in the Password box if you want to associate a password with the exported certificate. Retype the password in the Confirm password box.
6. Click OK.

Import a Digital Certificate

To import a digital certificate:

1. Open IIS Manager and navigate to the level you want to manage.
2. In the Features View, double-click Server Certificates.
3. In the Actions pane, click Import.
4. In the Import Certificate dialog box, type a filename in the certificate file box or click the browse button to navigate to the name of a file where the exported certificate is stored. Type a password in the Password box if the certificate was exported with a password.
5. Select "Allow this certificate to be exported" if you want to be able to export the certificate, or clear "Allow this certificate to be exported" if you do not want to allow additional exports of this certificate.
6. Click OK.

Managing FTP with IIS

Different from earlier versions of IIS, with Windows Server 2016, the FTP sites are managed with IIS 10.0. However, to use the FTP servers, you need to install the FTP Server role. The majority of FTP sites are used primarily to download files. In most of these situations, FTP uses anonymous authentication where a username and password are not required.

Install FTP

To install FTP on Windows Server 2016:

1. On the taskbar, click Start, point to Administrative Tools, and click Server Manager.
2. In the Server Manager hierarchy pane, expand Roles and click Web Server (IIS).
3. In the Web Server (IIS) pane, scroll to the Role Services section and click Add Role Services.

4. On the Select Role Services page of the Add Role Services Wizard, expand FTP Server.

5. Select FTP Service. (Note: To support ASP.NET Membership or IIS Manager authentication for the FTP service, you will also need to select FTP Extensibility.)

6. Click Next.

7. On the Confirm Installation Selections page, click Install.

8. On the Results page, click Close.

Configure FTP

To configure an FTP site for anonymous access:

1. Open IIS 10 Manager. In the Connections pane, click the Sites node in the tree.

2. Create a folder at "%SystemDrive%\inetpub\ftproot."

3. Set the permissions to allow anonymous access by opening a command and typing the following command:

    ```
    ICACLS "%SystemDrive%\inetpub\ftproot" /Grant IUSR:R /T
    ```

4. Close the command prompt.

5. Right-click the Sites node in the tree and click Add FTP Site, or click Add FTP Site in the Actions pane.

6. When the Add FTP Site wizard appears, enter **My New FTP Site** in the FTP site name box, then navigate to the %SystemDrive%\inetpub\ftproot folder that you created in the Prerequisites section. Note that if you choose to type in the path to your content folder, you can use environment variables in your paths. Click Next.

7. On the Binding and SSL Settings page, fill in the following:

    ▪ Choose an IP address for your FTP site from the IP Address drop-down, or choose to accept the default selection of "All Unassigned."

    ▪ Enter the TCP/IP port for the FTP site in the Port box. For this walk-through, choose to accept the default port of 21.

    ▪ For this example, do not use a host name. Make sure that the Virtual Host box is blank.

    ▪ Make sure that the Certificates drop-down is set to "Not Selected" and that they Allow SSL option is selected.

    Click the Next button.

8. On the Authentication and Authorization Information page, select Anonymous for the Authentication settings. For the Authorization settings, choose "Anonymous users" from the "Allow access to" drop-down, and select Read for the Permissions option. Click Finish.

Understanding Remote Access

Today, it is very common for an organization to use a remote access server (RAS). This enables users to connect remotely to a network using various protocols and connection types. By connecting to the RAS over the Internet, users can connect to their organization's network so that they can access data files, read email, and access other applications just as if they were sitting at work.

Certification Ready

How can you connect to servers when you are at home? 2.2

Virtual private networks (VPNs) link two computers through a wide-area network such as the Internet. To keep the connection secure, the data sent between the two computers is encapsulated and encrypted. In one scenario, a client connects to the RAS server to access internal resources from off-site. Another scenario is to connect two remote sites together by creating a VPN tunnel between an RAS server located at each site.

The four types of tunneling protocols used with a VPN/RAS server running on Windows Server 2016 include:

Point-to-Point Tunneling Protocol (PPTP) A VPN protocol based on the legacy Point-to-Point protocol used with modems. Unfortunately, PPTP is easy to set up but is considered to use weak encryption technology.

Layer 2 Tunneling Protocol (L2TP) Used with IPSec to provide security. L2TP is the industry standard when setting up secure tunnels.

Secure Socket Tunneling Protocol (SSTP) Uses the HTTPS protocol over TCP port 443 to pass traffic through firewalls and web proxies that might block PPTP and L2TP/IPSec.

Internet Key Exchange v2 (IKEv2) A VPN tunneling protocol that is built on IPSec. The primary advantage of IKEv2 is that it tolerates interruptions, by automatically restoring the VPN after the network connection is reestablished. With Windows, it is often referred to as *VPN Reconnect*.

When using VPNs, Windows 10 and Windows Server 2016 support the following forms of authentication:

Password Authentication Protocol (PAP) Uses plain text (unencrypted passwords). PAP is the least secure authentication and is not recommended.

Challenge Handshake Authentication Protocol (CHAP)   A challenge-response authentication that uses the industry-standard md5 hashing scheme to encrypt the response. CHAP was an industry standard for years and is still quite popular.

Microsoft CHAP version 2 (MS-CHAP v2)   Provides two-way authentication (mutual authentication). MS-CHAP v2 provides stronger security than CHAP.

Extensible Authentication Protocol (EAP)   A universal authentication framework that allows third-party vendors to develop custom authentication schemes, including retinal scans, voice recognition, fingerprint identifications, smart cards, Kerberos, and digital certificates. It also provides a mutual authentication method that supports password-based user or computer authentication. It is often combined with MS-CHAPv2.

Protected Extensible Authentication Protocol (PEAP)   Encapsulates the EAP with an encrypted and authenticated Transport Layer Security (TLS) tunnel.

Load Remote Access and Routing

To make a computer running Windows Server 2016 load Remote Access and Routing:

1. Click Start, and click Server Manager.
2. Open the Manage menu, click Add Roles and Features.
3. In the Add Roles and Features Wizard on the Before You Begin page, click Next.
4. In the Installation Type page, click Next.
5. On the Server Selection page, click Next.
6. On the Server Roles page, select Remote Access. Click Next.
7. On the Features page, click Next.
8. On the Remote Access page, click Next.
9. On the Role Service page, select DirectAccess and VPN (RAS) and Routing options. When you are asked to add features, click the Add Features button. Click Next.
10. On the Confirmation page, click Install.
11. When the installation is complete, click Close.

To open IIS manager, you use one of the following methods:

- Start ➤ Windows Administrative Tools ➤ Routing and Remote Access
- Using Server Manager, open the Tools menu and select Routing and Remote Access.

A configured Routing and Remote Access console is shown in Figure 7.6.

FIGURE 7.6   Routing and Remote Access Server console

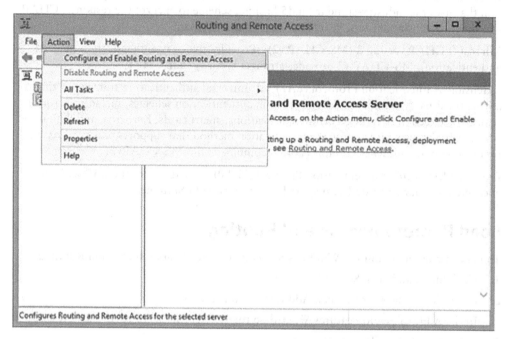

Configure a VPN Server

To enable RRAS and configure it as a VPN server:

1. Open the RRAS MMC Snap-in.

2. Right-click the server name for which you want to enable routing and then click Configure and Enable Routing and Remote Access. If you are using Server Manager, right-click Routing and Remote Access and then click Configure and Enable Routing and Remote Access.

3. On the Welcome page, click Next.

4. On the Configuration page, click Remote Access (dial-up or VPN) and then click Next.

5. On the Remote Access page, select Virtual private network (VPN) access and NAT and click Next.

6. On the VPN Connection page, select the network interface that is connected to the public Internet from which remote VPN clients will connect to this server.

7. To configure packet filters that restrict network access through the specified public network adapter to only the ports required by VPN clients, select "Enable security" on the selected interface by setting up static packet filters.

8. On the Network Selection page, select the private network to which remote VPN clients are to be granted access. The network adapter and its IP address are displayed to help you determine which to select.

9. On the IP Address Assignment page, specify the way in which the RRAS server will acquire IP addresses for the remote VPN clients. If you have a DHCP server with a range of addresses available, click Automatic. If you want the RRAS server to manage the IP addresses, click "From a specified range of addresses."

10. If you did not select Automatic on the Address Range Assignment page, click New and type starting and ending IP addresses to create the range from which remote VPN clients are assigned addresses. You can enter multiple ranges if required. Click Next when you have created the address ranges.

11. On the Managing Multiple Remote Access Servers page, select whether you want to use a centralized RADIUS server for authentication of your network clients. If you select No, then RRAS uses its local account database or, if the RRAS server is joined to an Active Directory domain, the RRAS server uses the domain account database. Note: To use Active Directory Domain Services (AD DS), you must join the RRAS server to a domain and add the computer account of this server to the RAS and IAS Servers security group in the domain of which this server is a member. The domain administrator can add the computer account to the RAS and IAS Servers security group by using Active Directory Users and Computers or by using the netsh ras add registeredserver command.

12. On the Completing page, click Finish.

Create a VPN Tunnel

To create a VPN tunnel on a computer running Windows 10 so you can connect to a Remote Access Server:

1. From Control Panel, select Network and Internet to access the Network and Sharing Center.

2. From the Network and Sharing Center, choose "Set up a new connection or wizard."

3. On the Set Up a Connection or Network page, choose Connect to a workplace.

4. On the Connect to a Workplace page, answer the question "Do you want to use a connection that you already have?" Choose to create a new connection or choose an existing connection.

5. On the next page, choose Use my Internet connection (VPN).

6. On the next screen, choose your VPN connection or specify the Internet Address for the VPN Server and a Destination Name. You can also specify the options to use a Smart card for authentication; Allow other people to use this connection; or Don't connect now, just set up so I can connect later.

You may need to do additional configuration to your VPN connection, such as specifying the type of protocol, authentication protocol, and the type of encryption.

In Windows 10 or Windows Server 2016, to connect using the VPN once the VPN connection is created and configured, open Windows Settings and click Network & Internet ➢ VPN. Then, click your VPN connection and click the Connect button. See Figure 7.7.

FIGURE 7.7   VPN connection

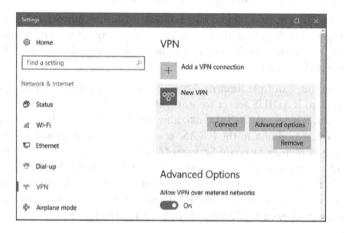

By default, when you connect to a VPN using the previous configuration, all web browsing and network traffic goes through the default gateway on the Remote Network unless you are communicating with local home computers. Having this option enabled helps protect the corporate network because all traffic also goes through firewalls and proxy servers, which prevents a network from being infected or compromised.

If you wish to route your Internet browsing through your home Internet connection rather than going through the corporate network, you can disable the Use Default Gateway on Remote Network option. Disabling this option is called using a split tunnel.

Enable a Split Tunnel

To enable a split tunnel:

1. Right-click a VPN connection and click Properties.

2. Click the Networking tab.

3. Double-click the Internet Protocol Version 4 (TCP/IPv4).

4. Click the Advanced button.

5. Deselect "Use default gateway on remote network."

It can be a lot of work to configure multiple clients to connect to a remote access server, and it may be too complicated for a computer novice.

If you have to configure multiple clients to connect to a remote server, it can be a lot of work, and it can be easy to make an error. To help simplify the administration of the VPN client into an easy-to-install executable, you could use the Connection Manager Administration Kit (CMAK), which can also be installed as a feature in Windows Server 2016.

Introducing Remote Administration

With early networks, users utilized dumb terminals (systems consisting of a monitor and keyboard without a processor) to connect to a mainframe. Later, computers could use telnet to connect to a server and execute commands at a command prompt. *Remote Desktop Services*, formerly known as Terminal Services, is one of the components of Microsoft Windows that allows a user to access applications and data on a remote computer over a network.

Certification Ready

Can you list and describe the various ways to manage a server remotely? 2.2

By default, Windows Servers are configured to use Remote Desktop for Administration licensing mode, which supports up to two remote sessions, and is primarily used to connect to a server to manage it. However, if you want to run applications that require more than the standard two remote sessions, you will need to first load and configure the computer running Windows Server 2016 as a Remote Desktop Session Host server role. You will also need an RD licensing manager to keep track of the licenses used, and you will have to purchase and install Remote Desktop Server licenses.

To access a computer running Remote Desktop Services, you would use Remote Desktop Connections to access a computer's graphical user interface including the desktop, start menu, and programs just as if you were sitting in front of the computer. See Figure 7.8. Two technologies that allow you to remotely access a computer's desktop are Remote Desktop and *Remote Assistance* over TCP port 1389.

FIGURE 7.8  Remote Desktop connection

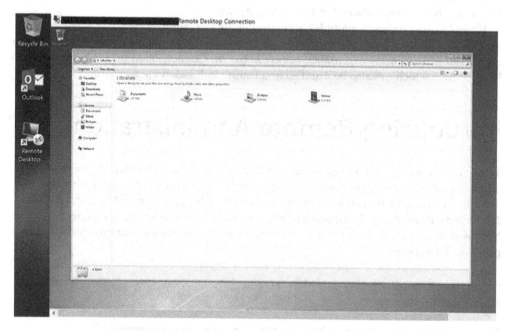

To connect to a remote computer:

- The computer must be turned on.
- It must have a network connection.
- Remote Desktop must be enabled in the System Properties.
- You must have permission to connect (be a member of the Administrators group or the Remote Desktop Users group).

Enable Remote Desktop

To enable Remote Desktop:

1. Right-click the Start button, and click System.
2. In the System window, click Remote settings.
3. Select one of the following options:
   - Allow connections from computer running any version of Remote Desktop (less secure).
   - Allow connections only from computers running Remote Desktop with Network Level Authentication (more secure) options.
4. If you are prompted for an administrator password or confirmation, type the password or provide confirmation.

5. Click Select Users. If you are enabling Remote Desktop for your current user account, your name will automatically be added to this list of remote users and you can skip the next two steps.

6. In the Remote Desktop Users dialog box, click Add. This will add users to the Remote Desktop Users group.

7. In the Select Users dialog box, enter the user's name and click OK.

Access Remote Desktop

To start Remote Desktop on the computer you want to work from:

1. Open Remote Desktop Connection by clicking the Start button, selecting Windows Accessories, and selecting Remote Desktop Connection. You could also run the mstsc.exe command.

2. In Computer, type the name of the computer that you want to connect to and click Connect. (You can also type the IP address instead of the computer name if you want.)

For more advanced options before the connection, click the Options button. See Figure 7.9.

FIGURE 7.9   Configuring Remote Desktop connections

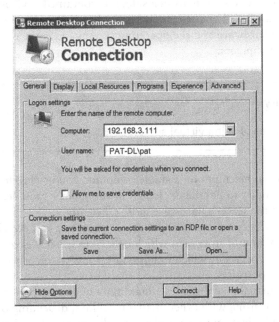

    If for some reason the Explorer taskbar is not available, you can also press the Ctrl+Alt+End keys to open the same window in Task Manager, from which you can start explorer.exe.

RemoteApp is a special mode of Remote Desktop Services that allows you to run an application in its own window instead of opening a session with Remote Desktop Connection. For the most part, the application looks like a normal application running on your local computer but in reality it is running remotely on a server. A RemoteApp can be either packaged as a .rdp file or distributed via an .msi Windows Installer package.

Besides using a VPN tunnel, you can use a Remote Desktop Gateway (RD Gateway) role service to enable authorized remote users to connect to resources on an internal private network over the Internet using a Remote Desktop Connection (RDC) client. RD Gateway uses the Remote Desktop Protocol (RDP) over HTTPS to establish a secure, encrypted connection between remote users on the Internet and the internal network resources on which their productivity applications run.

Understanding Server Virtualization

Virtualization has become quite popular during the last few years. By using *virtual machine* technology, you can run multiple operating systems concurrently on a single machine, which allows separation of services while keeping cost to a minimum. It can also be used to create Windows test systems in a safe, self-contained environment. Microsoft Hyper-V is a hypervisor-based virtualization system for x64 computers. The *hypervisor* is installed between the hardware and the operating system and is the main component that manages the virtual computers.

Certification Ready

What are the advantages of using virtual servers? 2.5

To run several virtual machines on a single computer, you need to have sufficient processing power and memory to handle the load. However, since most servers often sit idle, virtualization utilizes the server's hardware more efficiently.

To keep each virtual server secure and reliable, each server is placed in its own partition. A partition is a logical unit of storage in which operating systems execute. Each virtual machine accesses the hypervisor, which handles interrupts to the processor and redirects them to the respective partition.

In Hyper-V, each virtual machine uses a maximum of one processor; however, it may share the processor it is using with other virtual machines, depending on the number of processors on the physical computer and the number of running virtual machines. In addition, each virtual machine requires enough memory to run the operating system and applications, plus approximately 32 MB for the emulated video RAM and code cache. A motherboard and BIOS that supports virtualization are also required.

By default, Hyper-V stores all the files that make up a virtual machine in one folder with the same name as the virtual server for simple management and portability. Renaming a virtual machine does not rename the virtual machine folder. By default, these folders are located in the Shared Virtual Machines folder, which is located in Documents and Settings\ All Users\Documents\Shared Virtual Machines.

In Hyper-V, each virtual machine uses the following files:

- A virtual machine configuration (.vmc) file in XML format that contains the virtual machine configuration information, including all settings for the virtual machine.

- One or more virtual hard disk (.vhd) files to store the guest operating system, applications, and data for the virtual machine. So if you create a 12-GB partition for the virtual machine's hard drive, the virtual hard disk file will be 12 GB.

In addition, a virtual machine may also use a saved-state (.vsv) file, if the machine has been placed into a saved state.

A "saved state" virtual machine backup is also referred to as an "offline backup" as it requires some downtime for the virtual machine. Saved state means that the Hyper-V VSS writer places the virtual machine in a "hibernated" state. When the saved state method is requested the virtual machine is placed in saved state during the PrepareForSnapshot event.

Snapshots are taken of the appropriate volumes, and then the virtual machine is returned to the previous state, which is handled with the PostSnapshot event.

The saved state method generally translates into a couple of seconds or more where the virtual machine will not be responsive while the PrepareForSnapshot event is taking place.

A saved state backup is generally not recommended for production backups due to the fact that they:

- Requires downtime of the virtual machine

- Are not application aware

To install Hyper-V, you need:

- An x64 version of Windows Server 2016.

- 64-bit processors and BIOS that support hardware-assisted virtualization (Intel VT or AMD-V) technology.

- Hardware Data Execution Prevention (DEP), which Intel describes as eXecuted Disable (XD) and AMD describes as No eXecute (NS) it is a technology used in CPUs to segregate areas of memory for use by either storage of processor instructions or for storage of data.

In future versions of Windows, virtualization may not require the processor and motherboard supporting the hardware-assisted virtualization technology.

Install Hyper-V

To add the Hyper-V role:

1. Open Server Manager.

2. In the Server Manager window, open the Manage menu and click Add Roles And Features.

3. When the Add Roles and Features Wizard opens, on the Before You Begin page, click Next.

4. On the Installation Type page, Role-based or feature-based installation is already selected. Click Next.

5. When the Select Destination Server page appears, select the server on which you want to install Hyper-V and click Next. The Select Server Roles page appears.

6. Select the Hyper-V role. When you are prompted to add features, click the Add Features button. Click Next.

7. When the Hyper-V page appears, click Next.

8. On the Create Virtual Switches page, select the check box for a network adapter and click Next.

9. When the Virtual Machine Migration page appears, click Next.

10. When the Default Stores page appears, specify alternatives to the default locations for virtual hard disk and virtual machine configuration files, if desired, and click Next.

11. On the Confirm Installation Selections page, select Restart the destination server automatically if required and then click Yes. Click Install. The host may restart several times as the system is rebooted.

Creating Virtual Machines

After installing Hyper-V, you are ready to create some virtual machines and install the operating system on each virtual machine that you create.

Create Virtual Machines in Hyper-V

To create and set up a virtual machine:

1. Open Hyper-V Manager from the Administrative Tools. See Figure 7.10.

2. From the Action pane, click New and then click Virtual Machine.

3. From the New Virtual Machine Wizard, click Next.

4. On the Specify Name and Location page, specify what you want to name the virtual machine and where you want to store it.

5. On the Memory page, specify enough memory to run the guest operating system you want to use on the virtual machine.

FIGURE 7.10   Hyper-V Manager

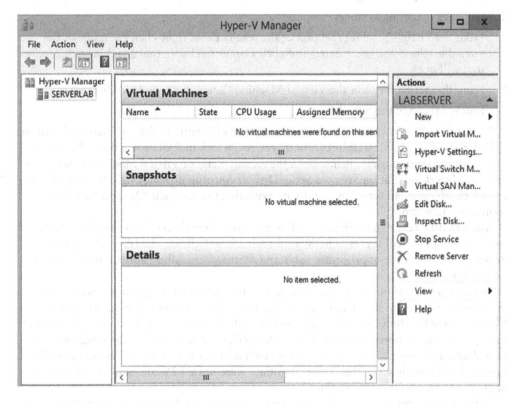

6. On the Networking page, connect the network adapter to an existing virtual network if you want to establish network connectivity at this point. If you want to use a remote image server to install an operating system on your test virtual machine, select the external network.

7. On the Connect Virtual Hard Disk page, specify a name, location, and size to create a virtual hard disk so you can install an operating system on it.

8. On the Installation Options page, choose the method you want to use to install the operating system:

   - Install an operating system from a boot CD/DVD-ROM. You can use either physical media or an image file (.iso file).

   - Install an operating system from a boot floppy disk.

   - Install an operating system from a network-based installation server. To use this option, you must configure the virtual machine with a network adapter connected to the same network as the image server.

9. Click Finish.

Install the Operating System on a Virtual Machine

To install the operating system:

1. From the Virtual Machines section of the results pane, right-click the name of the virtual machine you just created and click Connect. The Virtual Machine Connection tool will open.

2. From the Action menu in the Virtual Machine Connection window, click Start.

3. Proceed through the installation.

Some of the Windows built-in drivers do not run efficiently under a virtual environment. Therefore, you need to install Integration Services, which includes some basic drivers. To install the integration components, open the Action menu of Virtual Machine Connection and click Insert Integration Services Setup Disk. If Autorun does not start the installation automatically, you can start it manually by executing the %windir%\support\amd64\ setup.exe command.

You are now ready to configure and manage the virtual server just as if you were working on a physical server. This would include configuring the IP, enabling remote desktop, installing the appropriate roles and features, installing additional software, and so forth.

In many organizations, you may want to consolidate several physical servers to one machine running multiple virtual servers. Microsoft System Center Virtual Machine Manager (VMM) allows you to convert existing physical computers into virtual machines through a process known as *physical-to-virtual (P2V) conversion*. VMM simplifies P2V by providing a task-based wizard to automate much of the conversion process. Since the P2V process is completely scriptable, you can initiate large-scale P2V conversions through the Windows PowerShell command line.

While many companies use virtual servers to consolidate their servers, there may be an occasional need to convert a virtual server to a physical server. However, Hyper-V does not include any tools to convert a physical server to a virtual server (known as virtual-to-physical (V2P) conversion). Instead, you will have to use a third-party tool.

Physical to Virtual (P2V)

Physical to virtual (P2V) is a term that refers to the migration of physical machines to virtual machines (VMs), also called hardware virtualization.

Data migrated in P2V includes an OS, applications, programs, and data from a computer's main hard disk to a VM or a disk partition. The end result of a P2V migration is a VM with the same data, applications, and system configurations as the physical server being virtualized.

P2V enables developers to transfer their physical environment into a digital one, using less hardware and physical space, while giving developers the advantages of VMs, such as more flexibility since VMs can run on multiple platforms.

How Physical to Virtual Works

A P2V tool will save a physical machine's state as an image. This means the data that makes up a physical server or system is electronically copied, similar in concept to how a Docker container saves data by creating an image. The image is installed by a hypervisor in the specified storage space. A person or hypervisor can then determine the location of each required resource.

There are three main strategies for P2V migration:

- Manually - P2V can be done manually by creating or defining a virtual environment and then reinstalling the operating system, applications, and data. This can be a monotonous and uncertain process, especially if the new environment contains substantially different hardware than the old environment. The migration can partially or automatically carried out using special programs known as migration tools. By using these migration tools, P2V is much faster than manually rebuilding the contents.

- A semi-automated tool assists the user in migrating a physical machine to a VM.

- Fully automated P2V tools can migrate a physical machine to a VM without any assistance from the end user.

Managing Virtual Hard Disks

In addition to virtual networks, an administrator needs to manage virtual hard disks that will be attached to virtual machines. A virtual hard disk in Hyper-V, apart from a pass-through disk, is a VHD or VHDX file that basically simulates a hard drive on a virtual machine.

Types of Hard Disks

Depending on how an administrator want to use the disk, Hyper-V offers various types

Type of Disk	Description	When to use it.
Dynamically expanding	This disk starts with a small VHD file and expands it on demand once an installation takes place. It can grow to the maximum size you defined during creation. Can use this type of disk to clone a local hard drive during creation.	This option is effective when you don't know the exact space needed on the disk and when you want to preserve hard disk space on the host machine. Unfortunately, it is the slowest disk type.

Type of Disk	Description	When to use it.
Fixed size	The size of the VHD file is fixed to the size specified when the disk is created. This option is faster than a dynamically expanding disk. However, a fixed-size disk uses up the maximum defined space immediately. This type is ideal for cloning a local hard drive.	A fixed-size disk provides faster access than dynamically expanding or differencing disks, but it is slower than a physical disk.
Differencing	This type of disk is associated in a parent-child relationship with another disk. The differencing disk is the child, and the associated virtual disk is the parent. Differencing disks include only the differences to the parent disk. By using this type, you can save a lot of disk space in similar virtual machines. This option is suitable if you have multiple virtual machines with the same operating systems.	Differencing disks are most commonly found in test environments and should not be used in production environments.
Physical (or pass-through disk)	The virtual machine receives direct pass-through access to the physical disk for exclusive use. This type provides the highest performance of all disk types and thus should be used for production servers where performance is the top priority. The drive is not available for other guest systems.	This type is used in high-end data centers to provide optimum performance for VMs. It's also used in failover cluster environments.

Nested Virtualization

Nested virtualization allows administrators to create virtual machines within virtual machines.

Nested virtualization requirements:

- Operating system that allows nested virtualization (Windows Server 2016).
- Minimum of 4 GB RAM available to the virtualized Hyper-V host.
- The processor needs to use Intel VT-x.
- 2 virtual processors for the container host VM.

Managing Virtual Machines

When you work with physical servers, there may be times where you have to add a network card, add or expand a hard drive, or move a network card cable from one switch to another. Virtual servers have the same needs, but you must perform these tasks virtually.

Managing Disks

When you create a virtual hard drive, you can define the virtual hard disks as:

Fixed Size Virtual Hard Disks   Take up the full amount of disk space when created, even if there is no data using parts of the hard disk.

Dynamically Expanding Hard Disks   Expands as it needs space up to its full space.

One of the strengths of virtual servers is the ability to take snapshots. A *snapshot* is a point-in-time image of a virtual machine that you can return to. So, if you make a change to the system, such as loading a component or installing an update, that causes problems, you can use the snapshot to quickly revert to the point before the change was made.

The snapshot files consist of:

- A copy of the VM configuration .xml file.

- Any saved state files.

- A differencing disk (.avhd) is the new working disk for all writes and is a child of the working disk prior to the snapshot.

With Hyper-V, you can create 50 levels of snapshot per virtual server.

To create a snapshot in Hyper-V, select Snapshot from the Action menu or panel or by clicking the snapshot button in the toolbar. When you create a snapshot, a dialog box will appear that allows you to enter a name for the snapshot. You can dismiss this dialog and have the snapshot use an auto-generated name if you prefer. This auto-generated name will consist of the name of the virtual machine followed by the date and time when the snapshot was taken.

Managing Virtual Networks and Network Cards

Virtual networks consist of one or more virtual machines configured to access local or external network resources. The virtual network is configured to use a network adapter in the physical computer.

If a network adapter in the physical computer is selected, then any virtual machines attached to the virtual network can access the networks to which that physical adapter is connected. If the virtual network is configured not to use a network adapter, then any virtual machine attached to the virtual network becomes part of the internal virtual machine network. An internal virtual machine network consists of all virtual machines attached to a virtual network that is configured to use a network adapter. Each internal virtual machine network is completely isolated from all other internal virtual machine networks.

Add a Virtual Network

To add a virtual network:

1.   Open Hyper-V Manager.

2.   From the Actions menu, click Virtual Network Manager. See Figure 7.11.

FIGURE 7.11   Virtual Network Manager

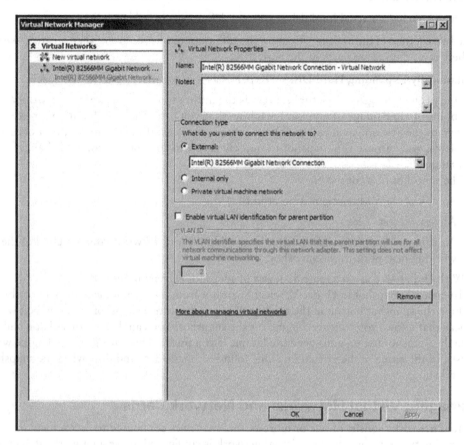

3. Under "Create virtual network," select the type of network you want to create.

4. Click Add. The New Virtual Network page appears.

5. Type a name for the new network. Review the other properties and modify them if necessary.

6. Click OK to save the virtual network and close Virtual Network Manager, or click Apply to save the virtual network and continue using Virtual Network Manager.

Modify a Virtual Network

To modify a virtual network:

1. Open Hyper-V Manager.

2. From the Actions menu, click Virtual Network Manager.

3. Under Virtual Networks, click the name of the network you want to modify.

4. Under Virtual Network Properties, edit the appropriate properties to modify the virtual network.

5. Click OK to save the changes and close Virtual Network Manager, or click Apply to save the changes and continue using Virtual Network Manager.

Remove a Virtual Network

To remove a virtual network:

1. Open Hyper-V Manager.

2. From the Actions menu, click Virtual Network Manager.

3. Under Virtual Networks, click the name of the network you want to remove.

4. Under Virtual Network Properties, click Remove.

5. Click OK to save the changes and close Virtual Network Manager, or click Apply to save the changes and continue using Virtual Network Manager.

Add a Network Adapter

To add a network adapter:

1. Open Hyper-V Manager. Click Start, point to Administrative Tools, and click Hyper-V Manager.

2. In the results pane under Virtual Machines, select the virtual machine that you want to configure.

3. In the Action pane under the virtual machine name, click Settings.

4. In the navigation pane, click Add Hardware.

5. On the Add Hardware page, choose a network adapter or a legacy network adapter.

6. Click Add. The Network Adapter or Legacy Network Adapter page appears.

7. Under Network, select the virtual network you want to connect to.

8. If you want to configure a static MAC address or virtual LAN identifier, specify the numbers you want to use.

9. Click OK.

More Information

For more information about Hyper-V, visit the following Web site:
https://docs.microsoft.com/en-us/virtualization/hyper-v-on-windows/about/.

Skill Summary

In this lesson you learned:

- When you view web pages, you are connecting to the web server using TCP port 80.

- SSL, short for Secure Sockets Layer, uses TCP port 443, which uses a digital certificate to encrypt data sent to and from a Web site so that it cannot be read by anyone except the source and target. When you are using SSL, the browser URL will start with https.

- File Transfer Protocol (FTP) is a standard network protocol used to transfer a file from one host to another over a TCP/IP-based network.

- Microsoft's web server/application server is Internet Information Services (IIS).

- To support multiple Web sites, you can assign additional IP addresses and assign a site to each IP address by using different ports for each site or host headers.

- To configure the IP address, port, and name a Web site will respond to, you must configure the site binding.

- A virtual directory is a directory used in a Web site that corresponds to a physical directory elsewhere on the server, on another server, or on a Web site.

- An application is a grouping of content on a Web site that is defined at the root level or in a separate folder that has specific properties, such as the application pool in which the application runs and the permissions that are granted on the folder.

- An application pool is a set of resources (a worker process or a set of worker processes) used by a Web site or application that defines the memory boundaries for the Web site.

- The Default Documents feature allows you to configure the list of default documents that will automatically be presented to a browser if a document is not specified.

- A virtual private network (VPN) links two computers through a wide-area network such as the Internet. To keep the connection secure, the data sent between the two computers is encapsulated and encrypted.

- To access a computer running Remote Desktop Services, you use Remote Desktop Connections to access a computer's graphical user interface including the desktop, start menu, and programs just as if you were sitting in front of the computer.

- Remote assistance is similar to remote desktop except it is used to connect to another user's session so that you can see what the user is seeing and interact with that session.

- By using virtual machine technology, you can run multiple operating systems concurrently on a single machine, which allows separation of services while keeping cost to a minimum.

- The hypervisor is installed between the hardware and the operating system and is the main component that manages virtual computers.

- Some of the Windows built-in drivers do not run efficiently under a virtual environment. Therefore, you need to install Integration Services, which includes some basic drivers.

- Microsoft System Center Virtual Machine Manager (VMM) allows you to convert existing physical computers into virtual machines through a process known as physical-to-virtual (P2V) conversion.

- A snapshot is a point-in-time image of a virtual machine that you can return to.

Knowledge Assessment

Fill in the Blank

1. The _____ is a system of interlinked hypertext documents known as web pages that are browsed with a web browser.

2. The predominant markup language for web pages is _____.

3. Microsoft's web server is known as _____.

4. In IIS, a _____ is a directory used in a Web site that corresponds to a physical directory elsewhere on the server, on another server, or on a Web site.

5. HTTPS uses port _____.

6. _____ is the most widely used digital certificate.

7. Microsoft's virtual machine technology is _____.

8. A _____ is a point-in-time image of a virtual machine that you can return to.

9. You typically use _____ to remotely connect and manage a server, which allows you to run programs directly on the desktop.

10. _____ is a special mode of Remote Desktop Services that allows you to run an application in its own window.

Multiple Choice

1. Which protocol is used to transfer files between computers?
   A. DNS
   B. HTTP
   C. FTP
   D. Telnet

2. Which port does SMTP use?
   A. 21
   B. 25
   C. 80
   D. 443

3. Which port does HTTP use?

   A. 21

   B. 25

   C. 80

   D. 443

4. A(n) _____ defines a set of resources used by a Web site or application that defines the memory boundaries of a Web site.

   A. Virtual directory

   B. Root directory

   C. Application pool

   D. Port forwarder

5. Which authentication sends username and password that is not encrypted?

   A. Anonymous

   B. Basic authentication

   C. Digest authentication

   D. Windows authentication

6. When configuring VPN, L2TP uses _____ for encryption.

   A. SSTP

   B. PPTP

   C. MPE

   D. IPSec

7. Which authentication method used with VPN clients can be used with retinal scan and fingerprint identifications?

   A. PAP

   B. CHAP

   C. MS-CHAPv2

   D. EAP-MS-CHAPv2

8. By using _____ technology, you can run multiple operating systems concurrently on one machine.

   A. Virtual machine

   B. Virtual directory

   C. Terminal server

   D. Remote access

9. After you create a virtual server in Hyper-V and install the operating system, you then need to install _____ so that the virtual server can run more efficiently.

   A. VMWare client tools

   B. Remote Desktop tools

   C. Integration Services Setup

   D. P2V Disk tools

10. Which protocol is used to send out email?

    A. POP2

    B. IMAP

    C. HTTP

    D. SMTP

True/False

1. When typing in a URL that does not specify a directory, your browser will always return a 404 error.

2. If you are using Basic Authentication, you should use digital certificates to encrypt.

3. To copy a digital certificate that includes the public and private key pair, use CSR.

4. Today, PTTP is the recommended VPN tunneling protocol.

5. The .vhd file holds the virtual machine configuration information.

Competency Assessment

Scenario 7-1: Allowing Work from Home

You just started working as a system administrator for the Acme Corporation. Your company decides that as a benefit to its employees, some employees can work from home one day a week. Explain what can you do to help make this happen, what key technology you would use, and how would you configure it.

Scenario 7-2: Isolating Server Applications

You have two network applications—a network accounting application and a network HR application—that are not processor hungry. Both of these applications must be kept totally isolated, and both will access a centralized database server. What do you recommend?

Proficiency Assessment

Scenario 7-3: Create a Web Site

1. Install IIS.
2. Create a Web site that responds to contoso.com and www.contoso.com using port 80 that points to c:\Inetpub\wwwroot\contoso.
3. Add an entry in the host file that points contoso.com to the IP address of your server.
4. Create a folder called virtual in the c:\inetpub folder.
5. Create a virtual directory that points to c:\inetpub\virtual.
6. Create an application pool called contoso.
7. Change the contoso Web site to use the contoso application pool.

Scenario 7-4: Using Remote Desktop

1. Make sure remote desktop is enabled on your computer.
2. Connect to another windows computer using Remote Desktop.

 **Real World Scenario**

Workplace Ready: Exchange and SQL Server

This lesson covered popular network application and services that are included with Windows Server 2016. However, Microsoft and many other companies have created other applications or services that use or depend on the applications and services that come with Windows Server 2016. For example, Microsoft Exchange depends on Active Directory for authentication, authorization, and name resolution for mailboxes. It also uses IIS to allow access to web-based versions of Microsoft Outlook and to allow mobile devices such as smart phones to sync email including calendar items and tasks. SQL Server also uses Active Directory and IIS to access and run reports. As you get deeper into being a system administrator, you will see that you are just getting started.

Appendix

Answer Key

Lesson 1: Server Overview

Answers to Knowledge Assessment

Fill-in-the-Blank Answers

1. role
2. processor
3. 64-bit
4. RAM
5. motherboard
6. ROM
7. BIOS
8. flashing
9. Server Core
10. answer file

Multiple-Choice Answers

1. D
2. A
3. C
4. D
5. E
6. C
7. B
8. B
9. D
10. D

True/False Answers

1. False
2. True
3. False
4. False
5. True

Answers to Competency Assessment

Scenario 1-1: Server Analysis

You should have at least two servers for a front end running the web server role and at least one server for a back end to run SQL. You may need additional servers, such as domain controllers and DNS servers. Each server should be running Windows Server 2016. You should have dual processor, 4 GB of RAM for the front-end servers and quad core, and 16 GB of RAM for the back-end SQL server.

Scenario 1-2: Identify Ports

Answers will vary. Users should be able to identify video ports, USB ports, and network ports.

Answers to Proficiency Assessment

Scenario 1-3: Installing Windows Server 2016

Many students will be new to computers and servers. Therefore, they may need assistance on how to burn a DVD from an ISO and how to make the server bootable from a DVD. You should also emphasize not to use the entire hard drive for the C drive/Windows installation since you will use the remaining space when working with disk management.

The steps to install Windows Server 2016 are:

1. Insert the Windows Server 2016 disc into the DVD drive and turn on the computer. Press any key to boot from the DVD (if necessary).

2. The computer switches to the Windows graphical interface, and the Windows Setup page appears. Using the drop-down lists provided, select the appropriate language to install, the time and currency format, and the keyboard or input method. Then, click Next.

3. On the Windows Server 2016 Install Now page, click Install Now.

4. When the Activate Windows page appears, in the text box, type the Windows Server 2016 activation key and then click Next.

5. On the Select the Operating System To Install page, select Windows Server 2016 Data-center (Desktop Experience). Click Next.

6. On the License Terms page, select the "I accept the license terms" option and then click Next.

7. Click the Custom: Install Windows only (advanced) option.

8. The Where Do You Want To Install Windows? page appears. From the list provided, select the partition on which you want to install Windows Server 2016, or select an area of unallocated disk space where the Setup program can create a new partition. Then click Next.

9. After several minutes, during which the Setup program installs Windows Server 2016, the computer reboots. When the Customize Settings page appears, in the Password and Reenter Password text boxes, type **Pa$$w0rd**. Click Finish.

Scenario 1-4: Using Windows Updates

No answer is needed. Depending on how long Windows is out, you can have a handful of updates, or you can have over a hundred updates. You should also tell students that they may need to perform updates two or three times before they can get all of the updates.

Lesson 2: Managing Windows 2016

Answers to Knowledge Assessment

Fill-in-the-Blank Answers

1. Settings, Control Panel
2. User Account Control (UAC)
3. unique
4. domain
5. Remote Desktop
6. date and time
7. Device drivers
8. Plug and Play (PnP)
9. signed driver
10. Device Manager

Multiple-Choice Answers

1. B
2. C
3. D
4. A
5. B
6. A
7. B
8. B
9. D
10. C

True/False Answers

1. False
2. False
3. False
4. True
5. False

Answers to Competency Assessment

Scenario 2-1: Managing Server Core

You can execute commands at the Cmd.exe or PowerShell.exe, and you can use the Sconfig.cmd to configure networking, workgroups, domains and Windows Firewall. To configure IIS after it is installed, you can use an MMC to connect to the computer and manage the service or application remotely.

Scenario 2-2: Configuring Services

You should only choose an account with minimal access to accomplish what it needs to accomplish. Therefore, you can use Local Service or Network Service, which will give minimal permissions much like a user in the Users group. If the service needs full access to the system, you can use the Local System account. If you still need more, you can create a local user account or domain user account, grant the appropriate rights and permissions to the group, and then have the service run under that account.

Answers to Proficiency Assessment

Scenario 2-3: Using Device Manager

No answer is needed. If students are installing on an OEM system such as Dell, IBM, or HP, they will most likely need to locate some drivers that are not included with Windows. This will require them to go to the vendor site to locate those drivers. Sometimes, one of the drivers that they have to update is the network card driver. In this case, they will need to go to the vendor web site and download using another PC. Then transfer it to a USB flash drive or CD and then install the driver. After that, they can then connect to the Internet to get any remaining drivers.

1. Click the Start button, right-click Computer, and select Properties.
2. Click Device Manager.
3. Identify problem devices and install the correct drivers (precise steps will vary).
   - View the devices under the tree and look for disabled devices (down black arrow) and devices with errors (black exclamation on a yellow field.

- Look for and identify devices in the Other devices folder.
- Open the Network adapters folder, Monitors, Network adapters, and Sound, video and game controllers and look for generic devices.

Scenario 2-4: Using EFS

No answer is needed. Since some students tend to do these types of labs blindly, you should also use some of the common troubleshooting tools (such as ipconfig and ping) to make sure they have configured everything properly. They can also try to ping localhost, 127.0.0.1, their own address, and the address of another computer on the same network (assuming the systems are configured to use the same IP address subnet).

1. Click the Start button and select Control Panel.
2. Click "View network status and tasks" under the Network and Internet option.
3. Click the "Change adapter settings" option.
4. Right-click Local Area Connection and select Properties.
5. Double-click the Internet Protocol Version 4 (TCP/IPv4) option.
6. Click "Use the following IP address" and input the following information:

   IP address: 172.24.1.XX where XX is your student number. If you do not have a student number, use .31.

   Subnet Mask: 255.255.255.0

   Default Gateway: 172.24.1.20

   DNS Server: 172.24.24.1.30

7. Click the OK button to close the Internet Protocol 4 (TCP/IPv4) Properties dialog box.
8. Click OK to close the Local Area Connection Properties dialog box.
9. If necessary, change your settings back to DHCP and save your settings.

Lesson 3: Managing Storage

Answers to Knowledge Assessment

Fill-in-the-Blank Answers

1. RAID
2. RAID-0
3. Hot spares
4. Storage area network
5. iSCSI

6. Resilient File System (ReFS)

7. File system

8. exabytes

9. Diskpart.exe

10. mirrored volume

Multiple-Choice Answers

1. A

2. D

3. C

4. D

5. B

6. C

7. B

8. C

9. C

10. C

True/False Answers

1. False

2. False

3. True

4. False

5. True

Answers to Competency Assessment

Scenario 3-1: Planning Your Disks

You need to add a second 80 GB hard drive to mirror the C drive. You should then add 3 more drives with a minimum of 80 GB each configured in RAID 5 to hold the mailboxes or connect to a SAN for the drive space. The SAN will use RAID 5 or a higher derivative. Of course, you will need additional network cards and cables to support a connection to a SAN. Since the 80 GB drives arranged in RAID 5 configuration will give 160 GB of usable disk space, you have plenty of space for growth.

Scenario 3-2: Researching Disks

Answers will vary.

Answers to Proficiency Assessment

Scenario 3-3: Connecting a Second Hard Drive

1. Physically connect the hard drive to the computer including the power.
2. Turn on the computer.
3. Click the Start button and select Computer and select Manage.
4. Expand Storage in Server Manager and select Disk Management.
5. Right-click the disk you want to initialize, and then click Initialize Disk.
6. In the Initialize Disk dialog box, select the disk(s) to initialize. Select the master boot record (MBR) and click the OK button.
7. Right-click an unallocated region of a basic disk and click New Partition.
8. When you choose to create a new partition or logical drive, the New Partition Wizard appears. Click Next to continue.
9. Specify 20000 MB for the disk size and click the Next button.
10. Specify the size of volume.
11. Assign a drive letter or mount to empty NTFS folder and click the Next button.
12. Specify the File System, allocation unit size, and volume label. You can also select a quick perform and enable file and folder compression if desired and click the Next button.
13. When the wizard is complete, click the Finish button.

Scenario 3-4: Create a Striped Volume

1. Right-click Basic Disk and select Convert Dynamic Disk.
2. Select both disks and click the OK button.
3. Click the Convert button.
4. When asks if you are sure to convert, click the Yes button.
5. Right-click the second unallocated space and select New Striped Volume.
6. When the Welcome screen appears, click the Next button.
7. Select the remaining disk and click the Add button. Click the Next button.
8. Assign the F drive and click the Next button.
9. When it asks to format the volume, click the Next button.
10. When the wizard is complete, click the Finish button.

Lesson 4: Monitoring and Troubleshooting Servers

Answers to Knowledge Assessment

Fill-in-the-Blank Answers

1. MBR
2. Safe Mode
3. System Configuration
4. paging
5. Teaming
6. cluster
7. active-passive
8. node
9. uninterruptable power supply (UPS)

Multiple-Choice Answers

1. C
2. A
3. B
4. D
5. B
6. A
7. A
8. C
9. A
10. C

True/False Answers

1. True
2. False
3. False
4. False
5. True

Answers to Competency Assessment

Scenario 4-1: Using a Troubleshooting Methodology

First you need to identify and document the problem symptoms, which are pretty obvious since you turn the power button on and nothing happens. You would next evaluate the system configuration, which nothing most likely changed. Next you would list or track possible solutions. This could be caused by the system not being plugged in, no power to the AC outlet where the server connects, faulty power supply, faulty motherboard or memory, or a short or power overload. You would check each component one by one usually from easiest to hardest. After you try isolating or replacing each component, you then move on to the next one. After you find and fix the problem, document the changes and notify the customer or client of the problem and its fix.

Scenario 4-2: Planning a Backup Strategy

It is obvious that you should back up daily since the data is important and changes often. You should perform a full backup on the weekends and differential backups or incremental backups daily. You could also isolate the programs and data and back up the data each night while backing up everything on the weekends.

Answers to Proficiency Assessment

Scenario 4-3: Looking at Backups

After you schedule backups, you must then make sure that backups occur. Second, you need to test your backups. To test backups, you need to delete an unimportant file and try to restore the file from time to time. Lastly, you should occasionally create a test server built from backups. This will test backups, and it will also test your recovery steps in case a disaster occurs.

Scenario 4-4: Looking at Event Viewer

The Event Viewer will often give you insight on events occurring on your system. However, to get the most of the Event Viewer, you should occasionally look at the Event Viewer. Similar to monitoring performance, you need to have a baseline so you know what type of errors and warning are in there. Therefore, when you start having problems, you may then notice new or different errors that did not show before. Second, by looking at the Event Viewer from time to time, the Event Viewer may show you potential problems so that you can fix them before they become noticeable or cause server failure.

Lesson 5: Essential Services

Answers to Knowledge Assessment

Fill-in-the-Blank Answers

1. hosts
2. PTR
3. DHCP
4. LDAP
5. FSMO
6. organizational unit (OU)
7. objects
8. SAM
9. groups
10. account operators

Multiple-Choice Answers

1. C
2. D
3. B
4. C
5. C
6. B
7. D
8. B
9. A
10. C

True/False Answers

1. False
2. True
3. False
4. True
5. True

Answers to Competency Assessment

Scenario 5-1: Designing Active Directory

You can use one domain with two different approaches (depending on your management needs). One approach is to have five OUs for each department with OUs for sites inside each department or to have an OU for each department with OUs for each site in the department OUs. When creating OUs, you should try not to make it too deep.

Scenario 5-2: Designing AD Physical Structure

You can use one domain with two different approaches (depending on your management needs). One approach is to have five OUs for each department with OUs for sites inside each department or to have an OU for each department with OUs for each site in the department OUs. When creating OUs, you should try not to make it too deep.

Answers to Proficiency Assessment

Scenario 5-3: Installing Active Directory

Remember that students first need to install Active Directory services. Then students need to run the dcpromo command to start the Active Directory wizard.

To install a new forest by using the Windows interface:

1. Open Server Manager. Click Start, point to Administrative Tools, and then click Server Manager.
2. In Roles Summary, click Add Roles.
3. If necessary, review the information on the Before You Begin page and then click Next.
4. On the Select Server Roles page, click the Active Directory Domain Services check box, and then click Next.
5. If necessary, review the information on the Active Directory Domain Services page, and then click Next.
6. On the Confirm Installation Selections page, click Install.
7. On the Installation Results page, click "Close this wizard" and launch the Active Directory Domain Services Installation Wizard (dcpromo.exe).
8. On the Welcome to the Active Directory Domain Services Installation Wizard page, click Next.
9. On the Operating System Compatibility page, review any warnings and then click Next.
10. On the Choose a Deployment Configuration page, click "Create a new domain in a new forest," and then click Next.
11. On the Name the Forest Root Domain page, type the full Domain Name System (DNS) name for the forest root domain, and then click Next.

12. If you selected "Use advanced mode installation" on the Welcome page, the Domain NetBIOS Name page appears. On this page, type the NetBIOS name of the domain if necessary or accept the default name, and then click Next.

13. On the Set Forest Functional Level page, select the forest functional level that accommodates the domain controllers that you plan to install anywhere in the forest, and then click Next.

14. On the Set Domain Functional Level page, select the domain functional level that accommodates the domain controllers that you plan to install anywhere in the domain, and then click Next.

15. On the Additional Domain Controller Options page, "DNS server" is selected by default so that your forest DNS infrastructure can be created during AD DS installation. If you plan to use Active Directory–integrated DNS, click Next. If you have an existing DNS infrastructure and you do not want this domain controller to be a DNS server, clear the "DNS server" check box, and then click Next.

16. On the Location for Database, Log Files, and SYSVOL page, type or browse to the volume and folder locations for the database file, the directory service log files, and the SYSVOL files, and then click Next.

17. On the Directory Services Restore Mode Administrator Password page, type and confirm the restore mode password, and then click Next. This password must be used to start AD DS in Directory Service Restore Mode for tasks that must be performed offline.

18. On the Summary page, review your selections. Click Back to change any selections, if necessary. When you are sure that your selections are accurate, click Next to install AD DS.

You can either select the "Reboot on completion" check box to have the server restart automatically or you can restart the server to complete the AD DS installation when you are prompted to do so.

Scenario 5-4: Managing a Domain

No answer is needed. However, this is something that can be demonstrated in class.

To create an organizational unit, right-click where you want to place the organizational unit and select New. Then select Organizational Unit. Then type in the name of the organizational unit and click OK.

To create a group, right-click the organizational unit where you want the group to be, select New, and then select Group. Specify the name of the group. Select the group scope, type the name of the group, and then click OK.

To create a user:

1. Right-click the organizational unit where you want the user account to be, select New, and then select User. Type a first name, last name, and a user login name. Then click Next.

2. Type a password in both boxes and click Next.

3. Click Finish.

Lesson 6: File and Print Services

Answers to Knowledge Assessment

Fill-in-the-Blank Answers

1. print
2. traverse folder
3. Windows Explorer
4. inherited permissions
5. effective permissions
6. EFS
7. network discovery
8. administrative
9. take ownership
10. C:\Windows\System32\Spool\Printers

Multiple-Choice Answers

1. A
2. A
3. B
4. C
5. D
6. D
7. B
8. A
9. B
10. A

True/False Answers

1. True
2. False
3. False
4. False
5. True

Answers to Competency Assessment

Scenario 6-1: Using a Troubleshooting Methodology

Create a Manager group with all of the managers as members. You should create a Data folder. Share the Data folder. Change the Everyone to Allow Full Control share permission. Then grant the Allow Modify NTFS permissions to the Managers group.

Scenario 6-2: Auditing the Managers folder

You need set up auditing. You must first enable object access auditing using group policies or local security policies for the computer where the folder is located. Then you need to enable Full Control successful and Failed access. You will then occasionally search the security logs in the Event Viewer from time to time.

Answers to Proficiency Assessment

Scenario 6-3: Managing a Folder

No answer is needed. This can all be demonstrated in class. If possible, students should be able to log in as different users and try to access the folders. They should try to access the folder directly or by using the UNC (\\servername\sharedname).

To create a folder:

1. Right-click where you want to place the folder using Windows Explorer, select New, and then select Folder.
2. Type the name of the folder and press Enter.

To share a folder:

1. Right-click the folder and select Properties.
2. Select the Sharing tab.
3. Click Advanced Sharing.
4. Select the Share this folder option. Type the name of the share and click OK to accept your changes and exit the Advanced Sharing option.
5. Click Close to close the Properties dialog box.

To modify NTFS permissions:

1. Right-click the folder and select Properties.
2. Select the Security tab.
3. Click Edit.
4. Click Add, specify the user you want to add, specify the permissions, and then click OK to accept your changes and close the Permissions dialog box.
5. Click Close to close the Properties dialog box.

Scenario 6-4: Manage Printers

No answer is needed. This can be demonstrated in class.

To install a printer:

1. Open Devices and Printers from the Start menu.
2. Click "Add a printer."
3. Select "Add a local printer."
4. With "Use the existing port" already selected, click Next.
5. Select a printer manufacturer and printer and click Next.
6. Specify the name of the printer and click Next.
7. Don't share at this time and click Next.
8. Click Finish.

To share a printer:

1. Right-click the printer in Devices and Printers and select Printer Properties.
2. Select the Sharing tab.
3. Select "Share this printer."
4. Click the OK button.

To manage permissions of a printer:

1. Right-click the printer in Devices and Printers and select Printer Properties.
2. Select the Security tab.
3. Select Everyone and click Remove.
4. Click the Add button, add Managers, and then click OK.
5. Click OK to accept your changes and close the Printer Properties dialog box

Lesson 7: Popular Windows Network Services and Applications

Answers to Knowledge Assessment

Fill-in-the-Blank Answers

1. World Wide Web
2. HyperText Markup
3. Internet Information Server (IIS)
4. virtual directory

5. 443
6. X.509
7. Hyper-V
8. snapshot
9. remote desktop
10. RemoteApp

Multiple-Choice Answers

1. C
2. B
3. C
4. C
5. B
6. D
7. D
8. A
9. C
10. D

True/False Answers

1. False
2. True
3. False
4. False
5. False

Answers to Competency Assessment

Scenario 7-1: Allowing Work from Home

The primary technology you will need to use is to VPN. Therefore, you will need to install a remote access server on a computer running Windows Server 2016. You should configure L2TP with IPSec for the best security. You will then have to configure the client computers to access the remote access server. In addition, depending on the applications that the user needs to access, he will use the applications on his laptop computer or he will have to use remote desktop to access servers or client computers within the organization.

Scenario 7-2: Isolating Server Applications

Some advantages of using virtual servers include isolating server applications and utilizing computer resource more efficiently. Therefore, you should use create two virtual servers on a single physical server. Although the applications will access a centralized database server, the applications themselves will run on the individual servers, keeping them totally isolated.

Answers to Proficiency Assessment

Scenario 7-3: Create a Web Site

No answer is needed. This can be demonstrated.

To install IIS:

1. Click Start, point to Administrative Tools, and then click Server Manager.
2. In Roles Summary, click Add Roles.
3. Use the Add Roles Wizard to add the web server role.
4. To open IIS Manager, click the Start button. Then select All programs, select Administrative Tools, and click Internet Information Services (IIS) Manager.

To create additional Web sites:

1. Open IIS Manager.
2. In the Connections pane, right-click the Sites node in the tree and then click Add Web Site.
3. In the Add Web Site dialog box, type a friendly name for your Web site in the Web site name box.
4. Click Select if you want to select a different application pool than the one listed in the Application Pool box. In the Select Application Pool dialog box, select an application pool from the Application Pool list and then click OK.
5. In the Physical path box, type the physical path of the Web site's folder, or click the browse button (. . .) to navigate to the file system to find the folder.
6. If the physical path that you entered in Step 5 is to a remote share, click Connect to specify credentials that have permission to access the path. If you do not use specific credentials, select the "Application user (pass-thru authentication)" option in the Connect As dialog box.
7. Select the protocol for the Web site from the Type list.
8. The default value in the "IP address" box is All Unassigned. If you must specify a static IP address for the Web site, type the IP address in the "IP address" box.
9. Type a port number in the Port text box.
10. Optionally, type a host header name for the Web site in the Host Header box.
11. If you do not have to make any changes to the site and you want the Web site to be immediately available, select the "Start Web site immediately" check box.
12. Click OK.

Scenario 7-4: Using Remote Desktop

No answer is needed. This can be demonstrated.

To make sure Remote Desktop is enabled, click the Start button, right-click Computer, and select Properties. Select "Remote settings." Make sure that one of the "Allow connections" options is selected under Remote Desktop and click OK.

To connect to another computer, click the Start button, click All Programs, select Accessories, and then select Remote Desktop Connection. Type the name or IP address of the host you want to connect to and click the Connect button.

Index

Note to the Reader: Throughout this index **boldfaced** page numbers indicate primary discussions of a topic. *Italicized* page numbers indicate illustrations.

S

9781119650744: Networking Fundamentals

- Understand wired and wireless networks
- Work with fiber optic and twisted pair cables
- Learn Internet protocol (IP) and categorize IPv4 Addresses
- Validate your skills and knowledge with MTA Certification

9781119650669: Security Fundamentals

- Gain knowledge of essential IT security concepts
- Learn physical, Internet, and wireless security
- Identify different types of hardware firewalls
- Validate your skills and knowledge with MTA Certification

9781119650515: Windows Operating System Fundamentals

- Install and upgrade Windows 10 client
- Setup user accounts and account controls
- Customize user profiles
- Configure LAN settings and remote assistance and management
- Validate your skills and knowledge with MTA Certification

9781119650652: Windows Server Administration Fundamentals

- Install and manage Windows Server
- Use Disk Management Tools
- Manage devices and drivers
- Optimize server performance
- Configure Windows Network Services
- Administer remote and virtual servers
- Validate your skills and knowledge with MTA Certification